THE END OF LEARNING

Milton and Education

Thomas Festa

Routledge
New York & London

Routledge
Taylor & Francis Group
711 Third Avenue,
New York, NY 10017

Routledge
Taylor & Francis Group
2 Park Square,
Milton Park, Abingdon,
Oxfordshire OX14 4RN

First issued in paperback 2014

Routledge is an imprint of the Taylor and Francis Group, an informa business

© 2006 by Taylor and Francis Group, LLC

ISBN 978-0-415-97839-2 (hbk)
ISBN 978-0-415-76291-5 (pbk)

Visit the Taylor & Francis Web site at
http://www.taylorandfrancis.com

and the Routledge Web site at
http://www.routledge-ny.com

STUDIES IN MAJOR LITERARY AUTHORS

Edited by

William E. Cain
Professor of English
Wellesley College

A ROUTLEDGE SERIES

STUDIES IN MAJOR LITERARY AUTHORS

WILLIAM E. CAIN, *General Editor*

For my parents

Contents

List of Figures

List of Abbreviations

CM	John Milton, *Works*, ed. Frank Allen Patterson et al., 18 vols. (New York: Columbia University Press, 1931–38)
ET	*Euripidis Tragoediae*, ed. Paulus Stephanus, 2 vols. (Geneva, 1602), Bodleian Library shelfmark don. d. 27, 28
Geneva Bible	All quotations of the marginal glosses and text of the Geneva translation are taken from the most fully annotated edition (London, 1599) unless otherwise noted.
KJV	*The Bible: Authorized King James Version with Apocrypha*, ed. Robert Carroll and Stephen Prickett (Oxford: Oxford University Press, 1997)
LCL	Loeb Classical Library
NRSV	*The Holy Bible: New Revised Standard Version* (New York: Oxford University Press, 1989)
OED	*The Compact Edition of the Oxford English Dictionary*, 2 vols. (Oxford: Oxford University Press, 1971), checked against the revisions and updates posted to the online edition.
Poems	John Milton, *Complete Shorter Poems*, ed. John Carey, 2nd ed. (London: Longman, 1997)
Poems AM	Andrew Marvell, *The Poems of Andrew Marvell*, ed. Nigel Smith (London: Pearson / Longman, 2003)
PL	John Milton, *Paradise Lost*, ed. Alastair Fowler, 2nd ed. (London: Longman, 1998). This is the main edition cited throughout unless otherwise noted.

PR   John Milton, *Paradise Regained* in *Poems*, ed. Carey.

YP   *Complete Prose Works of John Milton*, ed. Don M. Wolfe et al., 8 vols. (New Haven: Yale University Press, 1953–82)

Acknowledgments

Thankfully, this book stands as evidence that the mind is not, as Satan imagines in *Paradise Lost*, its own place. Over the years of researching and writing, I have become ever more greatly aware that, without the help and encouragement of several individuals and institutions, this effort would have landed me in a Paradise of Fools. An earlier version of this book was submitted to Columbia University in 2004 as a Ph.D. dissertation. First of all I must therefore thank my dissertation advisors for their unfailing generosity and magnanimity. I only began to imagine that I could accomplish so daunting a task when I met and studied under Edward Tayler, whose work in the field of Milton studies has contributed immeasurably to the thought of a generation of scholars. I feel especially privileged to have had the opportunity to work with him at the end of his distinguished career. Professor Tayler taught me by example the very nature of scholarly virtue. David Kastan has, from my first day as a graduate student at Columbia, welcomed me with unmatched grace and wisdom into the larger world of intellectual life. Without his continued support, learned encouragement, and unparalleled wit, this project would never have seen its proper "end." I was fortunate enough to have been Professor Kastan's student as his many years of teaching and thinking about Milton came to fruition in his recent edition of *Paradise Lost* for Hackett Publishing, and, as our ongoing exchanges about the text of the epic during that process confirm, I am certain to remain his student for a long time to come.

I must also thank several other kind teachers who, having read and commented on drafts of my work on Milton, have sustained and challenged me: Douglas Brooks, Julie Crawford, Michelle Dowd, Richard DuRocher, Kathy Eden, Alan Farmer, Andrew Hadfield, Bruce Holsinger, Jean Howard, William Kolbrener, Albert Labriola, Zachary Lesser, Elisabeth Liebert, Paula Loscocco, Laura McGrane, Thomas Olsen, Douglas Pfeiffer, Peter Platt,

Anne Prescott, Jason Rosenblatt, Alan Stewart, Daniel Swift, Henry Turner, and Adam Zucker. In the English Department at the State University of New York at New Paltz, where I teach, I would like to acknowledge Stella Deen, the current department chair, and my colleagues Nancy Johnson, Daniel Kempton, Christopher Link, and Thomas Olsen. A little farther afield, I owe special thanks to Kimberly Benston and James Boettcher, who have discussed my work with me and have expanded my idea of the nature of this undertaking more than they can know. Two other scholars deserve special mention for help and guidance of a more general kind: Christopher Grose, who first introduced me to the writings of Milton and inspired me to continue in my studies; and Anthony Low, who provided an excellent model of humane learning at a crucial point in my graduate education. I have been fortunate in my friends.

I should like to express heartfelt gratitude to the staff at the Bodleian Library; the British Library; the Folger Shakespeare Library; and Butler Library at Columbia University. Generous grants from Columbia and from the Folger Institute made much of my early research possible.

Two of the chapters first appeared as journal articles. Chapter 1 reprints with a few changes "Repairing the Ruins: Milton as Reader and Educator," from *Milton Studies* XLIII, Albert C. Labriola, ed. © 2003 by University of Pittsburgh Press. Reprinted by permission of the University of Pittsburgh Press. An earlier version of Chapter 2 first appeared as "Milton's 'Christian *Talmud*'" in *Reformation* 8 (2003), published by Ashgate. The article that became Chapter 2 won the William Tyndale Prize for 2004, awarded by the Worshipful Company of Stationers and Newspaper Printers, London. I am humbled by the honor, and wish to thank Andrew Hadfield, editor of *Reformation*, for this much needed encouragement. I am grateful to the editors and anonymous readers for both of these journals, whose assistance allowed me to improve and refine my arguments.

In bringing this book to the light, I have benefited greatly from the patient professionalism and benevolent solicitude of everyone at Routledge. I am especially grateful to my editors Max Novick and William Germano for all their help in this process. Professor William Cain, the academic editor of the series to which this book belongs, was enormously supportive and encouraging, and it is fair to say that without his indispensable help this book would never have appeared in its current form. In the last stages of its completion, Jonathan Munk, my copyeditor, performed deeds above heroic and saved me from many errors.

Finally I must thank my wife, Vicki Tromanhauser, whose love and support have taught me more than I can say.

Introduction

In the original sense of the word, education is a leading out, a drawing out, or a bringing up. Liberation of the mind is also at the very heart of the concept. Education has its roots, conceptually and linguistically, in the human aspiration to greater freedom, so that the bond between education and political enlightenment is as intimate as it is ancient. John Milton instinctively grasped this primal power of learning, a recognition that lent particular moral shading to his imagination. In the creative act, Milton's effort to lead the members of his fit audience toward their greatest intellectual and spiritual fitness irradiated the mind through all its powers: education thus constitutes the central trope for Milton's political and poetic writing.

Sublime as Milton's creative powers were, his theory of education, like the material universe in his account of creation, was not forged out of nothing. The substance of Milton's educational thinking remains available to us in the record of his thought, but we can also expand our awareness of its elemental structures by analyzing his own practices as a student, reader, and teacher. I take up the crucial matter of Milton's reading in Chapter One, in the analysis of books from his personal library, books undoubtedly used in teaching pupils at his home. If thinking about how Milton read helps us to understand what he expected of his audience, then piecing together the relationship between his practical pedagogical thought and his theoretical assumptions about the educative function of literature will clarify the nature of his intervention in his own context and allow us to reconsider the place he has in our curriculum. Milton, from work to work, has a unity of purpose underlying his exigent points, a didactic intention that of necessity changes for him but becomes more vital over time; this unity is not, however, identical to the one Milton sets forth in his autobiographical writings as his intention. His own perception of, or argument for, the intentional shape of his teachings riddles his works, yet Milton is notoriously contradictory and even manipulative in his interpretation of his achievement. Nonetheless, analysis of Milton's concept of education must take into account the intentions he avows in his writings, at least as an inaugural topic. When such authorial claims have the relative consistency that Milton's thoughts on education exhibit over the course of about thirty-five years of publication, the assertions themselves may be said to exercise a powerful force over the texts in which they appear. This is even, or perhaps especially, true where the intention to educate seems to distort rather than to clarify what the text is really about on more explicit or practical levels.

Milton's instincts for pedagogy, and the habits of inculcation everywhere visible in his writing, take on a larger political function in his use of education as a trope for the relationship between an individual and the authority of tradition. In this, Milton's educational thinking is consonant with the best minds of his age. Questions of epistemological authority occupied a central position in the thought of Bacon before him and of Locke after him, though the political significance of this branch of philosophy has not always received the attention that it deserves. For instance, although it has long been recognized that John Locke's *Some Thoughts Concerning Education* (1693) made a major contribution to the philosophy of education, it has only recently been shown that the educational writings form an integral part of Locke's political philosophy by uprooting the reliance upon customary authority and showing how a responsible polity could be inculcated outside of patriarchal structures of government.[1] Milton's educational project in the poetry and the prose, I contend, played an important part in the formation of this revolutionary attitude toward tradition, if from a different set of premises than those followed by the most influential early modern philosophers.

Milton's argumentative resourcefulness works as a literary strategy to emancipate readers from the tyrannical bonds of their political innocence, most immediately in the context of the failure of successive revolutionary regimes to establish lasting institutions. But his fluidity of argument is present in *Paradise Lost* as well as the political tracts and ought, therefore, to encourage us to place the epic in the complementary contexts of its outright educational claims and more subversive countervailing measures. Analysis of this feature of Milton's rhetoric will show how he dramatizes the nicely ambiguous "end of learning," which is to say both its objective and its abandonment. Milton's works investigate the humane and intellectual yearning for justice in response to the problem of evil, a problem not easily overcome by educational, or political, means. Yet his enduring faith in the power of education to train the citizens of a sophisticated polity suggests an ideology not simply directed by the needs of the institutionally empowered but rather committed to the empowerment of a public forum in which dissent will be integral.

Addressing the members of the Long Parliament on just this issue in *Areopagitica* (November 1644), Milton rails against religiously and politically motivated prepublication censorship, since it discourages learning. Milton reveals a predilection for open inquiry as a backdrop against which to measure the oppressive tendencies of his political moment. But this concept—for which, according to the *OED,* he coined the adjective in the tract's phrase "*Philosophic* freedom"—is notoriously slippery, exclusive, hedged in by doubt. Even this phrase stands not as a positive model of English liberty, but rather an ironic indictment of encroachments upon it seen through the eyes of unsuspecting "Italian wits" (YP 2:537–38). Although "lerned men" abroad have counted Milton "happy to be born in such a place of *Philosophic* freedom, as they suppos'd England was," Milton offers us a glimpse of their assumption only to retract this view as mistaken, merely "suppos'd." Learning is always at risk of having fallen into a "servil condition," he implies, at home as well as abroad.

What sort of thing, then, is Miltonic education? The present study endeavors to answer this question from multiple perspectives: historical and philosophical, practical and poetic. At the simplest level, Milton asks how one can realize the truth as a spiritual connection to Christ. If a person can lay claim to an authentic knowledge of Christ, does it follow that one can teach another to share this understanding, and if so, how could such an inward discovery be communicated or, indeed, confirmed? For "inward ripeness doth much less appear," Milton maintains in Sonnet 7 (*Poems,* p. 153). The urgent question asked by educators from classical times to the seventeenth century was whether something deeper than superficial knowledge, something more than "learning," something spiritual, could finally be taught. In other words, can virtue be taught, or must it be innate? Reciprocally, we might ask whether virtue is the proper register of knowledge.[2] Moreover, what is the relationship between learning and teaching, especially since, in this relationship, a politics as well as a form of ethical reflection may be said to inhere? Milton's attempts to answer these and other questions draw us toward a fuller consideration of his politics, his ethics, and his poetry as we locate his educational thought across several genres and discursive modes.

The value of teaching no doubt consists in the ability of education to address the constituents of a specific society in a particular time and place and to empower them to act more effectively. Conflicting models of political order and of the educational practices within them, as Milton and his contemporaries recognized, develop out of opposing theories of truth: the ends toward which they aspire. Hobbes saw that his political theory requiring submission to the authority of the sovereign could only take root when his discourse was "profitably taught in the Universities," which "are the Fountains of Civill, and Morall Doctrine."[3] The political truth that Hobbes envisaged would lead naturally to a reconfiguration of the universities, which would in turn ensure the transformation of the government. Czech philosopher John Amos Comenius, perhaps the most influential educational thinker of the seventeenth century, imagined a reformation of society by conceiving a system of universal education in which boys and girls alike would be compelled to attend school. "For those who are in any position of authority," writes Comenius, "it is as necessary to be imbued with wisdom as it is for a guide to have eyes. . . . Similarly, those in subordinate positions should be educated that they may know how to obey their superiors wisely and prudently, not under compulsion. . . . For a rational creature should be led, not by shouts, imprisonment, and blows, but by reason."[4] The coherence of Comenius's system of "pansophy" relied upon the availability of all knowledge for synchronic comprehension and distillation. From this encyclopedic digest of truth, the diachronic scheme of educating the young could be restructured more harmoniously and synoptically. For Comenius, the nature of truth was such that it could be calibrated to all members of a society at whatever stage of their intellectual development. Therefore Comenius "may undoubtedly be considered," according to Jean Piaget, "as one of the precursors of the genetic idea in developmental psychology, and as a founder of a system of progressive instruction."[5] For Comenius as for Hobbes, formulating an educational philosophy meant establishing the proper conduit between a student's psychology and a systematic approach to truth, with the further end of creating a social dynamic that would foster the political arrangement.

For Milton, to clarify the theoretical problem of education is to engage in a process that represents the contingency of truth, according to the allegory in *Areopagitica*:

> Truth indeed came once into the world with her divine Master, and was a perfect shape most glorious to look on: but when he ascended, and his Apostles after him were laid asleep, then strait arose a wicked race of deceivers, who as that story goes of the *AEgyptian Typhon* with his conspirators, how they dealt with good *Osiris*, took the virgin Truth, hewd her lovely form into a thousand peeces, and scatter'd them to the four winds. From that time ever since, the sad friends of Truth, such as durst appear, imitating the carefull search that *Isis* made for the mangl'd body of *Osiris*, went up and down gathering up limb by limb still as they could find them. We have not yet found them all, Lords and Commons,

nor ever shall doe, till her Masters second comming; he shall bring together every joynt and member, and shall mould them into an immortal feature of lovlines and perfection. (YP 2:549)

The allegory seems poised to suggest a method by which we might construct an educational response, spiritual and intellectual, to the loss of Truth, perhaps a war against "a wicked race of deceivers" to be fought by the "warfaring Christian" referred to elsewhere in the tract (YP 2:515). By its end, however, this passage asks us to sustain our efforts to re-member the hewn body of Truth while acknowledging that we never shall find all the pieces until the end of time. Over the course of the passage, the depiction of Truth gradually undermines our ability to rest certain in the knowledge that we have attained it. If truth is not precisely indeterminate, the concept as Milton presents it here remains steadfastly contingent, unverifiable, and interrogative.

Given our epistemological predicament, we might well wonder why Milton shifts to the obliquity of allegorical narrative to represent something as absolute as truth. At this crucial juncture in his argument, the rhetorical deflection is perversely unyielding. Allegory is a conventional method for discovering truth, a mode that Milton elsewhere reserves for the depredations of tradition and for hollow mechanistic representations of the literal. Hence the allegory of Custom that begins *The Doctrine and Discipline of Divorce* (in the second edition of 2 February 1644) or the residue of allegorical figures such as Sin and Death, Chaos and Old Night in *Paradise Lost*. When illustrating how a representation loses substance, Milton habitually enters his metaphors on an allegorical register.[6]

That Milton has chosen to break down the impediments to education from within this mode of representation invites further reflection. For allegory operates on both sides of the literary transaction: it is a means of encoding a text and of decoding or processing that text's potential meanings. The allegory of Truth in *Areopagitica* compresses several levels of Miltonic education because it embodies, in its rhetoric, the problem that it appears to have been set forth to remedy. Using a conspicuous and conventional method for determining meaning, the allegory draws our attention to its conventionality. The passage thereby denatures the intention that it ostensibly articulates. In this way, Milton teaches us the meaning of our very pursuit of meaning. Fidelity to truth, in this conception, requires that we remain faithful to what we must acknowledge is oblique to us. Miltonic education encompasses this critical effort of the mind, yet it further demands that we honestly confront the limited circumference of our understanding.

Allegorical representation is especially implicated in religious history since, as C. S. Lewis remarked, "the twilight of the gods is the mid-morning of the personifications."[7] As a mode of expression, allegory therefore has a special genetic link to a transitional moment in the history of religious thought. Allegorical interpretation of Scripture, above all the fourfold exegesis of medieval scholastic philosophy, provides a method of divination. The four layers exist simultaneously on the divine page of sacred writings: the literal (or historical), the allegorical (or typological), the moral, and the anagogical (or eschatological).[8] Precisely because of the narrative Milton relays, the allegory may be schematically represented according to this method. Milton locates the allegory of Truth *historically* in the decay that follows the death of the Apostles. False prophets arose, according to this version of early church history, as "a wicked race of deceivers," after Christ "ascended, and his Apostles after him were laid asleep." The *allegorical* level unfolds from Milton's source, Plutarch's *Moralia*. Milton most likely knew Plutarch's version of the story, as his references to the *Moralia* in other places suggest.[9] According to Plutarch, Typhon "tears to pieces and scatters to the winds the sacred writings, which the goddess [Isis] collects and puts together and gives into the keeping of those that are initiated into the holy rites." Plutarch immediately uproots the Egyptian myth and turns it into an allegory of "the effort to arrive at the Truth, and especially the truth about the gods," "the end and aim of which is the knowledge of Him who is the First, the Lord of All, the Ideal one."[10] The *moral* application of Milton's allegory speaks directly to his moment: to arrest the flow of books that might communicate sacred information is to inhibit the sacrosanct drive toward our comprehension, however limited, of divine Truth. On the fourth level of the *anagogical,* Milton offers his summation, that Truth shall not appear in its glorious likeness again until the end of time, the *parousia.*

The only piece Isis never finds, Plutarch tells us, is the male member of Osiris, which becomes the source of the fecundity of the Nile as well as the origin of the ancient phallic mystery cults.[11] In his use of the allegory, Milton tacitly equates the severance from Truth with castration. His narrative symbolically admits this absence, as it makes no mention of this part that he suggests could stand for the whole, or for the idea of wholeness.[12] In this respect, the narrative by which he represents the allure of a methodologically reassuring, coherent emblem of truth engenders an originary displacement of authority. Milton enacts an allegory of Truth to dramatize a misplaced desire for systematic coherence, for customary exegetical method, for certitude.

Yet Milton reaches for allegory precisely because the narrative of dismemberment gestures out toward the affective nature of the trauma, the primeval loss of truth. Dismemberment in the narrative signals displacement in time: "From that time ever since" provides the setting for the unresolved melancholic allegory. "Traumatic memories," as contemporary researchers in psychiatry remind us, "are the unassimilated scraps of overwhelming experiences, which need to be integrated with existing mental schemes, and be transformed into narrative language."[13] One symptom of the allegorical displacement in Milton's narrative is in the shift in gender, from a masculine Osiris as representative of Truth to a feminine "virgin" body—the "lovely form" of the primitive church as the virginal Bride of Christ. Placed in a spiritual framework, the dissociation increases exponentially. Each of us has been sundered from the mystical body of Christ, torn from our connection to Truth. The depiction of "the sad friends of Truth" thus questions us on a deeper, more therapeutic level as well. How does one recover from a lost connection to the truth? Miltonic education develops the historical sense, here "the carefull search that *Isis* made for the mangl'd body of *Osiris*." We must first recognize our distance from the origin—"We have not yet found them all," he says—in order to understand the situation in which we respond to its loss. What we can learn until Truth's reappearance at "her Masters second comming" is provisional, indirect, proper to reflection and critique of the self and of society in its concrete historical manifestation. Given the contingency of truth, Milton implicitly asks how, ethically, we may use the past as precedent. How do we reconcile historicism to the unattainable Truth, to faith itself? For Milton, education consists in teaching the proper attitude toward history, tradition, and authority.

Milton's paradigm of education unfolds gradually over the course of his works in relation to hermeneutic understanding. Based on the encounter with such remnants of sacred Truth as can be gathered from reading both text and world, the problem of education becomes one of understanding without external means of verification. This is why the problem of education is one of interpretation, of hermeneutics, a problem that we shall revisit with special attention in Chapter Four through a reading of *Paradise Lost*. Milton's notion of the contingency of truth has close affinities with the hermeneutic stance described by Hans-Georg Gadamer:

> Hermeneutics must start from the position that a person seeking to understand something has a bond to the subject matter that comes into language through the traditionary text and has, or acquires, a connection with the tradition from which the text speaks. . . . Given the intermediate position in which hermeneutics operates, it follows that its work is not to develop a procedure of understanding, but to clarify the conditions in which understanding takes place.[14]

The connection to tradition, for Milton, was to be achieved only by means of a struggle for rhetorical legitimacy in the "wars of Truth" (*Areopagitica*, YP 2:562). Given the historical context of the English Revolution, this connection (as we shall see) was fraught with political significance, as prelates, royalists, Presbyterians, and finally Cromwell adopted the symbolic trappings of customary authority in the effort to legitimate their rule. Milton would locate the struggle to define and possess truth against such monumental ideas of tradition, embracing instead a conflict of interpretations of history, politics, and self.[15] For Milton, as for Gadamer, the effects of tradition are as inescapable as they are irresistible. Thus hermeneutics discloses our historicity through the mediation of tradition.

As Milton shows in his allegory of Truth, the grounds of our historical being are themselves unstable because of our distance from the unrecoverable reality of the divine presence. The fractures within our understanding therefore become our true inheritance from a decimated origin in the past, a conceptual bearing that Gadamer dates to the Reformation. The hermeneutic circle does not teach a rehabilitation of authority and tradition so much as "the right use of reason in understanding traditionary texts. Neither the doctrinal authority of the pope nor the appeal to tradition can obviate the work of hermeneutics, which can safeguard the reasonable meaning of a text against all imposition."[16] At the same time, just as the authority of tradition cannot eclipse reason, neither can reason subjugate all other forms of authority—as it would in confident idealizations of the Enlightenment. As I will show in Chapter Two, this interpretive problem came to a head in Milton's reconsideration of the charitable teachings of the Mosiac Law in the divorce tracts. The hermeneutic enigma, which Milton so eloquently confronted as an educational challenge, becomes clearer when contextualized theologically. Considering the history of exegesis from the vantage of early modern Protestant readers, "the paradox of sacrifice," as Deborah Kuller Shuger has finely observed, "epitomized the pervasive ambiguities attached to humanist interpretation of the past as simultaneously authoritative and alien."[17] It is just this idea of history as at once "authoritative and alien," inescapable yet inescapably other, that drives Milton toward his particular understanding of his relationship to the past.

We need not, in other words, concede to T. S. Eliot that tradition is a totality and a "simultaneous" unity in order to observe this dynamic "perception, not only of the pastness of the past, but of its presence."[18] Milton harbored deep suspicions about essentialist metaphysics—about, for example, a representation's power to capture and contain the essence of the thing for which it stands.[19] The gravity of his doubt about metaphysics as a project for human thinking makes some of his ideas proximate to philosophy of the recent past.[20] This "philosophy without mirrors," as Richard Rorty describes it, is a way of doing philosophy that is poetic. It substitutes education for certainty of knowledge and does not, or cannot, construct a foundation upon which to erect a systematic theory of existence. Such philosophy is, as Rorty says, "therapeutic rather than constructive, edifying rather than systematic, designed to make the reader question his own motives for philosophizing rather than to supply him with a new philosophical program."[21] Similarly, hermeneutic understanding is "less knowing what the text means in itself than . . . knowing how we stand with respect to it in the situation in which we find ourselves."[22]

The story I shall tell in this book takes cues from philosophical hermeneutics insofar as I believe Milton's writings can help us understand our own concerns today with history, authority, and tradition—and because I think contemporary preoccupations with interpretation can help us understand the relationship to a literary past that I find exemplified in the writings of Milton. This study is thus an attempt to come to terms with a particularly Miltonic set of attitudes toward the past as articulated in the concerns of the present. Investigating Milton's approach to the philosophical problems that beset historical reflection will furthermore allow us to scrutinize some critical assumptions about the relations between historiography and literature and will in this way provide access to debates about the concept of modernity.[23]

In recent years, the project of dismantling the monolithic conception of scientific progress—a narrative that reached its peak of influence in the early and mid-twentieth century—has become a point of convergence for thinkers from across the disciplines. Stephen Toulmin, for example, attributes the twentieth-century conception of philosophical modernity to an earlier historic shift from practical to theoretical philosophy, from the non-dogmatic paradigm of rhetoric to the foundationalist imperatives of Cartesian rationalism. In response, Toulmin wants to resituate the origin of modernity in a skeptical, humanist moment prior to the rise of scientific "method" and to show how practical knowledge—as seen in such fields as jurisprudence, rhetoric, and diagnostic medicine—in fact offers an alternative paradigm for modernity. This pursuit of an alternative origin Toulmin parallels with the challenges that Wittgenstein, Dewey, and Rorty pose to the Cartesian ideal of certainty as the founding principle of modern philosophy.[24]

To some readers, the description of an alternative philosophical modernity—one in which I see Milton as a vital participant—will frankly not sound coherent enough to merit consideration as a form of philosophical thought. However, the conflict between rhetoric and science as principles of order within, and approaches to, human knowledge held a central importance for Milton and his contemporaries. Indeed, as Quentin Skinner has recently shown, this conflict between rhetoric and science remained a defining characteristic of Thomas Hobbes's philosophy, even as Hobbes transformed political theory into a science through the application of geometrical demonstration to political analysis.[25] The persistence of rhetorical models of truth among such diametrically opposed political thinkers as Hobbes and Milton suggests a greater continuity of ideas when viewed in historical context than the history of philosophy has traditionally allowed, and this ought to extend our category of the philosophic appreciably so that it comprises the tensions produced by rhetorical thought in an increasingly scientific age. Nonetheless, it is true that the disposition I attribute to Milton has closer connections to rhetoric than to philosophy as it is usually described, or is closer perhaps to "humanist logic" than to the philosophy of the schools.[26] The best scholarly work reconstructing Milton's own education has elucidated precisely this connection to classical rhetoric in the humanist curriculum, which Milton studied while a young man at St. Paul's School in London.[27] We shall return to the definitive influence of humanism upon Milton's thought in Chapter Three.

Attention to the history of educational theory and practice in the age of Milton will refine the questions I seek to ask at length of Miltonic education. Milton's first recorded comments on the subject place him squarely in the tradition of humanist educators. Under the heading "On the Education of Children" in his Commonplace Book, in an entry dated circa 1635–38 by the Yale editor, Milton writes: "The nature of each person should be especially observed and not bent in another direction; for God does not intend all people for one thing, but for each one his own work; whence comes Dante's: 'And if the world down there put its mind on the foundation that nature lays,' &c. See Paradiso cant: 8." (YP 1:405).[28] Nature and God's vocation unite in this humane concept of pedagogy, which promotes cultivating natural proclivity rather than violently bending it, or imposing artificial social constructs upon it. "God and nature," as Abdiel tells Satan in *Paradise Lost*, "bid the same" (6.176). Milton's early formulation is grounded in practical or experiential knowledge, and as such has a clear if implicit antecedent in Aristotle: "Education on an individual basis is superior to education in common, as in the case of medical care. . . . It would seem that particular cases are treated with greater subtlety if there is attention to individuals, since each person is more likely to obtain what suits him."[29]

In the early modern period, the prospect of fashioning an intellect often took on the harsher attributes of discipline, even within the mainstream of humanist thought. Erasmus says: "Nature is an effectual thing, but education, more effectual, overcommeth it."[30] Milton's disagreement on this point reveals perhaps a difference of degree rather than of kind, but from this formulation we can see that the divergence begins with the idea of nature. For Milton, as he says in the *De Doctrina Christiana,* "nature cannot mean anything except the wonderful power and efficacy of the divine voice which went forth in the beginning, and which all things have obeyed ever since as a perpetual command" (YP 6:340–41). The theological conviction that each person has "his own work," as Milton puts it in the Commonplace Book entry, tames the impulse to shape pupils against their natural inclination. In Sir Thomas Elyot's conception, which seems to have influenced Milton, this is the first duty of an educator: "The office of a tutor is firste to knowe the nature of his pupil, that is to say, where to he is mooste inclined or disposed, and in what thyng he setteth his most delectation or appetite."[31]

Against the idea that natural inclination toward learning provokes an impious curiosity, Milton repeatedly emphasized the way in which inquiry into the universe could breed knowledge that is both natural and godly. Receptivity to this aspect of what is perceived as the divine intention informs the idea of learning in Milton's paradigm. Indeed, attentiveness to God's design for the universe demands that education be pursued so that God may be more deeply understood and therefore more profoundly worshiped. In an early academic oration, most likely presented near the end of his time at Cambridge (around 1630–31), Milton defends learning against stupidly pious ignorance:

> God would indeed seem to have endowed us to no purpose, or even to our distress, with this soul which is capable and indeed insatiably desirous of highest wisdom, if he had not intended us to strive with all our might toward the lofty understanding of those things, for which he had at our creation instilled so great a longing into the human mind. Survey from every angle the entire aspect of these things and you will perceive that the great Artificer of this mighty fabric established it for His own glory. The more deeply we delve into the wondrous wisdom, the marvelous skill, and the astounding variety of its creation (which we cannot do without the aid of Learning), the greater grows the wonder and awe we feel for its Creator and the louder the praises we offer Him, which we believe and are fully persuaded that He delights to accept.
> (*Prolusion 7,* YP 1:291–92)

The impetus must be to survey "from every angle the entire aspect"—an unfathomably steep ascent, but Milton wishes to reassure his audience that a deep harmony unites the study of God with the study of His creation. As in the Commonplace Book entry, Milton expresses his intellectual ambition by admiring and respecting "the astounding variety" of all creation, a quality he lauds equally in his estimation of the natural wonders of the physical universe and in the spirit of each human being. The "peculiar sway of nature," he reminds us, "also is Gods working" (*Of Education,* YP 2:363).

Like many humanists who preceded him, Milton found no conflict in the study of spiritual, physical, and political sciences. In his brief tractate *Of Education* (June 1644), Milton synthesizes a multifarious program of study that "would trie all [the students'] particular gifts of nature, and if there were any secret excellence among them, would fetch it out, and give it fair opportunities to advance it selfe by" (YP 2:413). As when Roger Ascham seized upon the connection between serving God and serving one's country, Milton urges the political benefit to the polity of educating "our noble and our gentle youth" (2:406). Ascham sums up the humanist political insistence upon the *vita activa* thus: "if to the goodness of nature be joined the wisdom of the teacher in leading young wits into a right and plain way of learning, surely children, kept up in God's fear and governed by his grace, may most easily be brought well to serve God and country both by virtue and wisdom."[32] Although Milton disagreed with the monarchical inclinations of such thinkers as Ascham and Elyot, he believed that the effort to educate the meritorious if not hereditary elite "could not but mightily redound to the good of this nation" (YP 2:414).[33] Milton advances his theory of education to rectify shortcomings that he believes inhibit the reformation of the spiritual and political nation. Hence he sets out in the midst of the Civil War "to write now the reforming of Education . . . for the want whereof this nation perishes" (YP 2:362–63). Milton's radical humanism during the years of the English Revolution, which I describe at greater length in Chapter Three, fuses a commitment to political education with the spiritual project of reformation in the hope of forming a godly republic.

For the most part, historians of education have emphasized the unoriginality of Milton's tract.[34] His debt to humanist theories of education is well documented. Claims for his contribution to educational theory are usually brought forth on the basis of his connection to the experiments of the universal reformers.[35] Although *Of Education* is an aggregate of earlier theory and of Milton's own experience as a teacher, comparisons to the educational reformers who followed Comenius have tended to produce little insight into Milton's larger educational and philosophical project.[36]

Miltonic education, I submit, extends far beyond the bounds laid out in the brief tractate. *Of Education* was originally published, anonymously and without a title page, as a pamphlet of eight pages (see YP 2:357). It was cast as a familiar letter to the Prussian educational reformer (and translator of Comenius) Samuel Hartlib, who then resided in London and exercised wide influence over a circle of intellectuals. Milton shared certain ideals with the universal reformers, though he did not believe that education should be compulsory for all. While he had an interest and possibly a hand in some of the schemes advocated by the Hartlib circle,[37] Milton differed with them fundamentally and irreconcilably by asserting the centrality of classical literature to education.[38] Although Milton maintained that the study of the classics ought to remain the central feature of the curriculum, he critiqued the idea of learning foreign languages for their own sake, since "language is but the instrument convaying to us things usefull to be known" (YP 2:369). The innovation that Milton introduced into the humanist curriculum stems from his belief in the central importance of practical knowledge, natural science, and acumen derived from experiment.

Like Francis Bacon, whom Milton seems to have been reading with great care and only occasional disagreement since his Cambridge days, Milton differentiated between intellectual and moral curiosity. For Bacon,

> it was not the pure knowledge of nature and universality, a knowledge by the light whereof man did give names unto other creatures in Paradise, as they were brought before him, according unto their proprieties, which gave the occasion to the fall; but it was the proud knowledge of good and evil, with an intent in man to give law unto himself and to depend no more on God's commandments, which was the form of the temptation.[39]

The "sensible and material things" that remain to be explored by inductive scientific inquiry promote comprehension of God's works and of "creatures themselves," which, relative to an understanding of God, can only produce "wonder, which is broken knowledge."[40] Unlike Milton's allegory of Truth as the dismembered body of Osiris—in which an encyclopedic ambition destined to fail reveals the fallible desire for omniscience—Bacon contends that it is an error that "men have abandoned universality." When knowledge "is in aphorisms and in observations, it is in growth; but when it is comprehended in exact methods, it may perchance be further polished and illustrate." For Bacon, method presents a sure means of "progression" and works against those mere "intellectualists" who "disdain to spell out and so by degrees to read in the volume of God's works."[41] Bacon wishes to partition theology from philosophy absolutely, which in effect secures a fully secular space of scientific inquiry by means of a theological rationale, where Milton sees the two ineluctably intermingling. Milton's difference on this point, then, resides in his skepticism about the end toward which the Baconian method would take humanity. Often Milton's doubts, rather than his supposed certainties, convey a more profound layer of thought in his educational philosophy.

However, Milton could, like Bacon, cite Saint Paul's sayings in order to establish the neutralizing boundary between natural and divine science. Referring to Colossians 2:8, Paul's injunction that the faithful not succumb to the allurement of "vain philosophy," Bacon in *The Advancement of Learning* urged: "let those places be rightly understood, and they do excellently set forth the true bounds and limitations whereby human knowledge is confined and circumscribed; and yet without any such contracting or coarctation [i.e., restriction], but that it may comprehend the universal nature of things."[42] Echoing precisely this sentiment in the concluding sentences on the curriculum in *Of Education,* Milton explains that students ought to await "the right season" before beginning poetic composition, "when they shall be fraught with an universall insight into things" (YP 2:406). We may note, in passing, the fine distinction between the outward reach of empiricist diction in Bacon's phrase "comprehend the universal nature" and the inward flow of spiritualist diction in Milton's phrase "universall insight into things." Yet Milton desires that students should work inductively from "a reall tincture of naturall knowledge," which he seeks to ensure by employing groups of visiting experts, making pedagogical use of "the helpfull experiences of Hunters, fowlers, Fishermen, Shepherds, Gardeners, *Apothecaries;* and in the other sciences, *Architects,* Engineers, Mariners, *Anatomists*" (YP 2:393–94). Like Bacon, Milton urges "beginning with Arts most easie, and those be such as are most obvious to the sence" (YP 2:374).

Whatever may be said for the influence of Ramistic logical structure—commencing with the universal and branching out to the particular—on Milton's thought, his curriculum begins with empirical observation and basic grammatical training and then moves toward poetry and metaphysics. In *Of Education,* after all, he describes the condition of humanity in a moral universe as requiring an ascent toward God through "orderly conning over the visible and inferior creature" (YP 2:368–69). Inferior though it might be, the mortal part occupies a primary role in the "orderly conning" by which "sensible things" transmit knowledge of God to the invisible soul. The study of nature, like the study of human nature made possible by reading history, shows the way to ethical behavior governed by moral intelligence. In effect, the structure of Bacon's argument in *The Advancement* also moves on both

tracks at once, as Ramistic analytic diagrams of the book show.[43] In Milton's
case, the centrality of faith, perhaps surprisingly, does not suggest introducing students to "the highest matters of *Theology* and Church History" (YP
2:399–400) until they have completed courses in Latin and Greek grammar,
arithmetic, geometry, agriculture, modern authors on cartography and geog-
raphy, natural philosophy, astronomy, trigonometry, architecture, military
engineering, navigation, Hebrew, the ancient poets, moral philosophy,
household management, Italian, and law. Pupils are then to advance to logic,
rhetoric, and finally poetic composition, which, being more "simple, sensuous and passionate" than other intellectual endeavors, reflects the students'
"universall insight into things."[44] Following Bacon, then, Milton condemned
the fact "that scholars in universities come too soon and too unripe to logic
and rhetoric; arts fitter for graduates than children and novices." And Milton
also shares Bacon's belief that

> these two arts [logic and rhetoric], rightly taken, are the gravest of sci-
> ences; being the arts of arts, the one for judgment, the other for orna-
> ment. . . . The wisdom of those arts, which is great and universal, is
> almost made contemptible, and is degenerate into childish sophistry
> and ridiculous affectation. And further, the untimely learning of them
> hath drawn on by consequence the superficial and unprofitable teaching
> and writing of them, as fitteth indeed to the capacity of children.[45]

Milton's borrowings from Bacon are characteristic, in that *Of Education* at
once shares the Baconian emphasis on empirical observation leading to universals, but also reclaims the universal as the proper realm of the religious
poet.[46] Milton would concur with Bacon's judgment that "it disposeth the
constitution of the mind not to be fixed or settled in the defects thereof, but
still to be capable and susceptible of growth and reformation."[47] But Milton
also folds logic into the study of rhetoric, thus diminishing in a typically
humanist way the independent value of demonstrable analytic thought.
Moreover, Milton centers his entire project on the ultimate value of poetry, a
value famously depreciated through its identification with the faculty of the
"imagination" by Bacon in the second book of *The Advancement.*

   Milton clearly learned a great deal from Bacon's more rigorous treatment of education. As a result, Milton extended the range of his educational
agenda considerably in the dozen or so years between the Seventh Prolusion
and *Of Education.* The expanded scientific breadth, and the increased spiritual depth, of the mature educational project owed at least as much to Milton's sustained engagement with the educational thinking of Bacon as it did

to his personal friendship with Samuel Hartlib and other Comenian reformers such as John Dury.

In addition to the oversimplifications inherent in taking a linear historical approach to Milton's educational theory, another apparent contradiction plagues the critical conversation about *Of Education*. This involves a supposed incongruity between the two overt definitions of education in the tract:

> The end then of learning is to repair the ruins of our first parents by regaining to know God aright, and out of that knowledge to love him, to imitate him, to be like him, as we may the neerest by possessing our souls of true vertue, which being united to the heavenly grace of faith makes up the highest perfection. (YP 2:366–67)

> I call therefore a compleate and generous Education that which fits a man to perform justly, skilfully and magnanimously all the offices both private and publicke of peace and war. (YP 2:377–79)

To an extent, the tract thus defines education in a Janus-faced way, in that each definition deals with an aspect of the soul. The distinction between the first (which describes the purpose or result of education) and the second (which is more utilitarian and prescriptive) arises from the outlook on human action that each assumes. In the first definition, the Fall has brought about the decay of human faculties and consequently the ruination of learning. The intention of pedagogy, like the drive to reassemble the torn body of Truth, must be recuperative and memorial: "to repair the ruins of our first parents." Milton accentuates the belatedness and loss that haunt the effort to "repair" by "regaining." The dilapidated edifice of knowledge makes learning's "end" asymmetrical to the wish it articulates. Even as human beings may learn "to love" God "by possessing our souls of true vertue," Milton signals the circumscription of our ability "to imitate him." The end of learning is to be its limitation as well as its aim. If we wish "to be like" God, we ultimately cannot, though we may come "the neerest" to answering this longing by exercising our ethical intelligence, our virtue. We may say, with Levinas, that Milton here gives voice to the notion that, in the wake of the Fall, "The foundation of consciousness is justice and not the reverse."[48] In other words, we are not just because we are conscious human beings, but rather we express our consciousness through just action. Although the human will must be "united to the heavenly grace of faith" to make up "the highest perfection," this union ultimately cannot be an act of human will alone, and so our best resemblance is attained only through ethical action, by "possessing our souls of true vertue."

The limitation that inheres in our capacity to imitate God, then, opens the way for the second, more ideological definition of pedagogy, which has been called "a New Model Education."[49] In fact, the limitation that resulted from the Fall was, according to Milton, what necessitated the initial formation of political society.[50] If the goal in this second definition is unabashedly ideological, this is because Milton takes for granted that the fragmentation of human consciousness caused by the Fall initiated the aggressive ideologies that have riven human society.[51] This is to take "vertue" in another direction, in which a classical republican ideal of civic humanism takes precedence in the "offices" of the citizen. The greatness of the soul, or magnanimity, emerges from the social dimension of duty, "all the offices both private and publicke of peace and war."

How does the concept of pedagogy that emphasizes imitation and love of God overlap with this idea of the citizen? The two definitions, religious and political, converge in Milton's conception of liberty. No one, according to Milton in *The Tenure of Kings and Magistrates* (1649, 1650), "can be so stupid to deny that all men naturally were borne free, being the image and resemblance of God himself" (YP 3:198). Projecting a condition which, according to Quentin Skinner, "must be recognized as a God-given birthright, and hence a set of natural rights," this theory of the state of nature as a condition affording "primitive liberties" yields an idea of government designed to protect and uphold freedoms.[52] Since this notion of Christian liberty forms the principle around which society organizes itself, education therefore allows for intergenerational continuity of the political order. As John Rawls puts the matter with respect to a pluralistic secular democracy, "If citizens of a well-ordered society are to recognize one another as free and equal, basic institutions must educate them to this conception of themselves, as well as publicly exhibit and encourage this ideal of political justice." Although Milton restricts considerably the portion of the populace to be educated, I would argue that Rawls carries Milton's point to its logical extreme when he describes "the public role of educating citizens to a conception of themselves as free and equal."[53]

That Milton's educational views helped shape his poetry has long been accepted, but the ideological force of his moral didacticism has received less focused attention—an imbalance that I have aimed to redress in the chapters that follow. Readers of this book are in all likelihood familiar with the thesis of Stanley Fish's *Surprised by Sin,* that *Paradise Lost* is "a poem concerned with the self-education of its readers."[54] Drawing attention to the complexities of narrative and syntax as they relate to what he perceives as the poem's larger conceptual design, Fish persuasively describes certain local features of the epic in terms of didactic effects. All too often, however, he deductively imposes this idea of the poem's intentional design in order to proclaim the irrelevance of political interpretation.

In a groundbreaking essay, Mary Ann Radzinowicz dispelled the notion that seeing the epic as "paideutic" necessitates reducing the fullness of the poetic texture to a series of quickly unsurprising theological traps. "*Paradise Lost* constitutes a course in political education," Radzinowicz writes, "and political education serves in Milton's epic purposes that a political program might play in another kind of work," such as a prose tract. This is an especially astute remark given the period in which Milton began regularly to compose the epic. As we shall see in Chapter Three, Milton readily displaced the specific institutional recommendations of his later republican prose onto a more broadly construed ethical imperative that he thought would finally salvage the mission of the godly and meritorious few. In this sense, then, Radzinowicz must be right when she says that Milton sets problems "in the way a Socratic educator sets problems, the occasions for debate, and instances for correction." Modifying the more oppressive and totalizing view of "correction" by the epic narrator, Radziowicz notes that "Milton did not . . . calculate a magnificent plot to trap his readers into such misinterpretations and corrections as would lead them to salvation. His political paideia is overt and historical; it results in progressive enlightenment as to the very slowness and difficulty involved in human arrangements within fallen history." Milton's conception of the Bible corroborates this political reading of the epic, even as the concept of "progressive enlightenment" relays the proper skepticism about the experiential relationship between revelation and human political behavior. Milton's pedagogical efforts, while "overt and historical," are not simple or institution-bound: "Milton's method," she goes on to say, "is not that of the propagandist for this or that institution or program; his method is that of the teacher."[55] Even more than in the prose, Milton's poetry advocates the strenuous activity of right reason as the sine qua non of human regeneration, while at the same time emphasizing above all else the ethical attitude made manifest in self-sacrifice as the best possible means to achieve the public good. Barbara Lewalski has lucidly restated this argument, paying special attention to how Miltonic education affects the general political project of the epic:

> Milton's epic is preeminently a poem about knowing and choosing—for the Miltonic Bard, for his characters, and for the reader. It foregrounds education, a life-long concern of Milton's, and of special importance to him after the Restoration as a means to help produce discerning, virtuous,

liberty-loving human beings and citizens. . . . The Miltonic Bard educates his readers by exercising them in rigorous judgment, imaginative apprehension, and choice. By setting his poem in relation to other great epics and works in other genres, he involves readers in a critique of the values associated with those other heroes and genres, as well as with issues of contemporary politics and theology.[56]

My analysis of *Paradise Lost* in Chapter Four will not presume that Milton's intentions for his epic neutralize the effects of the text or definitively limit the range of its signification. Stanley Fish's presumption of "the" reader "in" *Paradise Lost* unhappily and artificially reduces Milton's possible, but also his historical, audience. Before I quarrel with Fish, let me say that I have myself been influenced by his work, and that I see the book's central thesis as a major landmark in the field of Milton criticism. But accepting the intuition at the heart of the thesis does not mean conceding to the premises of the argument. There are two key problems with the contention that "Milton's method is to re-create in the mind of *the* reader (which is, finally, the poem's scene) the drama of the Fall, to make *him* fall again exactly as Adam did and with Adam's troubled clarity, that is to say, 'not deceived.'"[57] First, Fish's assumptions tend toward an ahistorical conception of reading on which the "reader response" model, as much as the New Critical method it builds upon, finally depends.[58] We are told that "the" reader will be the same throughout time, a notion whose pernicious and exclusive ideology is immediately visible in the attribution of gender to that reader. This might be excused if the conception of education at work in Fish's reading were more historically informed. Fish argues that Milton writes in such a way as "to create problems or puzzles which the reader feels obliged to solve since he wishes, naturally, to retain a sense of control over the reading experience." Instead, readers repeatedly fall prey to "Milton's programme of reader harassment." The authoritarian pedagogue time and again countermands us, and we are "accused, taunted by an imperious voice." "The reader," in the manner of a severely punitive catechism, "is continually surprised by sin and in shame," but one wonders how long this "surprise" is supposed to last: if we feel reprimanded by the narrator's interpolated commentary upon the action in the first few books, which one of us will not learn to expect it as the narrative continues? Whether or not "Milton secures a positive response to the figure of God," it does not seem possible that, in a poem ever alert to the multiplicity of human experience and piously committed to faith in the absence of iconic resemblances, Milton should engender this effect "by creating a psychological (emotional) need for the authority he represents." The

potentially ambiguous antecedent of that last "he," given that it is not capi-
talized, suggests that Milton serves to enlarge chiefly his own authority, just
as his God does, and one cannot help but think in the light of Fish's preface
to the second edition of *Surprised by Sin,* Fish's own authority as a guide
through the poem.[59]

If Milton's poetry suffers a grave diminution from the effort to univer-
salize the experience of a single, idealized reader, then it stands to reason that
one important corrective to this tendency would be to enlarge the sense of
the responses of actual historical readers.[60] The second objection I have to
Fish's thesis is that, for all the emphasis he places upon education, the concept remains relatively inexplicit and uninformed by historical research into
the history of education in the period. In the important and provocative
study *Milton Unbound,* John Rumrich asks the critical question: "Does this
punitive and tedious didacticism actually have a place in Milton's own historical context?" Both my interpretation of Milton's writings and the
research I have conducted lead me to answer resoundingly no. Rumrich is
surely right to challenge Fish on this point, even if he does not quite go so far
as to refute directly the educational paradigm that Fish presumes for Milton.
Theoretically, I share Rumrich's general conception of Milton "as perhaps the
West's most challenging, uniquely integrated, philosophical poet." Although
I differ with Rumrich to some substantial degree in my concept of what it
means to call Milton a "philosophical poet," I also find myself in agreement
with his emphasis upon indeterminacy in *Paradise Lost.* Milton presumed the
rationality of his theodicy, which accords with his depiction of the unrecoverable origin of Truth. As *Areopagitica* demonstrates, the provisional nature
of knowledge in the postlapsarian world requires that the search for truth be
perpetual and progressive. This ideal, as Rumrich says, "may be understood
as a principle of dynamic coherence, one that allowed Milton room to make
theodical art out of his uncertainties."[61]

What we gain by seeing Milton in this way is a new set of problems, a
new vantage from which to challenge our own epistemological and ideological positions. This book has grown out of a long-standing effort to grasp the
conditions within which Milton conceived of, and rigorously adhered to, the
philosophical paradoxes of learning. As a process without end, education
paradoxically must strive to articulate its aims, even as it surrenders certainties to a contingent awareness of truth. Thus human consciousness must
learn to comprehend itself, all the while unsettled by the awareness that with
it consciousness does not end. As a result, the local and particular, instead of
being eradicated in favor of the universal, are restored to a greater dignity. In
this connection, Adorno's axiom on the morality of thinking offers a useful

point of departure: "Knowledge can only widen horizons by abiding so insistently with the particular that its isolation is dispelled. This admittedly presupposes a relation to the general, though not one of subsumption, but rather almost the reverse."[62] It is that "almost"—qualifying and even challenging as it does the effort absolutely to reverse deterministic relations between universals and particulars—which allows Adorno's philosophical stance to illuminate a pattern intrinsic to Milton's theology. As far as modern philosophical speculation will help to place Milton's thought in sharper definition, Wittgenstein, musing on the problem of definition itself, offers a useful insight into one of the recurrent themes of Milton's educational project: "The man who is philosophically puzzled sees a law in the way a word is used, and, trying to apply this law consistently, comes up against cases where it leads to paradoxical results."[63] Wittgenstein here identifies as puzzlement a confusion that stems from the presupposition of a systematic linguistic approach to creating meaning. Trying to articulate a consistent approach to the acquisition of knowledge led Milton to similarly paradoxical results early on. Milton's writings, starting with the divorce tracts, show that he understood this paradox as a condition of interpretation. Rhetorically, they refute systematic approaches to education in order to thwart the iconological dependence of intransigent minds upon the false security of custom. Over time, and in this way, Milton expresses a profoundly humane attitude toward the educable spirit in human beings, such that he seeks "to try, and teach the erring soul" according to the model of Jesus in *Paradise Regained:* "By winning words to conquer willing hearts, / And make persuasion do the work of fear" (1.222–24).

This book is organized as a series of chapters that explore Milton's developing attitudes toward education in his works from the onset of the Civil War to the completion of *Paradise Lost.* The four chapters stand in a structural relation to one another that goes beyond the chronology of the works examined, though the sequence of chapters does make some concession to chronological order in the interest of telling the story historically. In order, the chapters all address different aspects of the attitude Milton cultivates in himself and in his readers, an attitude toward history, authority, and tradition. The first chapter further critiques the reader response paradigm of interpretation through an analysis of Milton's own reading habits. This historical materialist approach to reading considers how Milton forms his identity as a writer through the material practices of reading and teaching. The next chapter focuses on appropriation: how Milton uses evidence to establish authority in the divorce tracts. There, Milton investigates and exposes the paradoxes of his historicism, attaining authority by reforming pedagogy as a metaphor for the vexed relation to the Law. In the third chapter, I set out to clarify Milton's idea of humanism by returning to the classical and early modern sources of his conception. This leads to a discussion of how he characterizes himself and his writing by creating an ethical and political persona, the subject in history as a speaker. Milton seeks, throughout the revolutionary period, to teach the nation through his own exemplary character and virtue, to acculturate the citizen of "the Commonwealth of learning," and to train the populace to grasp the significance of the emergent civic structures (YP 2:529). I have endeavored in the first three chapters to lay the contextual foundation for a new interpretation of the pedagogy of *Paradise Lost*. The fourth and final chapter addresses the epic as an act of creative synthesis, in which Milton interrogates the origins of our situation in history through a refashioning of the remnants of historical memory, political subjectivity, and sacred truth. In *Paradise Lost,* Milton teaches that liberty, or bondage to servitude, is an inward condition. Miltonic education reaches its most profound challenge in the discovery of what I term "inward archives." Understanding the situation in which we find ourselves means comprehending the myths of origin against which, and through which, we struggle in time.

Chapter One

Repairing the Ruins: Milton as Reader and Educator

Milton, like other teachers of literature, understood that education is essentially communal—not something that happens in isolation, but rather at the intersection of several minds, a collective endeavor. As Ben Jonson said, "hee that was onely taught by himselfe, had a foole to his Master."[1] Reading, too, involves not only a single reader, but a community, especially when it serves as the primary medium of an educational process, and is therefore like education at once expressive and constitutive of community. While recent formulations of this concept—such as Stanley Fish's "interpretive communities" and Roger Chartier's "communities of readers"[2]—will be of some use here, my present aim derives equally from an ancient concern of which Fish and Chartier are no doubt aware. Early in Plato's *Symposium,* when Eryximachus proposes the subject of the ensuing conversation, he quotes the tag "mine is not the tale" from Euripides' Melanippe to signal that his subject does not originate with himself but instead with his friend and fellow diner Phaedrus, suggesting that the idea, like the locution, originates with neither of them but nonetheless "belongs" to a far broader group than is, strictly speaking, in attendance at the feast.[3] The allusion to Euripides, by placing the speaker and his meaning at one more textual remove, dramatizes the sharing of texts as a means of encompassing hearers and readers alike in the formation of a community.

The largest question I take up in this chapter also begins with Euripides in order to ask, What do Milton's practices as a reader and his conception of the power of books tell us about his idea of education? In seeking answers to this question, I will argue for the importance of thinking about how Milton read specific texts and what material evidence we have of these encounters. The nature of this evidence and the processes it records relate to broader interpretive issues with far-reaching implications for comprehending Milton's thought, such as how he perceived the relative legitimacy of textual interpretations, the utility of such interpretations, and the formative contexts in which interpretations are valorized or debunked. While he holds the validity of an interpretation to be in the first instance absolute, its value ultimately depends upon its particular relation to other interpretations. Moreover, I hope these considerations will shed some new light on Milton's evolving conception of all texts, including his own, as heuristic, not ostensive—that is, leading to the discovery of an interpretation, not providing it.[4] By tracing the hermeneutic concept available and, indeed, advertised in Milton's reading practices, we can further refine our appreciation of fundamental epistemological positions taken and in some respects modified by Milton. I shall discuss how, by first considering Milton's annotating practices, we modern readers can deepen our understanding of what Milton says about books in *Areopagitica,* and what such theories might, in practice, look like according to Milton himself.

At some time in 1634, perhaps between the composition of *A Maske* and its performance, Milton bought his copy of Paulus Stephanus's edition of Euripides, as his autograph inscription on the flyleaf indicates.[5] It is clear from the different states of Milton's marginal handwriting that he read both quarto volumes in their entirety at least twice, once before and once after his return from Italy in 1639, before the onset of total blindness in 1652.[6] Even critics such as Samuel Johnson who have examined Milton's annotations have occasionally overlooked the care with which Milton read the books. "The margin," Johnson remarks in the *Life of Milton,* "is sometimes noted; but I have found nothing remarkable."[7] What is most remarkable about the attentiveness of Milton's reading, however, only becomes clear when his annotations are compared with the marginalia of other, later owners of the volumes. Notes in three other hands accompany the two stages of Milton's marginalia. The identity of one of the annotators is certain: Joshua Barnes, editor of Euripides in 1694 and fellow of Emmanuel College, Cambridge, who absorbed some of Milton's conjectures and emendations into his edition (without attributing them) and thereby introduced Milton into the historical collation apparatuses of modern critical editions. About a dozen of his proposed emendations remain accepted readings to this day in modern editions.[8]

The history of Milton's intervention into the mainstream of modern classical editing demonstrates the role of the material book in the transmission of the text and in what William Sherman refers to as "the intertextual and interpersonal quality of Renaissance reading."[9] Although Milton's hand appears to be the earliest to have marked the exemplum, he may not have been its first owner and, moreover, he likely knew himself not to be last. Marginal notation ranges, as Anthony Grafton has shown, from the cryptically idiosyncratic to the overtly discursive, a continuum that itself discloses a historical conception of the Renaissance book as material and intellectual property that differs radically from our own.[10] This historical conception of the book in turn relays an idea of authorship quite distinct from modern notions, evincing what Stephen Orgel has called "the legible incorporation of the work of reading into the text of the book."[11] Milton's Euripides marginalia present especially rich evidence of the habits of a seventeenth-century reader because they not only indicate his idea of and interaction with a classical text, but also imply his projection of a future audience for his notes.

The students Milton was tutoring when he reread the Euripides volumes comprise one such audience. Following his return from Italy, most likely "in the autumn of 1639 or early in 1640," Milton began to spend part of each day teaching his young nephews—John and Edward Phillips, then ages eight and nine.[12] From the start, the younger boy probably lived with his uncle, but later in 1640, when Milton found a larger house in Aldersgate, both lived with him, their education becoming a full-time responsibility. In April 1643, when it had become clear that Milton's first wife, Mary Powell, would not be returning any time soon from her "vacation" to her parents' home in Forest Hill (near Oxford), Milton took in more pupils.[13] In the spring or summer of 1645, Milton began searching for a larger house, and by September or October he had moved into a residence in the Barbican, where, as Edward Phillips recalled, "probably he might have some prospect of putting in Practice his Academical Institution, according to the Model laid down in his Sheet of Education."[14] Among the students Milton probably tutored were Cyriack Skinner, John Overton, Thomas Gardiner, Richard Barry, Richard Heath, Jeremy Picard, William Brownlow, and, later, Thomas Ellwood.[15] In addition, "tho the accession of Scholars was not great," he may have had other students whose names have been lost, since Phillips mentions Milton's "having application made to him by several Gentlemen of his acquaintance for the Education of their Sons, as understanding haply the Progress he had infixed by his first undertakings of that nature."[16] By August of 1647, however, Milton had given up the large house in the Barbican and moved to a smaller residence in High Holborn. The death of his own father and of Richard Powell, his father-in-law, had filled the house with relatives and in effect brought to an end what Samuel Hartlib was by then calling "Mr. Milton's Academy."[17]

In the portion of the biography devoted to his years at the Miltons', Edward Phillips memorialized his uncle's "excellent judgment and way of

Teaching" and, by extension, the reading practices involved. "By Teaching," Phillips says, "he in some measure increased his own knowledge, having the reading of all these Authors as it were by Proxy."[18] Milton would of course have deliberately formulated his curriculum based upon his own vast reading experience, but we can infer from Phillips's description that Milton was rereading "by Proxy" while instructing his pupils. Phillips depicts a pedagogical environment in which students, seated together in Milton's home, take turns reading from his annotated books, sharing their translations aloud, and participating in a conversation with and about the text that involves Milton's written memoranda and, certainly, his oral instruction. Phillips's account, therefore, suggests that Milton's books became communal property while he tutored his pupils and that he might have anticipated this when he wrote in them during this period.

Leaving aside for the moment assessments of the validity of Milton's readings of Euripides, of his metrical and philological proposals for the improvement of his Greek text, I want first to consider the kinds of comment Milton made and, more importantly, why he made them.[19] Throughout the two volumes, Milton writes out full, discursive comments in Latin where he makes his presence overt and thus the issue of his identity as reader an integral part of the comment. In his pre-1638 hand, he questions his own authority as he alters a word and thereby calls for a plainer sense to line 1145 of *Helena,* "The sense will be plainer, unless I am mistaken" (*ET* 2:584). Similarly, in another pre-1638 annotation, Milton wonders whether proper usage will allow him to change the position of a word in the Latin translation to clarify its syntax: "If linguistic usage permit, I would transfer *pedens*" (*ET* 1:525). These more tentative early comments show the young scholar self-consciously working through the volumes and commenting, most likely to himself, albeit with the knowledge that someone in the future may be reading critically over his shoulder and evaluating his judgments with superior knowledge.

In the earlier marginalia, Milton fashions his voice anxiously in relation to tradition, interjecting *puto ego* ("I think" or "I consider") primarily as a means of differentiating his interpretation from the printed scholia included with his edition. When he corrects the Greek text in his pre-1638 hand, Milton puts on display the same categories of discursive style that he will employ in future evaluations of his reading text, though he makes his own presence a less definite rhetorical feature of his statement: "This way the sense is plainer and more elegant" (*ET* 2:486). After 1638, he introduces one emendation by claiming, "I consider this to be more correct and elegant" (*ET* 1:484). The comment, in Milton's post-1638 hand, interjects the first person singular into the note with *puto* ("I consider"), rather than simply emending the text, as he does in so many other places. He systematically introduces *rectius* and *elegantus,* more correct and elegant, as if they were analytic categories emerging from his own interpretation, bearing witness to his critical judgment.

Positing an authorial identity in judgments announced by the post-1638 hand becomes a repetitive act of self-mythologizing analogous to the formulaic incantation of *cogito,* pronouncing "I think (this)" as a way to proclaim "I was capable of thinking (this)." The implication of authorial possessiveness surrounds the later notes, affecting their mode of address, as when a note marks ownership of an ingenious but suspect onomatopoetic etymology: "I think the word [i.e., διεκαναξε (*diekanaxe*)] comes from the sound of drinking wine" (*ET* 2:440). When he thinks a word should be omitted, Milton writes *ejiciendum puto* and explains his rationale instead of simply crossing out the word in his Greek text (*ET* 2:685). When he adds to a text, a rhetorical pause announces the weight of authority he wishes to grant his own marginalia: "The verse demands it, and I think it should be supplied" (*ET* 2:716).

Marginal annotations are not ordinarily read for their tone, but I would argue that this is because of modern assumptions about the place of marginalia in a volume that "belongs" to the "private" library of an "individual" collector, assumptions that have little to do with the actual reading practices of the sixteenth and seventeenth centuries. Applying the logic of modern consumption to a book owned by Milton implies a misconception about early modern libraries and a commensurate underestimation of marginalia's communal utility. Readers, it is sometimes assumed, tend to address only themselves in the margins of their books—by composing *aides-mémoire* in the form of topic heading and summary—though early modern (like many modern) readers were, of course, often adversarial in their annotating practices, disputing with their texts as if with the authors themselves and registering that active engagement in lively marks and comments.[20] While both verbal and nonverbal notation indicate the character of a reader's interaction with a text, the tone of verbal comments, as in Milton's Euripides marginalia, discloses the construction of a mode of address and thus an audience, which in turn proposes a conception of the material book as a communicative medium in excess of its printed text. Thus the book becomes the hub of a set of perceived relationships among readers extending beyond the horizon of a specific act of textual interpretation.

If these notes convey something of the tone of Milton's address, they nevertheless leave ambiguous the identity of his audience. Milton could, after all, be addressing himself to a time in which he would return to the volumes an older and more experienced reader. Conversely, he may be imagining a conversation with a future owner of his books. Again, the rhetoric of a certain kind of inclusion—where the information provided is, strictly speaking, unnecessary—hints at Milton's imagination of a broader audience for his conversation with the text. He begins an annotation to the Latin translation of *Suppliants,* line 530, "That verse should rather be rendered thus," instead of simply writing his correction alongside the faulty verse and crossing it out (*ET* 2:30). To whom does he write this?

Other kinds of comments in the post-1638 hand suggest another conception of the margins of texts: not merely a space for correction (even of self), they become a space of pedagogy. Milton's marginalia offer exemplary intellectual positions and thus demonstrate the processes at work in reflecting upon a text. Placing readers of his volumes at one remove from the text itself, Milton's comments and corrections attune readers to a debate about the text in order to prompt imitation. If the annotations reconfigure the margin of the book as a pedagogical space, they do so by defamiliarizing the intuitive recognition of meaning and thus making explicit the intellectual processes involved in the act of interpretation. In this way, Milton's marginalia provide a model for what he calls "a well continu'd and judicious conversing among pure Authors," in which "conversing" means not only "discussing," but also (from the Latin *conversari*) "associating" or living among (YP 2:373; cf. 1:883).

The correction to *Hippolytus,* line 998, shows Milton marking up his book with novice readers of the Greek in mind. Here, again in the post-1638 hand, Milton's annotation takes the form of a repeated Latin translation of his Greek correction to the Greek text (see figure 1). In this passage, Hippolytus—defending himself against his father's charge that he raped his stepmother, Phaedra—invokes his friends as character witnesses. Hippolytus assures his father that his friends are not the kind of people who seek to do wrong, that they are so blameless as to think it shameful merely to "report" shameful things or to perform wicked services in exchange for friendship. Milton changes the word *apaggellein* ("to report" shame) to *epaggellein* ("to order to do" shameful things). Changing the vague hint of evil gossip to a command to do evil, Milton renders the damning behavior in a crisper idiom, one that the editorial tradition has subsequently accepted.[21] By accommodating the sense of the word—adapting the diction to a more decorous relation with the play's overall design—Milton draws a more profound moral distinction in order to deepen the pathos of Hippolytus's response to the accusation.[22] Since Hippolytus is Artemis's "best friend among men" (l.1332), it is crucial to the tragic structure that Theseus makes the whole question of guilt hinge on the evidence of friendship when he laments, "If there were / some token now, some mark to make the division / clear between friend and friend, the true and the false" (ll.924–26).[23] As it happens, Theseus is as bad at interpreting moral character as he is at interpreting Phaedra's letter, since he has no recourse to the context Hippolytus, using Theseus' own criterion of friendship, tries to supply. Milton's emendation properly focuses the dramatic climax of the play on Hippolytus's severe, moralizing rectitude in contrast with the indecisive evidence of friendship. Thus Hippolytus tries to contradict "the dead, surest of witnesses [*marturos*]" (l.972) with a vain wish: "If I had one more witness [*martus*] to my character / if I were tried when *she* still saw the light, / deeds would have helped you as you scanned your friends / to know the true from the false" (ll.1022–25). Unfortunately, as the Nurse says, "words are wounds" (l.342), precisely because words have the power to indict Hippolytus and therefore to set in motion "deeds," as in his father's curse, which leads to his demise. The indeterminacy of verbal evidence—both the oral testimony of friends and the written accusation of the dead Phaedra—represents the epistemological crisis at issue in the play. The distinction emphasized by Milton's emendation is crucial: by focusing our attention on the force of indeterminate words to cause determinate action, as in a military order or a divine annunciation, Milton elucidates the tragic irony at the heart of Hippolytus's futile response to his father, since it is in fact his austere behavior that has convicted him in the minds of his accusers.[24]

Given that Milton was such a skilled reader of the ancient Greek as to be able to correct diction based on interpretation of context, idiom, and (sometimes) conventions of versification, one wonders why he was rereading the Latin translation at all, much less repeating a correction twice. In his early grappling with the original, he, like any Renaissance student of classical Greek, might well have relied upon the Latin from time to time as an aid to comprehension. Or he may have imagined that some later owner of the book would be helped along in this way. The repetition of his Latin translation *neque inhonesta petere* ("not to solicit shameful deeds") strongly encourages the student-reader to return to the Greek original and serves to illustrate the thrust of the emendation for the novice reading the Latin only as well as for the intermediate reader working primarily through the Greek at the top of the page. (The different functions of printed marginal glosses and paraphrastic footnotes in, say, Norton editions provide a modern analogue.) In all likelihood, as I mentioned earlier, he used these very books when working as a schoolmaster, particularly in the education of his nephews, whom he taught from his home with the volumes in his personal library.

The visual appearance of another set of corrections confirms the intrusive, meticulous, even obsessive, nature of Milton's reading practices in a way that cannot be communicated by mere transcription, as the modern edition of Milton's *Works* attempts to do (CM 18:309). When Milton redistributes lines 754–771 of *Suppliants* (see figure 2), he modifies the text by mechanically crossing out and rewriting the speech prefixes, with the explanation that "these speeches seem rather between Adrastus and the messenger speaking for the chorus, and so should be assigned to Adrastus" (*ET* 2:42). Likewise, when he redistributes lines in *Hippolytus* (ll.353ff.), Milton corrects the speech prefixes in both the Greek and the Latin texts (*ET* 1:527). These corrections, involving the deliberate modification of the reading text rather than simply altering the sense retrospectively by comment, seek to provide a continuity of reading experience while introducing editorial material, so that a person reading this book for the first time could incorporate the emendations into the primary experience of the text without pausing to read the editorial rationalization for them. At the same time, Milton's marginalia produce a de facto edition, illustrating the principles of exegesis by applying them for students.

Furthermore, the inclusion of corrections that do not alter the Greek text—that is, Latin corrections to the Latin translation—appears in this context to have been motivated by practical pedagogy, especially when the corrections carry on at some length. In this vein, Milton's annotations include a new translation of the opening five lines of *Rhesus* (*ET* 2:232). Milton excises the circumlocutions, removes the repetitive and verbose poeticisms, from the printed Latin translation, writing out a sparer literal crib that would act as a help to students interpreting the Greek.

Preparation for teaching was the most likely cause for another variety of marginalia, the cross-referencing note, which proves surprisingly scarce in the extant marginalia given the extent of Milton's reading. In the Euripides volumes, the only specific edition to which Milton alludes—he mentions Homer, but not an *edition* of Homer—is Scaliger's Manilius, a pioneering work of textual criticism (*ET* 2:29).[25] Another book that survives from Milton's library, the copy of Aratus with his marginal annotation, includes in his post-1638 handwriting the comparison, "Thus Lucretius II, 991, says we are all born of heavenly seed, and all have the same father, etc."[26] The note provides two forms of interesting evidence. First, given that, as Kelley and Atkins suggest, this may have been one of the notes that "were a part of preparation for teaching his nephews," the intertextual reference implies the similarity of Milton's practical curriculum to the theoretical proposal in *Of Education,* where he mentions the importance of "those Poets which are now counted most hard," including among others "*Aratus* . . . and in Latin *Lucretius*" (YP 2:394–95).[27] This account is further corroborated by the testimony of Edward Phillips, who includes both Aratus and Lucretius when he lists some of "the many Authors both of the Latin and Greek" that Milton had his nephews study.[28] Milton's cross-referencing in this instance seems particularly relevant to his teaching, since it links passages from two works he introduces together into the curriculum in *Of Education*. The second point to make about the note is that—like Phillips's description of Milton reading "by Proxy" when his students read or translated aloud—it helps flesh out our picture of the pedagogic environment in Milton's house, especially since Phillips mentions what must have been the edition of Aratus owned and annotated by Milton.[29] In other words, the reference may have been meant to inspire imitation. Milton handwrote the reference to Lucretius but did not mention the place where St. Paul adopts the thought from Aratus in his address to the Areopagus (Acts 17:28), perhaps thinking this too obvious for mention, perhaps wanting his students to remember the appropriation on their own.[30]

Euripides was one of Milton's most abiding literary interests, next to Homer and Ovid, and remained constantly in his thoughts, as the poet's daughter Deborah reported, even after his blindness prevented him from reading at his leisure.[31] As was shown above, Milton reread the volumes in their entirety in exactly the same years during which he acted as a schoolmaster to several young pupils. What effect did reading Euripides at that time have on Milton's writings, and what evidence can his marginalia provide of his conception of the efficacy and potency of books? Milton had rather self-consciously begun to figure his relations with a readership in explicitly pedagogical terms in the antiprelatical tracts published for "the honour and instruction of my country" in the early 1640s (YP 1:810). Milton's idea of the power of a book emerges most fully, however, when he actively and publicly responds to the Licensing Act of 1643. On 14 June 1643, the Long Parliament had issued an Order for Printing that mandated prepublication inspection by Presbyterian censors, an effort to stem the massive influx of dissent (both royalist and sectarian) that was adversely affecting parliamentary control in the capital and drawing momentum away from parliament's war effort. This largely ineffective Order merged with the Stationer's Company bid to secure rights of monopoly over the publishing trade.[32] *Areopagitica* represents Milton's response to the threat of constricted circulation impending as a result of the Order. How, then, did Milton conceive of readers responding to a book, whether of poetry or prose, "something so written to aftertimes, as they should not willingly let it die" (YP 1:810)?

We know from *The Reason of Church Government* that Milton thought of his own work and Euripidean drama as analogously "doctrinal and exemplary to a Nation," both as destined for an immediate occasion and as resurrected in posterity (YP 1:815). Since "the Apostle Paul himself thought it not unworthy to insert a verse of Euripides into the text of Holy Scripture, 1 Cor. XV.33,"[33] the Apostle's citation of the verse affirms the didactic potential of Milton's foray into the dramatic genre of the play from which it was quoted. In fact, as Milton says in the *Areopagitica,* Paul "thought it no defilement to insert into holy Scripture the sentences of three Greek Poets, and one of them a Tragedian," whereas "*Julian* the Apostat, and suttlest enemy to our faith, made a decree forbidding Christians the study of heathen learning" (YP 2:508). In *De Doctrina Christiana,* Milton—like Paul in the passage Milton was so fond of—cites Euripides as he discusses the nature of the soul and its fate after the death of the body: "Euripides in the *Suppliants* has given a far better interpretation of this passage than my opponents, without knowing it" (YP 6:407). The identical thought, expressed by the pagan tragedian, can resurrect a vital passage of Scripture through exact interpretation.[34]

If these allusions to Euripides reveal the way in which the tragedies could become "doctrinal," the quotation from *Suppliants* on the title page of *Areopagitica* indicates how they could become "exemplary." To put it in the language of the tract, where the allusions in the preface to *Samson Agonistes* and in *De Doctrina Christiana* affirm the activities of the "wayfaring Christian" reader, the epigraph seeks to energize the "warfaring" one. Theseus's retort to the Theban herald—who presumes that Athens, like Thebes, is under the rule of a *tyrannos* (l.399)—was glossed as a "vituperation of tyranny and praise of democracy" in one sixteenth-century edition:[35]

> This is true Liberty when free born men
> Having to advise the public may speak free,
> Which he who can, and will, deserv's high praise,
> Who neither can, nor will, may hold his peace;
> What can be juster in a State then this?
>   (*Areopagitica* [1644], title page; orig. in italics)

Milton himself marked the speech—though not precisely these lines—in his own copy. In his English version he effects a subtle, but interested, appropriation of Euripides, making the verses more didactic than in the original by changing the mood of the verbs from the Greek's more straightforward present active indicative to an auxiliary mood of permission, obligation, and condition. In effect, he shifts the mood from "does" to "can, and will." Milton intensifies the sense of civic duty by rendering the "Liberty" expressed by Theseus's hypothetical citizen—who "wishes" (*thelei*) to advise the city— as the native responsibility incurred by "free born men / Having to advise the public."[36]

Voluntary participation, intrinsic to any civic debate, moves to the center of Milton's translation, which accentuates the choice to speak out as a conscious act of reason. In the exordium that follows, proof of character, inhering in the speaker as in the audience, assures "civill liberty" through the practice of civic duty: primarily by means of "the strong assistance of God our deliverer"; secondarily through the exemplary leadership of parliament and its "indefatigable virtues"; and ultimately in the citizens who, "mov'd inwardly in their mindes," speak "a certain testimony" as a challenge to the "tyranny and superstition grounded in our principles" (YP 2:486–87).[37] Milton allies the ability to speak freely (the "can" of his epigraph), with the conscientious submission of "testimony" that becomes the subject of debate within public assembly (the "will" of his epigraph). When citizens pursue ethical action through political exigency "in Gods esteeme," "when complaints are freely heard, deeply consider'd, and speedily reform'd, then is the utmost bound of civill liberty attain'd" (YP 2:487). The excellence of parliament, the exordium repeatedly points out, is commensurate with its acknowledgment of and obedience to "the voice of reason from what quarter soever it be heard speaking": "there can no greater testimony appear" (YP 2:490). As Melanchthon said in his oration at Luther's funeral, God imparts his blessings upon humankind by calling "forth prophets, the Apostles, teachers and ministers. . . . Nor does He call only those to that warfare who have customary power, but often He wages war against them through teachers chosen from other ranks."[38] The "voice of reason" testifies willingly, is heard freely, and wars against papist "tyranny and superstition."

Milton's argument in *Areopagitica* centers on his conception of reason, which over the course of the tract undergoes something of a transformation, not unlike Truth, "untill she be adjur'd into her own likenes" at "her Masters second comming" (YP 2:543, 563). Books (such as Milton's own copy of Euripides) are instruments through which reason exercises itself in the educational process, when reason recognizes its likeness in a book: "as good almost kill a Man as kill a good Book; who kills a man kills a reasonable creature, Gods Image; but hee who destroyes a good Booke, kills reason it selfe, kills the Image of God, as it were in the eye" (YP 2:492). Just as the "eye" is the organ that perceives the "Image," the "reasonable creature" comprehends "reason it selfe," the analogy or correspondence between image and likeness; according to Erasmus, "What the eye is to the body, reason is to the soul."[39] As a result of this apparently iconographic exchange, Stanley Fish has attacked the encomiastic portion of *Areopagitica* as "decidedly *un*Miltonic," arguing that the logic of Milton's praise of books seems grounded in idolatrous practices or worship of the objects themselves.[40] But to characterize Milton's ethical defense of "that season'd life of man preserv'd and stor'd up in Books" as idolatrous is to think too literally about the action "that slaies an immortality rather then a life" (YP 2:493). Where Fish sees the "Image" of the letter that "killeth," Milton comprehends the "Image of God," which is to say the spirit that "giveth life" (2 Cor. 3:6). In this conception of the divine *logos* as the metaphorical "Image of God," Milton is close to contemporaries such as John Donne, Sir Thomas Browne, and Henry Vaughan, who explicitly deploy the trope during philosophical meditations and inquiries.[41] Futhermore, Milton had only recently revised his conception of the "Image of God" in such a way as to locate the residuum in the human capacity for choice. In *The Reason of Church Government,* as elsewhere in the course of the antiprelatical tracts, Milton had defended the scriptural justification for the Presbyterian "one right *discipline*" against the "English Dragon" of episcopacy on these very grounds: for "the Church hath in her immediate cure those inner parts and affections of the mind where the seat of reason is," the faculty which he refers to later in the pamphlet as "the dignity of Gods image" (YP 1:605, 857, 747, 842). But "the spurre of self-concernment" brought on in the following years by Milton's need to justify the freedom to divorce—ultimately a freedom of choice—refocused Milton's thinking about the place of interpretation (YP 2:226).[42]

In the second edition of his *Doctrine and Discipline of Divorce* (Feb. 1643/4), Milton approvingly cites a work that commences with exegesis of Genesis 1:26–27, "And God said, Let us make man in our image, after our likeness. . . . So God created man in his own image, in the image of God created he him" (KJV). In another connection (at YP 2:257), Milton shows that he knew Maimonides' *Guide of the Perplexed* in Johann Buxtorf the Younger's Latin translation, *Doctor perplexum* (Basel, 1629). Maimonides' argument, so influential in both the Jewish and Christian traditions, centers on explaining that the "image" of God is incorporeal, that is, that our "likeness" does not comprise a physical resemblance but rather our "intellectual apprehension," or "the divine intellect conjoined with man."[43] Milton, like Maimonides, partitions the "image of God" from idolatry, a division that is absolute. For Maimonides, it is paradoxically by means of this "image" and "likeness" that humanity upholds the Law, which is itself based on the destruction of idolatry and the worship of the one true God. In the exposition on Genesis 1:27 that commences *Tetrachordon*, Milton pursues a similar method to a different end. By "this Image of God," Milton explains, "wherein man was created,

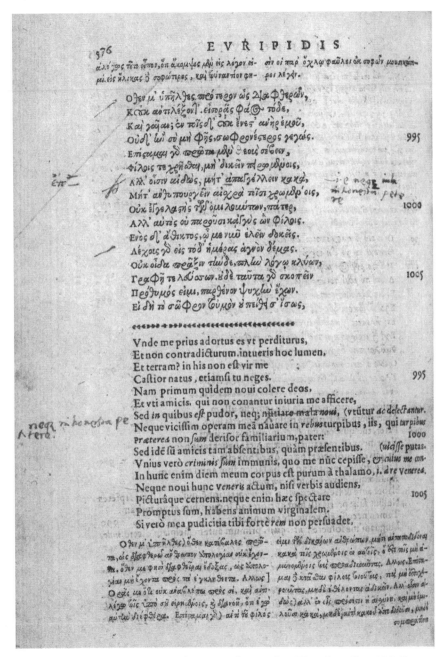

Figure 1. Milton's emendation to his copy of Euripides, *Hippolytus*, line 998. Reproduced by permission of the Bodleian Library, University of Oxford (Don d. 27, p. 576).

is meant Wisdom, Purity, Justice, and rule over all creatures. All which being lost in *Adam,* was recover'd with gain by the merits of Christ" (YP 2:587). Thus Milton explicates the phrase "Image of God" in the light of Pauline theology, favoring a typological interpretation that was common to diverse exponents of reformist doctrine throughout the seventeenth century.[44] In *De Doctrina Christiana* (1.18), Milton argues that "the inner man is regenerated by God through the word and the spirit so that his whole mind [*tota mente*] is restored to the image of God . . ." (YP 6:461; CM 15:366). Hence, "the faithful" have "God as their instructor [*edocti a Deo*]," and the regeneration of man's "intellect and will" emerges with "the restoration of the will to its former liberty" (YP 6:478, 462; CM 16:6; 15:370).

This "restoration," then, must be logically consistent with the effort to preserve "the pretious life-blood of a master spirit" since the ascent to spiritual regeneration results from the exercise of reason (YP 2:493). Milton makes the case in *Of Education* that all knowledge of God proceeds from observation of the "sensible" to the "intelligible": "[B]ecause our understanding cannot in this body found it selfe but on sensible things, nor arrive so cleerly to the knowledge of God and things invisible, as by orderly conning over the visible and inferior creature, the same method is necessarily to be follow'd in all discreet teaching" (YP 2:367–69). This passage makes explicit the epistemological assumptions underlying the educational system at work in *Areopagitica.* The intellect moves from material observation toward theoretical assertion, from inductive perceptions toward deductive demonstrations of truth.[45] Insofar as the theoretical takes the form of the theological in Milton's formulation, his logic descends ultimately from Aquinas:

> All creatures, even those lacking intelligence, are ordered to God as to their ultimate end, and they achieve this end insofar as they share some similarity with him. Intellectual creatures attain him in a more special manner, namely by understanding him through their proper activity. To understand God then must be the end of the intellectual creature. . . . A thing is more intimately united with God insofar as it attains to his substance, which comes about when it knows something of the divine substance, which requires some likeness of him. Therefore the intellectual substance tends toward divine knowledge as to its ultimate end.[46]

Aquinas here makes explicit the fundamental rationale for philosophical pursuits in the context of Christian piety, a rationale that is not, contrary to the assertions of Fish and others, considered idolatrous in most seventeenth-century

42   E V R I P I D I S

Πῶς δῆτ᾽ ἐσώθης; εἶπε τἄλλ᾽ ἐρήσομαι.

hac videntur αγ. Ἐπεὶ ταραγμὸς πόλιν ἐκίνησεν δορι,
potius inter
Adrastum et hunc Πύλας διῆλθον, ἥπερ εἰσῄει στρατός.
eum pro choro
itaque ponenda dyce. Ὧν δ᾽ οὕνεκ᾽ ἀγών ἦν, νεκρους κομίζετε;

αγ. Ὡς οἵγε κλύνοις ἔπτ᾽ ἐφέστασαν δόμοις.   755

χο. Πῶς φῄς; ὁ δ᾽ ἄλλ@ που κεκμηκότων ὄχλ@;

αγ. Τάφῳ δίδονται πρὸς Κιθαιρῶν@ πτυχαῖς.

χο. Τουκεῖθεν, τοίνυν θένδε; τίς δ᾽ ἔθαψέ νιν;   ⊬

αγ. Θησεὺς σκιωδης ἔνθ᾽ ἐλάθεεῖς πέξα.

χο. Οἷς δ᾽ ὀυκ ἔθαψε, πῇ νεκρους ἥκει λιπών;   760

αγ. Ἐγγύς. Πέλας γαρ πᾶν ὅ,τι σπουδαζ εται.

χο. Ἦ που πικρῶς νιν θεραπες ἦγεν ἐκ φόνου;

αγ. Οὐδεὶς ἐπέστη τῷδε δουλ@ ὢν πόνῳ.

      Φαίης αἄν, εἰ παρῆσθ᾽, ὅτ᾽ ἠγάπα νεκρούς.

χο. Ἔνιψεν αὐτῶν τῶν ταλαιπόρων σφαγάς;   785

αγ. Κάστρωσέ γ᾽ εὐνας, καὶ κάλυψε σώματα.

χο. Δεινὸν μὲν ἦν βάσταγμα, κ᾽ αἰσχώλω ἔρον·

αγ. ,,Τί δ᾽ αἰσχρὸν αὐθ ἐφ᾽ ποισι πέλλήλων κακα;

χο. αγ. Ὤμοι πόσω σφιν συνθανεῖν αἱ ἦθελον;

χο. Ἀκραντ᾽ ὀδύρῃ, ταῖς δὲ τ᾽ οξάγ-ς δάκρυ.   770

·««««««««««««««««««««««««««««»»«««««+

Quomodo sis seruatus:deinde alia interrogabo.
Nun. Poſtquam tumultus vrbem commouit haſta,
        Tranſij per portam qua intrabat exercitus.
Cho. Quorum verò cauſa certamen erat,*an Theſeus*,cadauera recepit?
Nun. Recepit,quia illi ſeptem *defuncti duces* in inclytas arcas ſunt conditi.755
Cho. Quomodo dicis?vbi verò *eſt* reliqua defunctorum turba?
Nun. Sepulturæ mandati ſunt ad Cithæronis valles.
cho. Illinc,an hinc?quis verò ſepeliit eos?
Nun. Theſeus,vbi eſt vmbroſa petra Eleutheris.
Cho. Quos verò non ſepeliit,vbi reliquit mortuos?   760
Nun. Hîc propè. propè enim eſt quicquid feſtinatur.
Cho. An ſerui tulerunt eos ægrè ex ipſa cæde?
Nun. Nullus ſeruus acceſſit ad hunc laborem:
        Dixiſſes,ſi affuiſſes,quòd *Theſeus* amaſſet mortuos.
Cho. Abluitne ipſorum miſerorum cruenta cadauera?   765
Nun. Quin etiam ſtrauit toros,& texit corpora.
Cho. Graue quidem erat geſtamen,& turpitudinem *aliquam* habens:
   a   Quid tamen turpia *dicis* hominibus communia mala?
Nun. Heu,quantò cum eis maluiſſem mori?
Cho. Fruſtra ploras,& iſtis elicis lachrymas.   770

Figure 2. Milton's emendation to his copy of Euripides, *Suppliants*, lines 754–71. Reproduced by permission of the Bodleian Library, University of Oxford (Don d. 28, p. 42).

English Protestant thought. The editors of the Yale prose works, in their annotations to the methodological passage in *Of Education,* surround Milton's sentence with echoes from Plato, Dury, Vives, Comenius, and others. Yet the "commonplace" derives the force of its conviction from Aquinas, who provides the logical connection between the Miltonic defense of "the Image of God" in books and the intellectual ascent from the inductive contemplation of the sensible to the deductive, if limited, comprehension of the intelligible.

Milton's emendations to the Stephanus Euripides demonstrate the principle in action. The "orderly conning" over the "visible and inferior" text employs the same logical progression as observation of the natural or "sensible" world, the Book of Nature. The hermeneutic circle—building a perspicuous context out of the aggregate of analytic details—represents an analogous process, as we have seen in Milton's emendation to *Hippolytus.* A venerable tradition of Christian hermeneutics has linked the operation of reason in this way to the speculative approach to truth.[47]

To the extent that readers exercise their reason, they approach the "end . . . of learning," for by this act only do they regain "to know God aright, and out of that knowledge to love him, to imitate him, to be like him, as we may the neerest by possessing our souls of true vertue, which being united to the heavenly grace of faith makes up the highest perfection" (YP 2:366–67). If in the imitation of Christ we strive "to repair the ruins of our first parents," then the specific form of that imitation consists in our exercising the remnant of divine "likeness," the "Image of God" that is reason. Arguing, as Maimonides did, against literal interpretation of Scripture, Milton reminds his readers that many "of most renowned vertu have sometimes by transgressing, most truly kept the law" (YP 2:588). By means of inspired transgression against the material letter of the book, a reader who repairs the ruins of a text by emendation—as Milton did in correcting his copy of Euripides—evinces godly reason. This means that errors (even of typography) relay to readers a didactic message, indirectly reminding them of a fall into print. Thus the duty of an educated reader is "to repair the ruins" of this textual fall. Restoring an Edenic "spirit" of the text, the reader must wrest it away from the "letter" of its manifestation, but always with the knowledge that this "spirit" remains accessible to us only through the material letter modified, emended with spiritual intent. Typography dovetails with typology.

It is as though, for Milton, the truth of a fallen text can only exist in the record of its correction, not in the correction alone. The very transmutability of the material text effects the transformation of its reader because perception of the "spirit" of a text so often registers in perception and modification of an "error" in a book. Milton depicts books as open to inspired modification, while still insisting on an essential conception of their verbal content, "the purest efficacie and extraction of that living intellect that bred them" (YP 2:492). If these two notions of textuality seem mutually exclusive, Milton asks us to remember that the essence of truth, like the intention of an author, can only be achieved provisionally after the Fall, by a reader who can only partially "repair the ruins" he or she has been bequeathed.

In consequence of the Fall, as Browne remarks in the *Pseudodoxia Epidemica,* there is no longer "a Paradise or unthorny place of knowledge." Our postlapsarian "understandings being eclipsed . . . we must betake our selves to waies of reparation, and depend upon the illumination of our endeavours. For thus we may in some measure repair our primary ruines, and build our selves men again."[48] Browne's epistemological argument bears a structural resemblance to the position Milton articulates with respect to knowledge in *Of Education* and *Areopagitica.* Just as Browne believes that there exist certain "waies of reparation," so Milton famously encourages the worldly virtue of the *vita activa:* "I cannot praise a fugitive and cloister'd vertue, unexercis'd and unbreath'd, that never sallies out and sees her adversary, but slinks out of the race, where that immortall garland is to be run for, not without dust and heat" (YP 2:515). Far from suggesting an idolatrous insistence upon the letter or indeed the object, Milton's ethical defense of books against prepublication censorship—his likening the intellectual content of books to the "Image of God"—emphasizes the active exercise of reason as a corrective measure against just such literal-mindedness.

To return to the language of *Areopagitica*'s epigraph, the ability to "speak free" stems from the right to interpret or differ in interpretation of Scripture and, therefore, depends upon the freedom to do so—the "can" of the epigraph. This makes for the apparent paradox expressed in the chapter of *De Doctrina Christiana* devoted to biblical hermeneutics (1.30). Even though "each passage of Scripture has only a single sense"—"the scriptures . . . are plain and sufficient in themselves," and "no inferences should be made from the text, unless they necessarily follow from what is written"— nevertheless "every believer is entitled to interpret the scriptures . . . for himself" (YP 6:580, 581, 583). Each believer "has the spirit, who guides truth, and he has the mind of Christ" (YP 6:583). Hence the centrality of scriptural interpretation: "If studied carefully and regularly, they [Scriptures] are an ideal instrument for educating even unlearned readers in those matters which have most to do with salvation" (YP 6:578–79). The problem of interpretation, however, broadens when considered in the context of *Areopagitica,* where the consideration of all books, not just sacred Scriptures, is at stake.

The category of "things indifferent," as against "those matters which have most to do with salvation," is therefore constitutive of the class of objects open to interpretation as an act of reason.

As soon as interpretation becomes necessary, so does justification. An interpretation, that is, will always be subject to challenge, and therefore must rise above other competing interpretations in order to sustain its own claim to validity. Interpretation, of course, first depends on recognizing the proper object of contemplation. The "neighboring differences, or rather indifferences" or "brotherly dissimilitudes" that Milton considers the objects under discussion in *Areopagitica* seem to have the ability to bring about "things not yet constituted in religion" and, moreover, to assist in the "reforming of Reformation it self" (YP 2:541, 553). The problem, then, is at least in part deciding what belongs in what category. In a tract heartily endorsed by Milton in *Areopagitica* (at YP 2:560–61), Robert Greville had collapsed the distinction between "things indifferent" and things necessary to salvation. Following the Smectymnuans, Greville writes that it is "Papall, Tyrannical" for the episcopacy to try to differentiate between indifference and necessity: "They will do more than *Adam* did: He gave names to Things according to their Natures; they will give *Natures* according to their owne fancies."[49] Greville asserts that "No Thing, No Act, is *Indifferent* . . . in it selfe, in the thing, but either *necessary* to be done, (if *Best*) or *unlawfull* to be done, if *Bad*." On the other hand, "if Right Reason have not, or cannot determine me; to which side soever I incline, and rest, I sin; because I act *Unreasonably*: being determined by humour, fancy, passion, a wilfull Will." The category of indifference is the province solely of right reason; the Prelates "have no power to determine what is *Indifferent*."[50] Greville goes further than Milton in arguing for what amounts to a libertarian agenda. Unlike the view Milton is developing in *Areopagitica*, Greville's *Discourse*—following his earlier treatise, *The Nature of Truth, its Union and Unity with the Soule*—propounds the belief that any man who knows the good will do it, that "recta ratio," as he argues circularly, can itself only be defined by "recta ratio": "But who shall tell us what is *Recta Ratio*? I answer, *Recta Ratio*."[51] Milton's earlier conception of virtue had, like Greville's, derived from the Socratic paradox that doing good is not an act of will, since no one knowingly does evil.[52] As he writes in *An Apology Against a Pamphlet*, "the first and chiefest office of love, begins and ends in the soule, producing those happy twins of her divine generation knowledge and vertue" (YP 1:892).[53] *Areopagitica* of course concentrates on a different but related pair of twins.

In *Areopagitica*, the whole matter turns on freedom of choice—the "will" of Milton's epigraph. At a critical moment, the speaker argues against those "who imagin to remove sin by removing the matter of sin" (YP 2:527). Milton's philosophical play on the word "matter" induces exactly the kind of consciousness for which he is arguing. The "matter of sin," he implies, is both the incarnation of fallibility that is the flesh and the pattern of thought that engenders such a lapse in spirit. "Matter," then, is both the problem and product of sinfulness in a fallen world, a concept that Milton represents when he collapses form into substance in a moment of ludic concentration, cause becoming interchangeable with effect. Mind, ordinarily held in contradistinction to matter, emerges indistinct from the material world; matter, charged with a vitality ordinarily reserved for descriptions of mind, becomes indistinguishable from the consciousness that saturates it. But the prose describing the desired removal of sin soon takes on language analogous at once to the expulsion of the cosmos from a divine first substance and to the expulsion of Adam and Eve from paradise: "Suppose we could expell sin by this means; look how much we thus expell of sin, so much we expell of vertue: for the matter of them both is the same; remove that, and ye remove them both alike" (YP 2:527). "Matter" is not merely the location of sin, as it is in more orthodox conceptions, but paradoxically manifests both "sin" and "vertue."[54] And we, in turn, merely discard meaning in the reduction of Milton's telling pun to one or the other possibility.

Reading matter, therefore, cannot be the origin of sin, no more than knowledge itself originates disobedience. If reason is the soul's very "being" (*PL* 5.487), and "reason also is choice" (*PL* 3.108), then in order for "each man to be his own chooser" (YP 2:514), "the Church" cannot have the seat of reason "in her immediate cure" (YP 1:747). On the contrary, the responsibility must fall upon the "umpire conscience" (*PL* 3.195). In the *Christian Morals,* Sir Thomas Browne appositely casts conscience in the role of judge: "Conscience only, that can see without Light, sits in the *Areopagy* and dark Tribunal of our Hearts, surveying our Thoughts and condemning their obliquities."[55] The only redress for what Milton calls "the fall of learning" is freedom of conscience: "Give me the liberty to know, to utter, and to argue freely according to conscience, above all liberties" (YP 2:520, 560). Individual conscience, guided by reason and the Holy Spirit, awakens the interpretive faculty to choice, serves as our connection to the divine *logos.* As he says in *De Doctrina Christiana,* "the phenomenon of Conscience, or right reason [*recta ratio*]" gives evidence of the existence of God (YP 6:132; CM 14:28). God wills that all may be saved, which is why Milton argues—following Arminius—that election is simply the salvation available to all believers: "The condition upon which God's decision depends . . . entails the action of a will which he himself has freed and a belief which he himself demands from men. If this condition is left in the power of men who are free to act, it is absolutely in keeping with justice and does not detract at all from the importance of divine grace" (YP 6:189). The argument of *Areopagitica* similarly inheres in the dilemma posed by freedom of choice. As he says, "many there be that complain of divin Providence for suffering *Adam* to transgresse, foolish tongues! when God gave him reason, he gave him freedom to choose, for reason is but choosing" (YP 2:527). God "trusts him [man] with the gift of reason to be his own chooser" because obedience to God, unless a conscious choice, is meaningless (YP 2:514; cf. *PL* 3.103–11).

Therefore, by analogy, human beings must have a certain capacity to will change if they are to learn. "He who makes you teachable," says Erasmus, "demands nonetheless your endeavor toward learning." It is "reason," for Milton as for Erasmus, "from which the will is born," and although "obscured by sin," it was "not altogether extinguished" by Original Sin; rather, as Erasmus argues: "If the power to distinguish good and evil and the will of God had been hidden from men, it could not be imputed to them if they made the wrong choice. If the will had not been free, sin could not have been imputed, for sin would cease to be sin if it were not voluntary, save when error or the restriction of the will is itself the fruit of the sin."[56] Not only sin, but also piety depends upon the freedom to taste what Erasmus pointedly refers to as "the fruit of the sin." The matter of them both is the same. For it is not the fruit but our intention that makes the sin what it is. If an omnipotent, omniscient, and benevolent God should not have created beings capable of choosing to transgress his law, then as Irenaeus argues "neither would what is good be grateful to them, nor communion with God be precious, nor would the good be very much sought after, which . . . would be implanted of its own accord and without their concern." Irenaeus finds his way out of the supposedly aporistic "trilemma" (God is benevolent and omnipotent, yet evil exists) by finding the benevolence of God redolent of his will to educate us: "being good would be of no consequence" if humankind "were so by nature rather than by will" and thus became "possessors of good spontaneously, not by choice."[57] God formed humankind, as the Father says in *Paradise Lost,* "Sufficient to have stood, though free to fall" (3.99). Our condition in this world necessitates choice, and choice depends on the presence of oppositions (or at least distinct alternatives) from which to choose: "Assuredly we bring not innocence into the world, we bring impurity much rather: that which purifies us is triall, and triall is by what is contrary" (YP 2:515). Milton's recognition of the dilemmas that necessarily face each person in this world fostered one of his most characteristic habits of thought, a pattern in his works memorably described by C. S. Lewis as "the co-existence, in a live and sensitive tension, of apparent opposites."[58] Given "the state of man," Milton asks, "what wisdom can there be to choose, what continence to forbeare without the knowledge of evill" (YP 2:514)? In recognition of this logical dilemma, "the question of censorship," as Edward Tayler puts it, becomes in *Areopagitica* "ultimately a question of reason in relation to freedom of choice."[59]

Milton therefore depicts the process of learning as a trajectory from choice to recognition, or, as he says in *Of Education,* employing Aristotelian terminology, from "that act of reason which in the *Ethics* is call'd *Proairesis*" (YP 2:396) to *anagnorisis.* Hence the figure of the teacher that ends the brief tractate: teaching is "not a bow for every man to shoot in . . . but will require sinews almost equall to those which Homer gave Ulysses" (YP 2:415). In a counterintuitive move, Milton figures the teacher as Telemachus, not Odysseus. Only Telemachus has "sinews almost equall" to Odysseus's in Book 21 of the *Odyssey,* which is, I think, Milton's way of suggesting that one is both taught and becomes a teacher in the act of recognizing likeness: Telemachus becomes most like himself when he demonstrates that he is most like Odysseus.

Because this comprehension of likeness requires a contrasting perception in order to achieve definition, Milton encourages the recognition of difference, or at least of "brotherly dissimilitudes" that come together to form the Temple of Solomon, the ruins that reformation seeks to repair. In short, the opportunity to correct error resides in its perception and therefore in the possibility of error's existence. Except in the recognition of difference—the differentiation between "cunning resemblances"—how can we come to see truth in its best likeness?

> Good and evil we know in the field of this World grow up together almost inseparably; and the knowledge of good is so involv'd and interwoven with the knowledge of evil, and in so many cunning resemblances hardly to be discerned, that those confused seeds which were impos'd on *Psyche* as an incessant labor to cull out, and sort asunder, were not more intermixt. It was from out the rinde of one apple tasted, that the knowledge of Good and evil as two twins cleaving together leapt forth into the World. (YP 2:514)

Except through the reading of books, how can we find the materials that instigate choice between one portion of truth and another, when the very structure of truth can only inhere in their composite? Therefore Milton encourages us, "Read any books what ever come to thy hands, for thou art sufficient both to judge aright, and to examine the matter" (YP 2:511). Repairing the ruins of England's "spirituall architecture" entails "an incessant labor" like that which Psyche faced: "to cull out, and sort asunder" (YP 2:555, 514). Thus the effort on behalf of truth by its very nature entails the considered sorting of opinion, so that what is for royalists the object of withering satire—proliferation of "plainly partiall" expression, even of "unchosen books"—is for Milton a mere statement of our condition in "this World" (YP 2:510, 530). For Milton, it is not the publication of controversial pamphlets but conversely the inquisitional Licensing Order that "may be held a dangerous and suspicious fruit, as certainly it deserves, for the tree that bore it" (YP 2:507). Like the fruit, books tempt with the dangerous knowledge of their arguments, but the fruit, Milton assures us, is not the sin. Book-like "Dragons teeth" may metamorphose into armed men, such as the "warfaring" *Spartoi* that sprang up before Cadmus—seeds, as it were, that sort themselves out.[60] But the chief labor of reformation activates a "Nation of Prophets, of Sages, of Worthies" working at the "defence of beleaguer'd Truth" in "the mansion house of liberty": "there be pens and heads there, sitting by their studious lamps, musing, searching, revolving new notions and idea's wherewith to present, as with their homage and their fealty the approaching Reformation: others as fast reading, trying all things, assenting to the force of reason and convincement" (YP 2:554).

When Milton translates or emends Euripides, as when he hopes for the "reforming of Reformation" through "books promiscuously read," he advances reasonable choice as the necessary condition for the pursuit of truth (YP 2:553, 517). Freedom of conscience demands freedom of choice, a condition that in turn entails a "perpetuall progression" of alternatives, if reason or virtue is to be exercised (YP 2:543). By a parallel logic, the closing verse of John's Gospel resists closure: "And there are also many other things which Jesus did, the which, if they should be written every one, I suppose that even the world itself could not contain the books that should be written" (21:25, KJV). That Parliament (in the very "mansion house of liberty") would pursue such a policy as represented by the Licensing Order—an even more literal effort at containment—inspired Milton's defense of the integrity of reason as a judge of knowledge's value. Milton's practices as a reader and annotator remain faithful to the paradoxical effort to sustain pure intentions in a fallen world. By scripting their own transmuting exchanges with and within books, readers participate in an ongoing textual conversation. Milton presents an excellent example of how that educational metamorphosis, provisionally repairing the ruins of our imperfect and fallen knowledge, arouses the "life beyond life" that is a book's progeny down through history.

Chapter Two

Milton and the Hebraic Pedagogue of the Divorce Tracts

Among the vast archives of the British Library there is a small artifact whose very form expresses the ambivalence characteristic of relations between Jews and Christians in early modern England. The volume is a compendium of twenty-one pamphlets bound together and entitled, *Tracts Relating to the Jews, 1608–1724*.[1] The contents of the volume range from virulent anti-Semitic invective to vagaries of conversion narrative to so-called philo-Semitic works. While the earliest pamphlet dates from the year of Milton's birth, the collection as a whole is the product of a later moment in which self-conscious scrutiny of Jewish and Christian relations was rapidly intensifying throughout Britain and Europe. On the inside of the back cover, on the lower left hand side, "BOUND 1940" is stamped.

On the eve of the *Shoah* the book was bound or, perhaps, "recollected." If the artifact is emblematic of the conflicting desires to authenticate, recuperate, tolerate, or convert the Jews, the gesture of its anonymous editor is also informed by the ambivalence legible in retrospect in its twentieth-century context. I begin the chapter with this anecdote not only because it indicates the historical situation in which Milton sought to rehabilitate the Mosaic Law in the divorce tracts, but also because the book represents two constitutive, mutually defining moments in the history of Anglo-Jewish relations. More specifically, both the 1640s and the 1940s witnessed complex and lasting shifts in the cultural imagination of these relations, as well as related changes in affective attitudes. It is, moreover, impossible to think about early modern attitudes toward the Jews and ideas of Jewishness without also calling to mind the Holocaust. What seem to be philo-Semitic attitudes in one period may have the most disastrous implications three centuries later.

It is in the light of this recognition that I examine the figure of the Hebraic pedagogue in Milton's divorce tracts. To begin with, Milton's philo-Semitic engagement with Hebraic tradition ought to be contrasted with the limited concept of toleration discernible in the following remark from *Observations on the Articles of Peace*: "while we detest *Judaism,* we know our selves commanded by St. *Paul, Rom.* 11. to respect the *Jews,* and by all means to endeavor thir conversion" (YP 3:326).[2] When Milton concedes to his audience that "we detest *Judaism*"—and recall that he has just referred to the accusation of toleration for Judaism as "A most audacious calumny"—he betrays his own difficulty reconciling intellectual commitment to compassion, sympathy to the conception of Christian succession (YP 3:326). In other words, "respect" and "conversion" would seem to be mutually exclusive. Milton imagines a scenario in which Christians are teaching the Jews, supplanting Christianity's living ancestor as pedagogue in order to bring about Jewish conversion. The desire to convert the Jews creates what I will call the paradox of learned succession: Milton insists that learned Christians cannot dismiss the Mosaic Law, but at the same time sees Christianity as a fulfillment of Judaism's promise.

Milton's conception of the role of the Jews tends to equate their time with the past, as Jeffrey Shoulson has convincingly argued, and thus to fossilize what was in fact a living culture.[3] However, the increased efforts during the 1640s to reappraise the origins of the Old Testament in the actual texts of Hebrew Scripture as well as to readmit the Jews to England and convert them to Christianity help elucidate Milton's attitudes toward the inheritance of Hebraic thought. Writers in England during the Civil War of the 1640s articulated a renewed intellectual commitment to the Mosaic Law and even at times a humanitarian interest in the continuing fates of the people of the Covenant. Intellectual positions staked out by Milton, attitudes and habits of thought cultivated particularly in the divorce tracts, contributed learned cultural motivation to the emerging readmission debate of the 1650s. Although as far as we know Milton participated in that debate only indirectly, his contribution was significant enough to draw the attention of several of his contemporaries. Milton's tracts function within the broader dogmatic environment as a kind of intellectual prehistory to the readmission movement. Having rethought the pedagogical inheritance of the Mosaic Law in the course of the controversy over divorce, Milton advocated the vindication of Hebraic thought as an especially radical adjunct to the foment of revolutionary ideas.

Throughout the divorce tracts, Milton employs the metaphor of the schoolmaster to represent continuity in the relations between Hebrew and

Christian scriptural traditions, referred to by synecdoche as the Law and the Gospel. Yet the metaphor of the Law as a teacher derives most immediately from St. Paul's letter to the Galatians, in which the Apostle argues for precisely the opposite valuation: "But before faith came, we were kept under the law, shut up unto the faith which should afterwards be revealed. Wherefore the law was our schoolmaster *to bring us* unto Christ, that we might be justified by faith. But after that faith is come, we are no longer under a schoolmaster" (Gal. 3:23–25, KJV). This identification of Hebrew Scripture with instruction and guidance can of course be traced to the fact that the "Law" (νομος) translates the Hebrew title *Torah,* which is based on a stem meaning "to teach, to guide."[4] But Paul introduces the metaphor of the schoolmaster so that he can argue for the irrevocable disruption of the Law's influence under the new covenant of grace. The Epistle to Galatians recommends the subordination, appropriation, and ultimate transumption of Hebrew Scripture.[5]

Thus the narrative of the schoolmaster extends into an allegory of inheritance: "the heir, as long as he is a child, differeth nothing from a servant, though he be lord of all; But is under tutors and governors until the time appointed of the father" (Gal. 4:1–2, KJV). The temporal dimension of pedagogy as a metaphor for succession is somewhat obscured by the translation of παιδαγωγος as "schoolmaster." In the Greek, *paidagogos* signifies a household servant or slave who escorted a boy to and from school and served as custodian and disciplinary figure until the child reached maturity.[6] Thus Paul explains that the Law, serving as a protection against transgressions, had a pedagogical function only temporarily, in the period before Christ appeared as Abraham's "offspring."[7] Recalling Isaac and Ishmael, Paul goes on to elaborate the transfer of the birthright from the firstborn to the heir, which confers onto the allegory the further significance held in the distinction between birth by "flesh" and birth by spiritual "promise." As the Geneva gloss of 1560 spells out, "Agar and Sina represente the Lawe: Sara and Ierusalem ye Gospel: Ismael ye Iewish Synagogue, and Isaac the Church of Christ" (marginal gloss at Gal. 4:22–24). The mothers are the two testaments, and their offspring embody the two communities of believers; the pupil or ward assumes his inheritance in a way that is analogous to the child of a lawful marriage rather than, as it were, the offspring of an adulterous affair.

Before turning to the divorce tracts, I want first to show briefly how Paul's metaphor of the schoolmaster functions in the writings Milton published the year before he entered the divorce controversy. In *The Reason of Church Government,* Milton adduces this passage from Galatians as a means of challenging the prelacy's claim to authority based in scriptural precedent. If Christianity might be said to be the student of Judaism, how then can the legitimacy or authenticity of the Christian faith be independently ensured for believers who do not subscribe to the institutions of the established church? Milton first needs to curtail the influence of the ancient Jewish priesthood, from Aaron on down, as a model that could be said to have informed the apostolic church and might therefore be used to justify the Episcopal form of church hierarchy.

In matters of discipline Milton asks "how the Church-government under the Gospell can be rightly call'd an imitation of that in the old Testament? for that the Gospell is the end and fulfilling of the Law, our liberty also from the bondage of the Law I plainly reade" (YP 1:763). In this interpretation, Milton is close to the early reformers, for whom preterite servility inheres in the bondage to outward or carnal forms of worship. "A son and a seruaunt are so contrary one to an other," says Luther, "that the same man can not be both a sonne and a seruaunt. A sonne is free and willing, a seruaunt is compelled and vnwilling: a sonne liueth, and resteth in faith: a seruaunt in works."[8] Thus the doctrine of faith is in Milton's argument aligned with the Presbyterians, the doctrine of works with the "Romish" bishops. By analogy, the prelacy for Milton is like "a schoolmaister of perishable rites," in that it imitates obsolete ritual and clings to an overly literal connection between the apostolic church and the earliest Jewish priesthood (YP 1:837). As one paraphrast put it in 1642, "Politique Lawes, Mens Traditions, Ceremonies of the Church, yea and the Law of *Moses,* are such things, as are without Christ, therefore they availe not unto righteousnesse before God."[9]

In *The Reason of Church Government,* Milton agrees with the reformers in his interpretation of Paul's metaphor of the schoolmaster. Milton explicitly denies that "the ripe age of the Gospell should be put to schoole againe, and learn to governe herself from the infancy of the Law, the stronger to imitate the weaker, the freeman to follow the captive, the learned to be lesson'd by the rude." (YP 1:763). None of "those principles which either art or inspiration hath written" can be used to show that the educational authority of the Law as schoolmaster endures (YP 1:763). Christianity, in this narrative, has graduated from the Law's school. John Donne vividly illustrates the idea of the relationship between traditions as matriculation: "The Jews were as School-boys, always spelling, and putting together Types and Figures," whereas "The Christian is come from school to the University, from Grammar to Logick, to him that is *Logos* it self, the Word."[10] In the antiprelatical tracts, Milton uses the metaphor of the schoolmaster to argue for the self-sufficiency of the Gospel,[11] thereby limiting the temporal reach of the Law's authority for Christians under the dispensation of grace.

Emphasizing the importance of recuperating and yet limiting the influence of the Law, Luther acutely documents the paradox that will preside over the compromise between finding corroboration in Jewish tradition and escaping its authority: "a good Scholemaster enstructeth & exerciseth his scholars in reading and writing, to the ende they may come to the knowledge of good letters & other profitable things, that afterwards they might haue a delite in doing of that, which before when they were constrained thervnto, they did against their willes."[12] The trope of the schoolmaster leads Milton, too, in *The Reason of Church Government*, to turn from reading to writing itself as metaphor for the precedence of the Gospel over even the moral authority of the Law: "besides what we fetch from those unwritten lawes and Ideas which nature hath ingraven in us, the Gospell . . . lectures to us from her own authentick hand-writing, and command, not copies out from the borrow'd manuscript of a subservient scrowl, by way of imitating" (YP 1:764). The sense of history itself appears to be at risk in this redeployment of the trope of education, as Milton all but calls for the abrogation of the Law. The Gospel speaks directly from Christ's *auctoritas,* bearing the divine signature as "authentick hand-writing," rather than slavishly copying out the "borrow'd manuscript" of the Jewish tradition. The scroll of the Torah here represents the monastic tradition, a text imperfectly transmitted on the authority of human tradition, whereas the Gospel pronounces a lecture that originates from the authority of divine command.

At the same time, Milton cannot dispense with the idea of an authoritative text of Hebrew Scripture, and he therefore advances the concept of God's "authentick" writing when he seeks to justify the fierceness of his own polemic in the *Animadversions* and elsewhere. Herein lies the basis for Milton's critique, in *An Apology Against a Pamphlet*, of the "Rabbinical *Scholiasts*" who "have often us'd to blurre the margent with *Keri,* instead of *Ketiv,* and gave us this insuls rule out of their *Talmud, That all words which in the Law are writ obscenely, must be chang'd to more civill words.* Fools who would teach men to speak more decently then God thought to write."[13] Milton recalls the tradition—from Masoretic textual criticism of the Hebrew Bible—of supplying vowel points, alternative spellings, synonyms, tropes, and euphemisms for vocalization (*qere,* Hebrew, "what is read") in the margins of the extant consonantal text (*ketib,* Hebrew, "what is written"). In a pejorative tone, Milton critiques the tradition of pronouncing a marginal emendation (*qere*) in place of the word or name of God as enshrined in the text (*ketib*). In this way, Milton distinguishes between the relative authority of something written over against a spoken utterance, investing the original transcription (*ketib*) with a primary power and devaluing the mark of editorial interference (*keri*).[14]

Yet this moment in the first edition presents readers with a revealing, self-reflexive irony. For, twenty-four pages later, the pamphlet ends by appending a single erratum that refers us back to the very sentence in which Milton has excoriated the Rabbis for their emendations. The alteration Milton wishes his readers to make to the text—"*for* speak *correct it* read"—removes any hint of authority from the oral tradition embodied in a "marginall Keri," denigrating the editors as "Fools who would teach men to [read] more decently then God thought to write."[15] This again recalls a comment by Luther, quoted above, in which the Law "like as a good Scholemaster enstructeth & exerciseth his scholars in reading and writing," though in this case what the Rabbis "teach" diminishes in authority precisely to the extent that it supplants text with tradition.[16] Milton's change emphasizes the act of interpretation that is required for any understanding of Scripture, the textual mediation that is necessarily involved in reading, even prior to reading aloud. As the mild irony of Milton's emendation to his own text demonstrates, the Talmudic distinction between "the textual Chetiv" and the "marginall Keri" does not, because it cannot, limit interpretation: Milton's own defense of his vituperation appropriates figures of thought from rabbinic traditions.[17] Characteristically Milton is dismissing the Rabbis in order to engage them on this point, not just engaging them in order to dismiss their practice.

Teaching, preaching, and prophesying are, of course, at their etymological roots very close to one another, and so Milton connects pedagogy as a metaphor for the relationship between traditions to the authority of the texts from which interpretations originate. If the schoolmaster is to teach reading and writing, he must do so from a textbook that does not contain errors. Milton again and again transposes the issue of interpretive, which translates in this context as spiritual, authenticity into the related topic of textual accuracy. Thus in *The Doctrine and Discipline of Divorce*, the earliest of his writings on divorce, Milton places himself in the position of a Christ-like iconoclast bringing down the members of a priestly hierarchy who merely support their own power by means of their traditional authority to interpret Scripture. Milton posits that, in forming his own argument, he imitates Christ, despite the fact that he objects to the expansive application of Jesus' rigorous interpretation of the Law in Matthew 5:31–32, which restricts interpretation of the Mosaic permission to divorce to what the King James Version calls "the cause of fornication."

Milton's objection to the use of this New Testament proof-text as a precedent for contemporary divorce law is historicist. His argument therefore reconstructs the proper context within which the passage must be inter-preted. Only the context of Christ's pronouncement can regulate its applica-tion, since exegetes must commit to a construction of His overall intention as the court of last appeal. Milton insists that Christ's injunction be read within the specific context of the laxity to which the rabbinic tradition's overly literal interpretation of the Law had led. Christ's stricture does not represent a universal precept that would repeal "one jot or one tittle" of the Law (Matt. 5:18). "For what can be more opposite and disparaging to the cov'nant of love, of freedom, & of our manhood in grace," Milton asks, "then to bee made the yoaking pedagogue of new severities" (YP 2:636)?

It is precisely the novelty of the pedagogues' "new severities" that betrays their ideological and political motivation for interpreting Jesus' response to the Pharisees as a cancellation of the Mosaic Law on the permis-sion to divorce. So Jesus does not correct the Pharisees, "whose pride deserv'd not his instruction." Instead, he "only returns what is proper to them. . . . But us he hath taught better, if we have eares to hear" (YP 2:307). This is why in Matthew 5:31, Jesus "cites not the Law of *Moses,* but the licencious Glosse which traduc't the Law" (YP 2:317). In Milton's historical reenactment of the New Testament debate, Jesus hoists the Pharisees on their own petard. He answers them in kind so that their spiritual error—a lack finally of charity—will be exposed. Paradoxically, the Pharisees' laxity in allowing modification of God's law has produced severity and diminished the charity of the Law by restricting freedoms that Moses protects. Current rigorists, Milton claims, adhere too rigidly to the letter of the wrong Law, which is why Jesus, in refuting the lax Pharisees, "cites not the Law of *Moses,* but the Pharisaical tradition falsely grounded upon that law" at Matthew 5:31 (YP 2:307).

Milton similarly co-opts the technical terminology of the rabbinic edi-torial tradition to fashion a metaphor for prophetic exegesis: "Ye have an author great beyond exception, *Moses:* and one yet greater, he who hedg'd in from abolishing every smallest jot and tittle of precious equity contain'd in that Law, with a more accurat and lasting Masoreth, then either the Syna-gogue of *Ezra,* or the *Galilean* School at *Tiberias* hath left us" (YP 2:231). The *OED*—in its rather uninspired explanation of the appropriated term, "Masoreth"—misses Milton's point altogether: "Milton seems (misled by the rendering 'tradition') to have supposed the word to be applicable to the exegetical traditions of the Rabbis, by which the severity of the Law was increased." But this is precisely what motivates Milton's remarkable diction: the received text is inextricable from the editorial tradition that produced it. Time and again Milton confounds tradition in this way, binding the act of interpreting or teaching to its codification or institutionalization. Masorah, or Milton's variant "Masoreth," signifies most broadly the rules established to govern the production of scribal copies of Hebrew Scripture; more narrowly, the term refers "to the corpus of notes in copies of the Masoretic Text which were prepared for scholarly use."[18] Thus "Masoreth" here is both text and tradition, and Jesus in his interpretation of the Law enacts its fulfillment through "more accurat and lasting" interpretation, generating as it were the best text, a new record of the Law. Christ the mediator, as Milton's trope indicates, interposes the lens through which we begin to see the Law clearly. Yet even Christ's "more accurat and lasting Masoreth" must be articulated in the terms of an interpretive tradition. Just as a "plain and Christian *Talmud*" would have to be at once a Christian "teaching" and the text of such instruction (in this case, Milton's own tract, *Tetrachordon*), so the "more accurat and lasting Masoreth" will figure as a different text (YP 2:635). This new text, then, is to be the text of "equity"—the technical hermeneutic term, derived from ancient forensic rhetoric, whose synonym has been *caritas* in the Christian lexicon at least since Augustine.[19]

Milton makes the accuracy of the text commensurate with its "precious equity," such that every "jot and tittle" of the new covenant may stand for a more enduring yet flexible text of the Law. To the extent that a "Masoreth" conforms to the rule of "plain sense and equity" dictated by "the all-interpreting voice of Charity" (YP 2:309), it is "more accurat and lasting" than the unstable, because not yet ameliorated, strictures of the Law. In *Tetrachordon* Milton inveighs against "crabbed *masorites* of the Letter" who will not "mollifie a transcendence of literal rigidity . . . but must make their exposition heer [Matt. 19:9] such an obdurat *Cyclops,* to have but one eye for this text, and that onely open to cruelty and enthralment" (YP 2:668–69). Lacking the depth of perspective gained by "a skilfull and laborious gatherer," who arrives at the meaning of a passage of scripture by "comparing other Texts," literalists subscribe to "*alphabetical* servility" (YP 2:338, 282, 280).[20]

Christ's "Masoreth" is set against the work of the Masoretes of Tiberias—renowned for their linguistic accuracy and credited with the codification of Hebrew grammar—and the Synagogue of Ezra, the scribe and prophet traditionally held to have established the canonical text of the Hebrew Bible, who symbolized authoritative interpretation.[21] Milton revisits the historical sites of authoritative canonization, codification, and editing in order to rewrite Christian succession from the authority of the Hebrew Scriptures in their standard form, the authentic tradition of the Holy Land passed on in an "unbroken line from the generation of Ezra" to the rabbinic grammarians of Tiberias.[22] As a result, Milton gives the impression that he is conducting a kind of comparative religious anthropology, employing the terminology of the Rabbis to corroborate a radical Protestant interpretation of scripture and lending his argument the patina of historicism.[23]

What is again at issue is metaphysical priority, which the paradoxical metaphor of temporal succession underscores. As one contemporary put it, "Every book and letter which the Prophets wrote as Divine Scripture, for the use of all Nations and Ages, Jesus Christ hath preserved by the diligence of the *Massorites*."[24] Hugh Broughton defended the Masoretic annotations, claiming that "God teacheth vs elegancie of the tongue, or sense of the text, by setting a word in the margine, to adorne the text, and this passeth the witt of man, and must needs be knowen to bee the worke of God."[25] Indeed, learned contemporaries, such as Broughton and his admirer John Lightfoot, doctored Talmudic texts so that all traditions would inexorably confirm Christian succession.[26] A combination of rabbinic lore and typological allegory drives the midrashim of these "Christian Hebraists" on Matthew 5:18, Jesus' troubling and apparently contradictory explanation of the conformity of his teachings to the letter of the law ("jot and tittle"), which Milton found so useful in his expansion on the Mosaic permission to divorce.[27] Citing the Jerusalem Talmud ("Sandarin, fol. 20"), Broughton embroiders his tale of inheritance: "The Iewes, to shew Gods care ouer euery letter in the Bible, bring in the Law co[m]playining of loosing Iod."[28] For "when *jod* is taken from *Saraj,* being the last letter of a womans name, [it] cometh first to make *Iesus,*" so that "*jod* appeareth not contemned."[29] Because "a Testament which faileth in a letter, faileth in all," when Sarai becomes Sara the threat arises that "*Iod* is gone, & the auctority of the Law is lost."[30] Consequently, "by way of Prosopopoeia," the Hebrew Doctors "bring in the Law as a Plantife before God, complaining of losing *Iod,*"[31] and "God answereth, thou hast no losse."[32] The story is then recycled through the filter of the Gospel: "our lord doth tell us, that *the least Letter or Tittle in the Law shall not faile:* but any man may see he borroweth this speech from the *Massorites* diligence, touching the letter *Iod.*"[33] Learned contemporaries of Milton found ways to mobilize rabbinic teachings in order to buttress their own versions of arguments from the Gospel on a range of interpretive issues. Even among those not conventionally educated the 1640s and 1650s, as Nigel Smith has shown, witnessed a rise in "the need to increase personal inspired authority by enunciating" Hebrew, however imperfectly understood.[34] It was in this climate that Milton extended a greater sympathy toward Hebraic thought, which became the central strand in his narrative of tradition and tuition.

Hence Milton's appropriation of the vocabulary of rabbinic textual tradition, while not necessarily unique in the period, nevertheless acquires a

radicalism absent from the doctrinal positions staked out by more orthodox divines. The conventional tropes of Christian succession gradually give
way to a searching inquiry into the ongoing relevance of Hebraic thought.
To an extent, Milton's use of rabbinic terminology participates in typological interpretation. But Milton, more than other practitioners, wants to
have it both ways. The "living historicity" that Erich Auerbach and others
have seen as the legacy of Jewish tradition in Christian figuralism provides
Milton with a way of revitalizing Jewish tradition without dispensing with
Hebraic thought. I reluctantly take issue with Auerbach's account of typology, from which I have learned much. The characterization of Christian
typological interpretation as "indirect, complex, and charged with history,"
does an injustice, in the final analysis, both to what is meant by "history"
and to the aims of those who practiced typology. My disagreement resides
in the equation of pattern with historiography. This tendency—to see history as anticipating Christ's triumph—was undoubtedly the normative
mode of regarding things scriptural for Milton and his Christian contemporaries. Typology always retroactively sees the past in terms of future
events, or at least events subsequent to the initial event. The integrity of
the initial event under scrutiny, then, gives way to the interpretive
demands of the future event, so that the inquiry becomes even more selec-
tive than historical analysis would permit. However, when treating a "thing
indifferent" to salvation, such as Milton believed the marriage bond to be,
Milton would not necessarily have resorted to typological exegesis where it
did not serve his purpose. Indeed, as I have been arguing, the nascent historicism at work in the divorce tracts forestalls typological (and ultimately
antinomian) tendencies. For typological habits of thought would ultimately erode the authenticity of Milton's claim to historical accuracy in his
appeal to Hebraic divorce law as precedent.[35]

"It is a paradox applying to all narrative," says Frank Kermode, "that
although its function is mnemonic it always recalls different things."[36] The
challenge to systems of typology remains: What, after all, becomes of the
Jewish history and prophecy upon which Christian fulfillment depends? As
popular manuals of typology such as William Guild's frequently reprinted
Moses Vnuailed make graphically legible, a firm line must be drawn between
traditions which theologians nevertheless find meeting on every page of
scripture.[37]

Thus Milton self-consciously alerts his readers to the entanglements of
traditional spiritual inheritance and, at the same time, disburdens us of the
fantasy that we might disinherit or opt out of the history to which our ideas
are indebted. As William Robertson put it in an edition of the Psalms and

Lamentations that featured parallel columns of the Hebrew text alongside a transliteration into the Roman alphabet:

> [I]t is most necessary, and most profitable, that Christians should know, themselves, to read, and understand their own rights, to their happiness, in the words of life, & not only by their Teachers neither only by the Translation of their Teachers, but by their own particular inspection and knowledge, to know, read, and understand their own rights and evidences to life, and that in the very self same Language and Words, which they were at first delivered in, as in the first, primitive, and original Copies of those rights and interests in eternal life: . . . the Rights and evidences of their heavenly Inheritance.[38]

The priestly teacher gives way to the congregation of individual believers, who at once disavow their relation to the clergy and also bypass the schoolmaster in order to receive directly the "authentick" writing of the prophet. Thus the Apostle's allegory of the pedagogue implicitly transforms into a justification for Protestant (and perhaps Independent) biblicism summed up in the oxymoron "original Copies." The populist appeal of Robertson's phonetic guide to the Hebrew original pushes the allegory in a direction characteristic of reformation humanistic learning: the return to the sources (*ad fontes*) will lead the saints from their captivity and bondage under the hieratic Latin text back to the Holy Land of Scripture in the original languages. As "The Translators to the Reader" of *The Holy Bible* [KJV] say: "we desire that the Scripture may speake like it selfe, as in the language of *Canaan*, that it may be vnderstood euen of the very vulgar."[39]

Exegesis is after all, like education, etymologically a "leading out"; this figure hovers over Milton's translations of Psalms 80–88 from April 1648:

> Thy land to favour graciously
> Thou hast not Lord been slack,
> Thou hast from *hard* captivity
> Returned Jacob back.   (Ps. 85, ll.1–4, *Poems*, p. 318)

Going back to the original language is like returning to the land of Israel. The Bible should "speake like it selfe": the concept is crucial as it plays out amid the radical sectarians of mid-seventeenth century England.[40] Nearly contemporaneous with Milton's renditions of the Psalms into English was *An Endeavour after the reconcilement of . . . Presbyterians, and Independents. With a Discourse touching the Synagogue of the JEWES.* And within a year of Milton's translations were *The Petition of the Jewes For the Repealing of the Act of Parliament for their banishment out of ENGLAND* and Edward Nicholas's *An Apology for the Honorable Nation of the Jews, and All the Sons of Israel,* possibly the most genuinely philo-Semitic tract in the period. [41] Nicholas, to whom Menasseh ben Israel favorably refers in his address to Cromwell,[42] links the fates of "all the sons of Israel": "The sufferings of many of the faithful friends of Parliament" parallel the "great indurings that honorable Nation hath suffered, what bloody slaughters have been made of them in *London,* in the North country of *England,* and divers other parts of this kingdom."[43] As Nicholas claims in his relatively early bid for the readmission of the Jews: "We have great and important cause to take heed, lest we of this Kingdom of *England,* putting from us and abandoning these people of God, we separate not our selves from Gods favor and protection, this being a greater aggravation of the sin, for that it is now more known." Nicholas goes on to document how "The rage of men in all countries of the world have been very extreme against the Jews . . . In *Spain* there were 120000 Jews cast out and banisht, in the year 1492. In *Italy* and other places, the like hardship they have endured."[44]

Nicholas was not alone in his condemnation of Christian attempts at forced conversion. A similar rethinking of Anglo-Jewish relations emerges inadvertently from entirely hostile accounts. As Thomas Edwards—who cites "*Miltons doctrine of divorce*" as a source of heresy to be contended with in the "Catalogue and Discovery of many Errours of the Sectaries"— describes in his corrosive *Gangræna,*

> The sectaries being now hot upon the getting of a Toleration, there were some meetings lately in the City, wherein some persons of the severall sects, some Seekers, some Anabaptists, some Antinomians, some Brownists, some Independents met; some Presbyterians also met with them . . . the Independents as well as the others holding together with the rest of the sects . . . some professing at one of the meetings, it was the sinne of this Kingdom that the Jewes were not allowed the open profession and exercise of their religion amongst us; only the Presbyterians dissented and opposed it.[45]

Edwards identifies toleration as the most acute of all dangers to the new orthodoxy as he dismisses sectarian heresies wholesale. Inadvertently offering a glimpse into the social vitality of the sects, Edwards wishes to enlist Paul in his cause, not surprisingly assailing heretics as "false Teachers, who broach false Doctrine."[46] Although he does not name Milton in the passage quoted above, Edwards does group Milton's writing on divorce with the sectarians who urge toleration of the Jews. Yet what for Edwards constitutes "false" teaching is for Milton essential to "the charity of patient instruction" (YP 2:567).

For Milton the reasonable power of the Mosaic Law derives in effect from historicizing the teachings of Christ within the tradition of Hebraic interpretation. This in turn leads Milton to recontextualize the Mosaic permission: divorce was not "permitted for the hardnes of thir [the Jews'] hearts . . . for the Law were then but a corrupt and erroneous School-master, teaching us to dash against a vital maxim of religion by doing foul evil in hope of some uncertain good" (YP 2:285). The metaphor of the schoolmaster remains the same as in the antiprelatical tracts, but its significance for Milton in the divorce tracts is the opposite. The Law is God's "reveled will" wherein "he appears to us as it were in human shape, enters into cov'nant with us, swears to keep it, binds himself like a just lawgiver to his own prescriptions, gives himself to be understood by men, judges and is judg'd, measures and is commensurate to right reason" (YP 2:292).[47] Milton must get beyond what Jesus says to the Pharisees in Matthew, which entails a return to Moses, in effect reversing typology.[48] Just as the binary opposition between nature and grace breaks down when Milton seeks to defend the "compulsion of blameles nature," so the narrative of succession is revised when the Law proves more charitable than a strict and decontextualized application of a precept from the Gospel (YP 2:355; cf. 2:279). Thus, in the divorce tracts, Milton finds "mercy" not only in the Gospel but also in Hebrew Scriptures. Rather than seeing the "Old Testament" as prefiguring the Gospel, Milton sees the Gospel in terms of the Hebrew Bible. He restores the ancient Hebraic interpretation of divorce law against the Gospel, thus claiming that the New Testament provides a contextual application of the Old, an application that does not abrogate the Mosaic Law but adheres to a broader interpretive precept of equity and love.

As a result of his advocacy of the right to divorce on grounds of intellectual incompatibility, Milton came to associate the Law with liberation.[49] In the divorce tracts, Milton refutes the idea that the Mosaic Law is a "most negligent debaushing tutor" and instead finds in the Law "the rules of all sober education" (YP 2:654).[50] Yet, by means of another paradox that opens onto a more profound meditation upon what might be called Christianity's intellectual history, Milton recasts the pedagogical metaphor rejected in *The Reason of Church Government* in the service of a diametrically opposed hermeneutics. Thus the figure of the teacher reappears in the divorce tracts with a difference. At the present time, Milton fears, "Custome still is silently receiv'd for the best instructer" (YP 2:222). "Custome" serves as the figure for intellectual sloth, the drudgery of inconsequential education commensurate with the "borrow'd manuscript of a subservient scrowl" monkishly copied out. "Custome" stands for "obstinate *literality*" (YP 2:279), which Milton deems a "Jewish obstinacy" (YP 2:319) not unlike "female pride": "Who can be ignorant that woman was created for man, and not man for woman; and that a husband may be injur'd as insufferably in mariage as a wife. What an injury is it after wedlock not to be belov'd, what to be slighted, what to be contended with in point of house-rule who shall be the head, not for any parity of wisdome, for that were somthing reasonable, but out of a female pride" (YP 2:324). On the face of it, this seems Milton's most egregious example of masculinist stereotyping. However, a predictable pattern of misogynist wish-fulfillment strains against a more striking admission that "parity of wisdome" is possible. For a brief moment, then, Milton reveals "somthing reasonable," an insight beyond prejudice. In such moments Milton exposes the limitations as well as the depths of his ideology of liberty: evidence of "parity of wisdome" he finds to be only "particular exceptions" (YP 2:589) to a general rule. But I would argue that this evidence suggests the relationship between an individual human being and tradition "writ large," an irony nicely conveyed in the pun at the heart of his sonnet resisting the "new" forcers of conscience and their "classic" hierarchy.[51] An individual, even as a representative of an alternative tradition, counters the unoriginality of historical inheritance by finding just such "particular exceptions." When Milton admits the possibility of a "parity of wisdome" among spouses, as when he recuperates the pedagogical role of the Mosaic Law, he implicitly rejects the Pauline text that he explicitly claims to endorse. Milton quotes Paul somewhat selectively: "*I suffer not* saith S. Paul, *the woman to usurp authority over the man*" (YP 2:324). What Milton has omitted from the verse is telling: "I suffer not a woman to teach, nor to usurp authority over the man, but to be in silence" (1 Timothy 2:12, KJV). One is tempted to see this omission as suggesting that "parity of wisdome" should authorize "a woman to teach," if not to "usurp." Whether figured as a liberating discovery of precedent or sloughed off as a hindrance to inspired thought, pedagogical authority for Milton signifies the ability to judge accurately, and thus defend historically, the validity of a tradition— whether a tradition corroborates truth or is contextually irrelevant. In this case, the notion that one tradition was (like Eve in one version of the Genesis myth) "created for" another would seem to endorse a rather literal-minded interpretation of those "priorities" Milton had dismissed in castigating the prelacy.

Amid the personal pain and special pleading of John Milton, as abandoned husband ("What an injury is it . . . not to be belov'd"), stands what may, however, be taken as a metaphor for the relation between Hebraic thought and Christian fables of succession. For, just as "particular exceptions" might reverse an assumed hierarchy obtaining in the marriage of a man and a woman, so the exigency of an argument against Christian tradition will open Milton to an unprecedented sympathy for traditions of Jewish thought. This sympathy Milton represents as a return to an originary relation with the Mosaic Law in the manner of Christ's response to the Pharisees on the question of divorce. Therefore *learned* succession is inherently paradoxical. It involves not only knowledge of legal and scriptural precedent, but also the ability to adjudicate flexibly between distinct contexts. And on such occasions as the debate over the legality of divorce—in which according to Milton the precedent, fully grasped, invites a legitimate resistance to customary interpretation—resistance to precedent is possible without violating the charitable spirit of the New Testament, even where the legal interpretation seems to reverse the literal sense of the Gospel text. The "Jewish obstinacy" of the post-Exilic rabbinic tradition is aligned with Episcopal, Presbyterian, even early reformist traditions that would hinder the domestic liberty of contemporary Protestants.

Thus "female pride" and "Jewish obstinacy" meet in a shocking image for the "pretious literalism" of his opponent, who would take Matthew 19:9 to signify that Christ prohibits divorce absolutely, except in cases of adultery: "let some one or other entreat him but to read on in the same 19. of *Math.* till he com to that place that sayes *Some make themselves Eunuchs for the kingdom of heavns sake:* And if he then please to make use of *Origens* knife, he may doe well to be his own carver" (YP 2:334). Milton's irony cuts both ways: Origen, who was said to have castrated himself because he interpreted Matthew 19:12 too literally, was also the strongest early advocate of Neoplatonic allegory as an exegetical technique.[52] Thus this passage—fusing "female pride" with "Jewish obstinacy"—suggests perversely that the father of patristic allegory was an emasculated literalist who conjoined pride with obstinacy to become a "Judaizing" eunuch, a neutered Jew.[53] Edward Gibbon's tart iteration of this historical irony has it thus: "As it was his general practice to allegorize scripture; it seems unfortunate that, in this instance only, he should have adopted the literal sense."[54]

The whole question of divorce seems to Milton essentially related to the integrity of his gender: to take away from a Christian husband the option of divorcing "were to unchristen him, to unman him, to throw the mountain of *Sinai* upon him, with the waight of the whole law to boot, flat against the liberty and essence of the Gospel" (YP 2:353). Just as a woman may exhibit "parity of wisdom" with a man, Christian exegetes may uncover new ways in which the Mosaic Law is "commensurat to right reason" (YP 2:292) above and beyond the prescribed customs of Christian tradition. Moreover, a "reasonable" resolution of conflict will illustrate the appeal to a higher interpretive principle. The most powerful injunction and the basis of the new covenant, charity provides the ultimate context within which to interpret a particular passage of Scripture. The rule of charity instructs the exegete to overturn the assumed hierarchies of gender and religion because it is reasonable to be charitable and charitable to be reasonable.

Nevertheless, Milton displays an ambivalent attitude toward his own instructors that resembles his outlook on gender relations in marriage. When Milton describes Christ's method of teaching as "not so much a teaching as an intangling," he insists that "it is a general precept, not only of Christ, but of all other Sages, not to instruct the unworthy and the conceited who love tradition more then truth, but to perplex and stumble them purposely with contriv'd obscurities" (YP 2:642, 643). Readers of Milton's prose are surely familiar with heuristically "contriv'd obscurities." In the space of a single sentence, Milton enacts just such a pedagogical exercise: if tradition corroborates truth—as when "all . . . Sages" other than Christ confirm the truth of his "general precept"—then the lover of truth need not fear the assent of tradition. But Milton's fear that he might himself be seen as one who loves "tradition more then truth" is everywhere visible in the divorce tracts. As Milton says in the preface to Parliament that begins *The Judgement of Martin Bucer*, "I may gratulat mine own mind, with due acknowledgement of assistance from above, which led me, not as a lerner, but as a collateral teacher, to a sympathy of judgment with no lesse a man then Martin Bucer" (YP 2:435–36; orig. in italics). Supposedly having discovered the similarity of his arguments for divorce to Bucer's after publishing the second edition of *The Doctrine and Discipline of Divorce*, Milton wishes to distinguish the inspired originality of his own thought from even the anti-traditional tradition of the reformers.

In doing so, he represses the authority of tradition while he weds it to his insight. Milton depicts this ambivalent relation to tradition as his own "collateral" pedagogical aptitude, "not as a lerner" but rather as one with an intuitive or native "sympathy of judgment" deriving unimpeachable "assistance from above." Milton likewise acts out his reluctance to cite the authority of Hugo Grotius: "First therefore I will set down what is observ'd by *Grotius* upon this point, a man of general learning. Next I produce what mine own thoughts gave me, before I had seen his annotations [on Judges

19:2]" (YP 2:329–30). Bolstered by Grotius, Milton can then claim the "subsequent, or indeed rather precedent" authority of a shared opinion that does not diminish his own originality of thought (YP 2:403).

This is the same anxiety palpable at the end of *Tetrachordon,* when Milton reluctantly ushers in the weight of patristic "testimony" corroborating "the words of Christ concerning divorce, as is heer interpreted" (YP 2:692; orig. in italics).[55] Accustomed "not to scanne reason, nor cleerly to apprehend it," some of the weaker sort of teachers who simply "follow authorities" have made it necessary for Milton to establish that "this opinion which I bring, hath bin favour'd, and by som of those affirm'd, who in their time were able to carry what they taught, had they urg'd it, through all Christendome" (YP 2:692–93). Because some of the "wisest heads" have "tended this way" but have been less full in their reason than in their "assertion," Milton says, "I shall be manifest . . . to meet the praise or dispraise of beeing somthing first" (YP 2:693). The habitual insistence upon what he calls in Sonnet 7 "inward ripeness" obsessively displaces an awkward usury of ideas, in which Milton, through the undisclosed interest of his appropriation, gains more credit than he gives:

> But herein the satisfaction of others hath bin studied, not the gaining of more assurance to mine own perswasion: although authorities contributing reason withall, bee a good confirmation and a welcom. But God, I solemnly attest him, withheld from my knowledge the consenting judgement of these men so late, untill they could not bee my instructers, but only my unexpected witnesses to partial men, that in this work I had not given the worst experiment of an industry joyn'd with integrity and the free utterance though of an unpopular truth. (YP 2:715–16)

Milton must "solemnly attest" to his own ethic, "industry joyn'd with integrity": more significant than the claim to testimonial corroboration from "unexpected witnesses" is his autobiographical narrative.[56] Milton relays how "God withheld" awareness of "the consenting judgement" of authorities so that he, as the champion of "an unpopular truth," might find a way of "beeing somthing first." In making such a claim for the original, or prophetic, status of his exegetical enterprise, Milton envisions himself "bearing the burden of zealous contempt," as befits a prophet.[57] Yet once more, when Milton argues through his sleight against the "partial men" who require authoritative "witnesses" in order to validate an argument, he demonstrates how the originality of his thought relates to the integrity of his gender—makes him a whole, as well as an impartial, man.

In his reluctance to admit his debt to his predecessors, his teachers, his sources, Milton assumes the role of "a collateral teacher" (YP 2:436). The gesture implies that, for Milton, from the divorce tracts onward, to resist authority intellectually is to wield it as a teacher. Even as one's own authority relies on a commanding knowledge of precedent, Jesus exemplifies charity as the ultimate pedagogy. And yet Milton in the divorce tracts found a more equitable solution to the hermeneutic dilemma he faced by returning to the charity of the Law. In his apparently contradictory celebration of the Law's continual pedagogical relevance and his disavowal of his own teachers, Milton assumes the paradoxical stance of the Christian Hebraist. The Hebraic pedagogue triumphs in the contest of teachers in play throughout the divorce tracts. As a Christian Hebraist, Milton crafted an inspired approach to the historic struggle for liberty, a "Christian *Talmud*" resolute in its union of heterogeneous materials.

In his disavowal as much as his effort to refashion and thereby lay claim to the power vested in Hebraic authority, Milton reveals the tension inherent in efforts to construct authorial stability out of the ruins of a textual inheritance. The contradictory impulse to establish a univocal sense of presence by appropriating multivalent Scripture is doubtless a reaction formed against the perceived incursions of slack custom. For Milton, traditions therefore must be contested by an enabling sociological "context" within which an author appropriates precedent. If a writer is formed as a reader responding to emergent occasions *against* other readers, then the intellectual culture toward which an individual reader directs his or her attention requires the fullest definition possible. In this regard, as we have seen, Milton re-imagines the debate over the use of scriptural proof-texts as a contest centered on the accuracy of a text, what he calls the text's "authentick handwriting." Later in the English Revolution, Milton would return to the metaphor of the pedagogue as figure of political authority, thereby creating a character of such ethical integrity that his resistance to the defenders of the monarchy on behalf of the fledgling republic would represent the highest form of heroism. If the Hebraic pedagogue triumphs, finally, as a model of reconstituted authority in the divorce tracts, then Milton's appropriation of a related legitimacy for his own authorial persona in the political tracts and later in *Paradise Lost* makes legible the social and literary implications of the interpretative strategy he refined during the English Revolution.

Chapter Three

The English Revolution and
Heroic Education

Criticism of Milton's politics has often been couched in dismissive remarks about his biography, but few censures in English literary history have achieved the rancor or notoriety of Samuel Johnson's criticism in the *Life of Milton* (1779). While political disagreement between these two figures is to be expected, the bitter sarcasm that Johnson reserves for Milton's efforts as a teacher during the opening years of the Civil War stands out:

> Let not our veneration for Milton forbid us to look with some degree of merriment on great promises and small performance, on the man who hastens home because his countrymen are contending for their liberty, and, when he reaches the scene of action, vapours away his patriotism in a private boarding-school. . . . Of institutions we may judge by their effects. From this wonder-working academy I do not know that there ever proceeded any man very eminent for knowledge.[1]

Even as Johnson's famous disdain for the "surly republican" manifests itself in this instance as a mocking dismissal of his results as a teacher, his criticism implicitly works at a deeper level to counteract the political intentions that underlie Milton's program of education. Although he claims that his digression is motivated by an unwanted intrusion of the natural sciences into Milton's curriculum, Johnson's emphasis upon "axioms of prudence" and "principles of moral truth" has a clear ideological agenda. The "first requisite" of education is, in Johnson's view, "the religious and moral knowledge of right and wrong." Thus when he launches his notorious attack on Milton's politics, Johnson articulates his objection in terms of a moral and psychological defect in the subject's character: "Milton's republicanism was, I am afraid, founded in an envious hatred of greatness, and a sullen desire of independence; in petulance impatient of all controul, and pride disdainful of superiority."[2] Envious, sullen, proud, and petulant, Milton failed in his political and his educational projects alike, according to Johnson, because he lacked the proper moral orientation.

Within a year, Francis Blackburne, clearly identifying the ideological motivation behind Johnson's *Life*, offered a rebuttal to this line of criticism. Johnson's moral condemnation of Miltonic pedagogy certainly deserved Blackburne's tart retort: "for the balance-master to reproach Milton for his pedantry is certainly betraying a strange unconsciousness of his own talents, unless he depends upon his reader's sagacity in discriminating a *great* pedant from a *little* one. He is obliged, however, to complete the humiliation of Milton, to put his prose-works into the scale."[3] Blackburne, a republican, objected to the royalist motivations for impugning "Milton the prose-writer, who, in that character, must ever be an eye-sore to men of Dr. Johnson's principles; principles that are at enmity with every patron of public liberty, and every pleader for the legal rights of Englishmen, which, in their origin, are neither more nor less than the natural rights of all mankind."[4] That Blackburne published his defense as an introduction to an edition of *Areopagitica* and *Of Education* indicates the political utility he found in Milton's educational strategies. Blackburne explains his rationale first for engaging Johnson and then for overseeing the republication of the tracts:

> We have only to add, that it has been thought convenient to subjoin to these Remarks, new and accurate editions of two of Milton's prose tracts; *viz.* his Letter to Mr. Samuel Hartlib on Education, and his Areopagitica. The first was grown scarce, being omitted in some editions, both of the author's prose and poetical works; but highly worthy to be preserved as prescribing a course of discipline, which, though out of fashion in these times, affords many useful lessons to those who may have abilities and courage enough to adopt some of those improvements, of which the modes of learned education in present practice are confessedly susceptible.
>
> The other will of course recommend itself to all advocates for the liberty of the press, and moreover may, in half an hour's reading, entertain some part of the public with a contrast between the magnanimity of Milton, in facing a formidable enemy, and Dr. Johnson's see-saw meditations, the shifty wiles of a man between two fires, who neither dares fight nor run away.[5]

Blackburne uses the metaphor of single combat to describe Milton's heroic work, a trope that, as we shall see, derives from Milton's own representation of his role as defender of the English republic. The "magnanimity" of Milton became the assurance of his political soundness for those who wished to endorse what they perceived as his defense of natural rights and his patronage of liberty. However, just as his blindness could be employed as a sign of divine punishment or of human virtue in action, Milton's representation of his labors as evidence of a new form of courage—of intellectual heroism—during the polemical years of the English Revolution would be used against him by his enemies.

Johnson and Blackburne quarrel over the political intentions beneath Milton's use of his learning, and both find in the ethical composition of the life an index to the political works' authenticity, though from diametrically opposite ideological perspectives. What this episode tells us about Milton's reception in the eighteenth century, during the American Revolution, is that for better or worse Milton's early readers followed the criteria that he himself established for judging his works. As we shall see, his personal virtue was the mark of authenticity Milton himself offered long before his early biographers drove the point home for future polemicists and ideologues. This effect, which he carefully cultivated throughout the revolutionary prose, reveals the profundity with which Milton conceived of his own pedagogical duty to his countrymen, a duty that carried on through the composition of the epic.

Arguing for the historical utility of literary representations, Christopher Hill remarks that, unlike other documentary evidence, literature "can convey the ethos of a society, what its members thought right and proper behaviour as well as what they thought outrageously possible."[6] Hill's comment serves as a crucial reminder of the dynamic interaction between the conceptual work—assumed in a culture's metaphors and analogies for heroic achievement—and the behavior of a person, such as Milton, seeking to create works that could be found, as he said in *The Reason of Church Government*, "doctrinal and exemplary to a Nation" (YP 1:815). In order to accomplish this heroic task, Milton had to dramatize not only his country's struggle to achieve the liberty he thought to be England's native inheritance, but also his own epic struggle to defend himself from the enemies of freedom.

CIVIL WAR AS POLITICAL EDUCATION

After the Restoration, a satirical poem by Thomas Jordan appeared twice, in 1662 and 1663, published for the second time in the collection *A Royal Arbor of Loyal Poesie* with the title "The Players Petition to the Long Parliament after being long silenc'd, that they might play again. 1642." The title, like the premise, relies upon what is in all likelihood a fictitious appeal to the

MPs of twenty years earlier—a context established to lend the irony of its Restoration publication more bite: "Your *Tragedies* more really are exprest, / You murder men in *Earnest,* wee in *Jest.*" When the player describes the actions of Parliament, the setting shifts momentarily away from the playhouse:

> Now humbly, as we did begin, Wee pray,
> Dear *School-masters,* you'd give us leave to play
> Quickly before the King come, for we wou'd
> Be glad to say y'ave done a little good
> Since you have sate, your Play is almost done,
> As well as ours, would have it ne'er begun;
> For we shall see e're the last Act be spent,
> *Enter* the King, *Exeunt* the Parliament.[7]

The Long Parliament, depicted here as an assembly of overweening schoolmasters, has prevented the "play" of state that the king will restore. The "tragic scaffold" erected for the execution of the "royal actor" outside Whitehall in Marvell's "Horatian Ode" (*Poems AM,* p. 276) has now become the stage for a comic triumph—a counterbalancing performance of power that Jordan celebrates: "up go we, who by the frown / Of guilty Consciences have been kept down" (ll.77–78). Jordan's comparison of stern MPs to "*School-masters*" bears a close resemblance to the aspersions cast on Milton by Peter du Moulin in *Regii Sanguinis Clamor ad Coelum Adversus Parricidas Anglicanos* (1652; *The Cry of the Royal Blood to Heaven Against the English Parricides*), later recycled by Dr. Johnson in his censure of the "acrimonious and surly republican."

In his own response to the cry of the royal blood, Milton fired back with his *Second Defense of the English People* (1654): du Moulin had accused Milton of being "some starveling little schoolmaster, who would consent to lend his corrupt pen to the defence of parricides" (YP 4.1:607).[8] Characteristically incensed by the accusation of insincerity and corruption, Milton responded with some of his most moving prose, in which, ironically and unfortunately, he dismantled the reputation of the wrong man.

For the duration of the commonwealth and protectorate, the critical dimension of education remains, in Milton's prose, the moral fitness of the polity. The entire basis of liberty, as opposed to license, is to be found in the moral health of the commonwealth. "For, my fellow countrymen," as Milton says in the *Second Defense,*

> your own character is a mighty factor in the acquisition or retention of
> your liberty. Unless your liberty is such as can neither be won nor lost

by arms, but is of that kind alone which, sprung from piety, justice, temperance, in short, true virtue, has put down the deepest and most far-reaching roots in your souls, there will not be lacking one who will shortly wrench from you, even without weapons, that liberty which you boast of having sought by force of arms. (YP 4.1:680)

Hence the emphasis on the political function of education arises from the interrelated obligations of the citizens within a republican polity—the mutual dependency of the meritorious upon each other. No doubt, the republican implications of Milton's educational proposals, as much as the educational implications of Milton's republican projects, occasioned Johnson's withering sarcasm about his success. Theoretically, the position advocated by Milton has at times surprising modern corollaries in the philosophies of education advanced by thinkers as diverse as Louis Althusser and John Dewey.[9]

The connection between the system of education and the polity it was designed to promote became clear in seventeenth-century England in a way that it had not before. In particular, given education's power to influence religious opinion, the subject concentrated political thought during Milton's lifetime. Although the implications that pedagogy held for the formation and maintenance of social order had occupied a central place in political philosophy since at least *The Republic,* the role of government in religious indoctrination took on new significance with the advent of radical sectarian dissent in the early modern era. Many of the most distilled political formulations of the seventeenth century therefore center on the power of education to alter the course of the nation's development. After the tumultuous years of civil war and faction, everyone understood that education had played a crucial part in the ideological ferment. Therefore, according to that part of the Clarendon Code called the Act of Uniformity (1662), schoolmasters as well as clergymen were forced to declare that taking arms against the king was illegal, to swear conformity to the Church of England, and to disavow the Solemn League and Covenant.[10] Both republicans and royalists consistently saw education as the cornerstone of the polity. As Marchamont Nedham put it, "Children should bee educated and instructed in the Principles of Freedom."[11] Both before and after the establishment of the protectorate, the specific commitments of educational reformers revolved around the dream of a "universal reformation" attainable by educational means.[12]

Reformation, personal and social, is at the heart of Milton's educational project as well as those of his friends in the Hartlib circle, even though (as we saw in the Introduction) they frequently disagree about the specific curriculum to achieve this end. In his preface to Parliament, added to the second edition of *The Doctrine and Discipline of Divorce,* Milton approaches the public dimension of reformation by returning to the first principle of education: "For no effect of tyranny can sit more heavy on the Common-wealth, then this houshold unhappiness on the family. And farewell all hope of true Reformation in the state, while such an evill as this lies undiscern'd or unregarded in the house. On the redresse whereof depends, not only the spiritfull and orderly life of our grown men, but the willing, and carefull education of our children" (YP 2:230). Milton registers the vital political stakes involved in the "carefull education of our children." The two senses of domestic government merge here: "houshold" economy functions as a metaphor for the Houses of Parliament. Education becomes the byword for nothing less than the ongoing viability of revolutionary ideals, though it represents somewhat disproportionately the connection between generational inheritance and "Allegiance" to the Long Parliament, between what is "unregarded in the house" and in the House. Thus Milton claims in the famous analogy from *The Doctrine and Discipline of Divorce,* "as a whole people is in proportion to an ill Government, so is one man to an ill mariage" (YP 2:229). England, he argues, ought to return to its historic role as the initiator of the Reformation, though it had been thought of as "the Cathedrill of Philosophy" by other nations since long before that (YP 2:231). "Let not England," he says, "forget her precedence of teaching nations how to live" (YP 2:232).

As a political strategy, therefore, Milton and his fellow republicans were fundamentally committed to reforming the moral constitution of the people (or at least of the meritorious few who would govern) rather than instituting a specific political constitution. Indeed, the movement toward a more educated polity can be seen as a general development in seventeenth-century English government. As Helen Jewell has recently shown, "Government was increasingly by the educated": in 1584 only 219 of 460 MPs (48 percent) had attended university or the Inns of Court, whereas in 1640–42 the total is 386 of 552 MPs (70 percent).[13] (So in referring to members of the Long Parliament as "*School-masters,*" Thomas Jordan was, ironically, not far from the mark.) This increase in the educational level of the parliamentarians may be the result of a "bulge in university entrants" in the late sixteenth century, though enlargement of the matriculating student body in the highest reaches of English education did not of course imply vast improvements in education for the poor or middling sort. In 1642 in the countryside, 70 percent of men on average were unable to sign their own names.[14] Nonetheless, the commitment to a morally indoctrinated constituency was surely stronger and more consistent than republican attachment to any specific institutions that would be established and stabilized by reforming government, despite the occasional proposal, such as Milton advanced with increasing desperation in *The Readie and Easie Way,* to inaugurate a perpetual senate.

Specifically ethical education was important to republicans because, as Jonathan Scott says, "in general republicanism defined itself not in relation to constitutional structures but moral principles."[15] For Milton in particular, as Blair Worden observes, "there can be no true political reformation which is not also a reformation of manners and morals, of the household, of education."[16] As Milton says in *The Tenure of Kings and Magistrates:* "For indeed none can love freedom heartily, but good men; the rest love not freedom, but licence; which never hath more scope or more indulgence then under Tyrants" (YP 3:190). The constitutive politics of personal reformation, central to Milton's argument on behalf of the regicide much as it had been in the earlier antiepiscopal and divorce tracts, remained a persistent emphasis even as his preoccupation with specific forms of political remedy changed.[17]

English national character, or the settled disposition of the populace as Milton perceived it, evinced a disturbing consistency that had disastrous political implications, though it was perhaps rectifiable by means of worldly education.[18] This indigenous weakness provided the basis for Milton's uncompromising critique of the Long Parliament and the bitter pronouncement on the English people in the manuscript digression in *The History of Britain,* one of the darkest parts of that gloomy book: "Valiant indeed, and prosperous to win a field; but to know the end and Reason of winning, unjudicious and unwise: in good or bad Success alike unteachable" (YP 5.1:450). Milton cannot have meant this claim "quite literally," as David Norbrook says, "for he was proposing a programme of republican education which he clearly believed could bear fruit if there were only time."[19] Thus in *The Tenure of Kings and Magistrates,* Milton defines his task precisely as an expedient pedagogical one, demanding that the mercurial (he would say "hypocritical") Presbyterians, and others who had turned loyalist, embrace parliamentary rule:

> Another sort there is, who comming in the cours of these affaires, to have thir share in great actions, above the form of Law or Custom, at least to give thir voice and approbation, begin to swerve, and almost shiver at the Majesty and grandeur of som noble deed, as if they were newly enter'd into a great sin; disputing presidents, forms, and circumstances, when the Common-wealth nigh perishes for want of deeds in substance, don with just and faithfull expedition. To these I wish better instruction, and vertue equal to thir calling; the former of which, that is

to say Instruction, I shall indeavour, as my dutie is, to bestow on them; and exhort them not to startle from the just and pious resolution of adhering with all thir [strength &] assistance to the present Parlament & Army, in the glorious way wherein Justice and Victory hath set them. (YP 3:194; brackets=added 2nd ed.)

Milton sought above all to inculcate fortitude in a nation fearful of the repercussions of killing a king. As Milton diminished the significance of appeals to precedents and specific forms of governance, he worked to separate an intrinsic morality of just action from a set of political circumstances. The justice or injustice of an action must be accountable first and foremost to the good of the many. Nonetheless, when *The Tenure of Kings and Magistrates* sets up a relationship between the leadership of the country and the people, Milton refrains from equating freedom with the "parricide" of which he was accused by his opponents. Teaching the public the meaning of "deeds in substance" entails teaching them the name of action, and the semantic distinction between a king and a tyrant therefore features prominently in Milton's argument.[20] Once a king becomes a tyrant, action on behalf of the public good becomes not simply just, but necessary in a state founded upon liberty. At the same time, Milton knew that the divines who had taught the laity and provided a coherent rationale for political action in the early 1640s had by 1649 long since abandoned the policy that allowed Parliament to unite disparate factions against monarchy. Yet the most effective argumentative strategy would always falter before an unswerving commitment to the ethical principle that must underlie just action: "To teach lawless Kings, and all who so much adore them, that not mortal man, or his imperious will, but Justice is the onely true sovran and supreme Majesty upon earth" (YP 3:237).

A people "endu'd with fortitude and Heroick vertue," as the regicides themselves had been, would redefine the very notion of heroism to match the "matchless valour" of the army under Cromwell's command (YP 3:191, 233).[21] Contrary to the "the tongues and arguments of Malignant backsliders," Milton advocates a civic republicanism along the lines of the great classical republicans, who provide exemplary instances of a more heroic ideal: "The *Greeks* and *Romans,* as thir prime Authors witness, held it not onely lawfull, but a glorious and Heroic deed, rewarded publicly with Statues and Garlands, to kill an infamous Tyrant at any time without tryal: and but reason, that he who trod on all Law, should not be voutsaf'd the benefit of Law" (YP 3:222, 212). By implication, in the regicidal tracts, as in his earlier tractate *Of Education,* Milton's educational proposals thinly veiled "a deep anxiety about the malaise afflicting the parliamentary cause and a conviction that the only cure for it was, in effect, a New Model education."[22] Milton envisioned his political pedagogy more consistently than has been generally recognized, and as late as the second edition of *The Readie and Easie Way* he was still rallying for "the heroic cause" of liberty, which he claimed to have celebrated "in a written monument," his *First Defense of the English People* (YP 7:420–21). The phrase is especially poignant in the face of the Good Old Cause's all but certain defeat, since Andrew Marvell, both as a student and friend of Milton, had praised the achievement of Milton's defense as a monument of learned triumph so worthy of admiration that "I shall now studie it even to the getting of it by heart." Echoing the conclusion of the *Second Defense,* Marvell writes, "When I consider how equally it turnes and rises with so many figures, it seems to me a Trajans columne in whose winding ascent we see imboss'd the severall Monuments of your learned victoryes. And Salmatius and Morus make up as great a Triumph as That of Decebalus."[23]

MILTON AND INTELLECTUAL HEROISM

The heroism associated with Milton, from his early Whig admirers down to the young Wordsworth, was consistent in emphasizing the strenuous intellectual combat at which he excelled, and the exemplary vigilance that his life represented:

> Milton! thou shouldst be living at this hour:
> England hath need of thee: she is fen
> Of stagnant waters: altar, sword, and pen,
> Fireside, the heroic wealth of hall and bower,
> Have forfeited their ancient English dower
> Of inward happiness.[24]

When John Toland defended his life of Milton, he underscored Milton's character (and his own) in novel-like terms: "SINCE therefore it was equally lawful for me to write whose life I pleas'd (when my Hand was in) the first Charge against me, one would think, should have bin, that I had not fairly represented my Hero."[25] In Milton's Defenses, there can be little doubt that educators—and, by extension, the educational process itself—have come to occupy heroic roles in the foundation and establishment of the commonwealth. It may be that, by the time he completed the *Second Defense,* Milton was, as Stephen M. Fallon has argued, "not merely a participant in heroism, or equal to those heroes who broke the yoke of tyranny; he is the lone heroic figure left."[26] Certainly the newfound heroism of the teacher figures prominently throughout

Milton's Defenses, such that heroism itself appears reconstituted or at least reconceived in order to include pedagogues. As he asserts in the *Second Defense,* "He alone is to be called great who either performs or teaches or worthily records great things" (YP 4.1:601). To teach the public how to praise, as well as how to recognize deeds worthy of praise or blame, is to rearticulate the classical ideals of ethical virtue.

If Milton's "learning has the effect of intuition," as Hazlitt says, Milton's intuition unfailingly leads him back to his learning when he narrates the events of his own life.[27] In keeping with his lifelong commitment to the moral fitness of the orator as an index of the justness of the orator's participation in public debate, when Milton seeks to defend the republic, he must also defend the rectitude of his character while he answers for the rightness of his cause. In this, Milton follows the ideals of the ancient Roman rhetoricians, particularly the ethical system as it was expounded in the *Institutio Oratoria* of Quintilian: "Surely every one of my readers must by now have realized that oratory is in the main concerned with the treatment of what is just and honourable [*aequi bonique consistere*]? Can a bad and unjust man speak on such themes as the dignity of the subject demands?"[28]

In advocating an ethical principle of judgment upon which to base the analysis of political discourse, Milton elevates the heroism of the moral agent to a level "above heroic." At the same time, as has often been remarked, the direction of Milton's thought can be observed in the drift of his Defenses' titles: from the first and second defenses of the English people, to a defense of himself. Nonetheless, when defending himself, Milton rises to the challenge of rhetorical combat. As he puts it, the English people had accomplished "the most heroic and exemplary achievements since the foundation of the world" (YP 4.1:549); subsequently he himself had slain the great Salmasius in single combat, a sublimated and ironic transformation of the classical *aristeia* as much as an appropriation of chivalric heroism for intellectual ends: "When he [Salmasius] with insults was attacking us and our battle array, and our leaders looked first of all to me, I met him in single combat and plunged into his reviling throat this pen, the weapon of his own choice. And (unless I wish to reject outright and disparage the views and opinions of so many intelligent readers everywhere, in no way bound or indebted to me) I bore off the spoils of honor" (YP 4.1:556). The Miltonic *aristeia* evidences not merely virtue or excellence of the warrior, but also the election of the godly. "There are," as Cicero argues in *De officiis,* a work extremely influential in the development of Milton's thought, "instances of civic courage that are not inferior to the courage of the soldier."[29] And Milton's victory reciprocally confirms the righteousness of the nation, as England's defender has yet once more repelled the incursions of what he styled in *The Tenure of Kings and Magistrates* an "outlandish King" (YP 3:214). Again, Milton figures intellectual debate through a metaphor of single combat, a trope that had a long history in humanist literature. Petrarch had depicted the pursuit of virtue as the destruction of a tyrant through valiant humanistic battle. In following the dictates of "sacred friendship," he would, like "Gophirus" in Herodotus, "stab with the point of my pen, even through its own breast, the impious grudge" that the tyrant envy was "clutching in its bosom in unequal embrace."[30] In essence humanistic combat, Milton's Defenses rearticulate the tropes of heroic literature as a means of conveying the scope and endurance of his, and the nation's, achievements.[31]

Milton repeatedly presents his decision to defend the commonwealth against royalist propaganda, in spite of the loss of eyesight that would ensue, as an act of epic heroism:

> The doctors were making learned predictions that if I should undertake this task, I would shortly lose both eyes. . . . I seemed to hear, not the voice of the doctor (even that of Aesculapius, issuing from the shrine at Epidaurus), but the sound of a certain more divine monitor within. And I thought that two lots had now been set before me by a certain command of fate: the one, blindness, the other, duty. Either I must necessarily endure the loss of my eyes, or I must abandon my most solemn duty. And there came into my mind those two fates which, the son of Thetis relates, his mother brought back from Delphi, where she inquired concerning him. (YP 4.1:588; CM 8:68)

Never one to shrink from self-mythologizing, Milton presents his choice as parallel to Achilles' choice. The common denominator is greater and subtler than it first appears. Between Milton's dilemma and the passage in Homer, there is the striking similarity of a decision to be made between duty and health, length of life and glory.

For Milton, the duties of the left hand (as he had said of his intervention in the pamphlet wars in *The Reason of Church Government*) outweighed the privilege of the right, so that prose called him away from poetry, just as civic duty had called him away from studious retirement. He expresses his recognition by referring to Achilles' famous speech in Book 9 of the *Iliad:*

> I carry two sorts of destiny toward the day of my death. Either,
> if I stay here and fight beside the city of the Trojans,

my return home [*nostos*] is gone, but my glory [*kleos*] shall be everlasting;
but if I return home to the beloved land of my fathers,
the excellence of my glory is gone, but there will be a long life
left for me, and my end in death will not come to me quickly.[32]

Milton's decision neatly allows for parallels between the self-sacrifice of two heroes, himself and Achilles, on behalf of the public good: the one fighting in military combat, the other a pamphlet war. Milton is spurred on by righteous self-assertion—if not self-righteous assertion—by the confidence he voices in the sonnet to Cyriack Skinner, despite his loss of sight in both eyes: "What supports me, dost thou ask? / The conscience, friend, to have lost them overplied / In liberty's defence, my noble task, / Of which all Europe talks from side to side" (*Poems*, p. 347, ll.9–12). But the rhetorical warfare that stands for civic duty—which Milton transforms in this passage from the *Second Defense* into a narrative of epic heroism—also provides a way for Milton to graft his autobiography onto the myth of the maker. Thus Milton's sacrifice of his eyesight on behalf of the Good Old Cause likens him not only to Homer's hero Achilles, but also to "blind Maeonides" himself (*PL* 3.35).

Milton's blindness therefore signifies the insight—commensurate with participation in epic writing and epic warfare—gained by the choice of losing external sight, which is in turn like the loss of life. (Death in the *Iliad* is always "dark": "a mist of darkness clouded both eyes / and he fell as a tower falls in the strong encounter" [*Iliad*, 4.461–62]). For Milton, the emphasis upon *choice* in this passage must have been paramount, and therefore the will of Achilles must be knowingly to commit to his brief but glorious life: to give up just as much of his present life, as it is figured in his *nostos*, or homecoming, in exchange for *kleos*, or everlasting glory or fame. And this is precisely what modern commentators see as the educational thrust of the *Iliad*, as when Cedric Whitman says that Achilles "is learning all the time. He is learning the meaning of his original choice, mentioned in his great speech in the *Embassy* of Book IX, learning, in fact, how really to make it."[33] Milton can relate this myth to his own life because he has gone blind, like the poet who sang Achilles' fame, thereby becoming the subject of his own myth in the process of favoring the *vita activa* over the *vita contemplativa*.[34] And Milton's intellectual heroism, which transcends the *merely* active life of the warfaring hero, places his efforts on a level with "the epic poet," as he says in the conclusion to the *Second Defense*, fulfilling his civic duty "to have celebrated at least one heroic achievement of my countrymen" (YP 4.1.685).

The structure of the *Iliad* leaves no doubt, from the first word, *menin*, that the "specifically divine wrath" of Achilles is divinely sanctioned—that, in effect, "the will of Zeus" is coextensive with the plot of the poem. [35] For Milton, "The more veracious a man is in teaching truth to men, the more like must he be to God and the more acceptable to him" (YP 4.1:585; CM 8:64). If Achilles proleptically figures the choice he will make when he reenters combat to avenge Patroclus—even as he offers to the Embassy in Book 9 the most extraordinarily damaging critique of the heroic code to which he will soon give his life—so, too, Milton wants to hedge the aggrandizement of his claim to heroism with a knowing critique. Milton goes so far as to concede: "although I should like to be Ulysses—should like, that is, to have deserved as well as possible of my country—yet I do not covet the arms of Achilles. I do not seek to bear before me heaven painted on a shield, for others, not myself, to see in battle, while I carry on my shoulders a burden, not painted, but real, for myself, and not for others to perceive" (YP 4.1: 595–96). Milton makes his remarks about divinely sanctioned soothsaying—what he calls "the sound of a certain more divine monitor within" (YP 4.1:588)—self-consciously as he adduces his list of blind worthies, among them Phineus the blind Thracian king, whom Apollonius of Rhodes depicts in the *Argonautica:*

> he had no scruples about revealing
> to men, precisely, the divine will of Zeus himself.
> So Zeus afflicted him with interminable old age,
> and took the sweet light from his eyes. [36]

Upon these lines Milton comments: "Because of no offence, therefore, does it seem that this man who was godlike and eager to enlighten the human race was deprived of his eyesight, as were a great number of philosophers" (YP 4.1:585; CM 8:64). No offence? While the *Argonautica,* by showing the readers of the poem the veracity of Phineus's prophecy, opens a new context for interpreting Phineus's situation—against, that is, the interpolated myth of his blinding—the Thracian king functions in Milton's narrative as an oddly less compelling example than Milton overtly states. After all, unlike Achilles (and, by extension, Milton in his comparison), Phineus does not abbreviate his plight but rather prolongs it by delivering his truth to men, "while I drag on a weary old age / whose end eludes me."[37] Phineus, unlike Achilles, makes his choice, if that is what it is, almost unwittingly, and ironically he suffers disfavor in the eyes of Zeus for his soothsaying. Unlike Achilles, Phineus will be condemned to a long and bitter life, tormented perpetually by the harpies until he is relieved by the Argonauts. Thus Phineus is an especially *bad* example of the righteous blind, afflicted as he is by divine wrath, and his blinding ought to serve as an ironic and cautionary tale for the kind of heroic truth-telling that Milton evokes in the *Second Defense*. Rather than serving as an admonition against the kind of critique that royal propagandists would have leveled against Milton, the example seems to undercut the structurally symmetrical narrative with which Milton ends the list of heroes, that of Achilles' choice.[38] Milton introduces Phineus's tale ironically to show that he is aware of the danger of assuming that his trial is over, that his suffering has been deferred and that he has found divine favor simply because he has sacrificed his eyesight in order to defend an unpopular truth.[39]

Like the micronarratives of heroic struggle that the passage allows Milton to bring into focus as he allegorizes his life, this episode in the *Second Defense* suggests something of the depth of Milton's engagement with the ethos of epic, the extent to which he internalized these tales and read their implications into his own lived experience. Milton employed the Phineus episode repeatedly, obsessively returning to the passage as his own eyesight gradually gave way. The crucial pattern that this use of Apollonius exposes in retrospect is the reluctance—or, better, the flat out unwillingness—of Milton to acknowledge the accursed condition of the blind seer, who foretold in an almost Promethean defiance the truth that the gods wished to keep from mortals. Indeed, Milton always revises the Phineus episode in *Argonautica* Book 2 in the direction of divine *sanction* or benediction. As Milton put it in his ode to the librarian of the Bodleian, John Rouse, *Ad Joannem Rousium* (1646 or 1647), which he included with a replacement copy of his "twin book" (*Gemelle . . . liber*), the 1645 *Poems:*

> Modo quis deus, aut editus deo
> Pristinam gentis miseratus indolem
> (Si satis noxas luimus priores
> Mollique luxu degener otium)
> Tollat nefandos civium tumultus,
> Almaque revocet studia sanctus
> Et relegatas sine sede musas
> Iam pene totis finibus Angligenum;
> Immundasque volucres
> Unguibus imminentes
> Figat Apollinea pharetra,
> Phineamque abigat pestem procul amne Pegaseo.
> (ll. 25–36, Strophe 2, *Poems*, pp. 303–4)

[If only some god or god-begotten man, moved to pity by the native talent of our ancient race—if we have made sufficient atonement for our past offenses and the degenerate idleness of our effeminate luxury—will take away these abominable civil wars and summon back our nourishing and sacred studies, recall the homeless Muses, now banished from nearly the entirety of England to the borders, and transfix with the arrows of Apollo the filthy birds, and drive Phineas's plague far from the river of Pegasus. (My translation.)]

Thus the divine wrath with which Phineus has been afflicted becomes the wrath of Apollo, god of poetry and prophecy, with which some god or god-like man shall, in Milton's optative subjunctive clause, drive away the harpies. Again, this revises Apollonius in the direction of divine favor, since it was in fact the Argonauts who drove the harpies away from the blind seer. The interjection of lines 27–28 suggests, further, the sacred context within which this pagan tale has been transposed. The verb *luere*—here *luimus*—means "to atone for," Milton's diction therefore suggesting a particularly reciprocal relationship between divinity and humanity. Although the sacral connotation of the word, in conjunction with the notion of discipline in the following line (*Mollique luxu degener otium*), suggests our responsibility for the plight which befalls us, the civil wars are *nefandos,* which carries a semantic range inclusive not only of "abominable," as I have translated it above, but also "impious." The point here is that Milton employs the Phineus myth in order to suggest the overwhelming role of divine judgment in every human action, whether the action finds favor or brings retribution. Even more significantly for our purpose, Milton chooses this episode—revised to suit his meaning—as a way to champion the return of sacred studies (*studia sanctus*) to England, thus ending the civil broils with which the native talent has been afflicted.[40] The sacred studies represent the active life, or *negotium,* of the poet favored by a benevolent deity.

Thus Milton again imposes the Achillean choice—the active life of civic duty versus the impiously contemplative retreat from it (*otium*)—only this time with the avowed intention of bringing about a reversal, a return of the "wandering Muse" of "At a Vacation Exercise" (l.53, *Poems,* p. 80). The rising poet of the 1645 collection has become the deliverer of the people of England, as Milton so explicitly would frame the issue in the *Second Defense,* though in *Ad Joannem Rousium* the remarkable difference is that poetry itself springs forth with the force of Apollo's arrows (which of course Book 1 of the *Iliad* sets up as a structural analogue, as well as precipitant cause, of Achilles' wrath). The change suggests that the will of the gods was not to punish Phineus so much as to rescue him.

The revision in the ode to John Rouse is clearly in line with another astonishing transformation that Milton brought about by way of the example of Phineus in the *Argonautica,* in a familiar letter concerning his blindness that dates from some three months after the *Second Defense.*[41] Milton tells his friend Leonard Philaras to seek the expert opinion of the Parisian physician Thévenot on his behalf, despite the fact that Milton is clearly dubious of the idea that he might regain his eyesight: "I shall do what you urge, that I may not seem to refuse aid whencesoever offered, perhaps divinely" (YP 4.2:869).[42] Milton again quotes lines from Apollonius, explaining that the effects of blindness made him "often think of the Salmydessian seer Phineus," this time selecting a passage drenched in pathos, concerning the experience of blindness itself (i.e., *Argonautica* 2.205–8). Milton uses the letter as an occasion to ask himself rhetorically, "If, as it is written, man shall not live by bread alone, but by every word that proceedeth out of the mouth of God, why should one not likewise find comfort in believing that he cannot see by the eyes alone, but by the guidance and wisdom of God" (YP 4.2:870)? Over the course of the letter, however, Milton switches his identification from Phineus to Lynceus, who, according to Apollonius, not only "excelled in sharpness / of eyesight—if the report be true that this hero could easily discern even what lay underground," but also was notoriously "overconfident" in his "mighty muscles."[43] Instead of a damned prophet awaiting rescue from his torment by the heroic Argonauts, Milton makes himself an Argonaut, his quest a metaphorical journey across "The mind, that ocean where each kind / Does straight its own resemblance find" ("The Garden," ll.43–44, *Poems AM,* p. 157). He bids Philaras farewell "with a mind not less brave and steadfast than if I were Lynceus himself."[44] Hence Milton returns full circle to his valorization of the humanistic employment to which he had been called by Parliament as a form of epic heroism, revising and allegorizing the struggles of epic protagonists in order to bestow divine favor upon them—even where their original contexts had urged quite the opposite. Movingly, the blind poet revises his predecessors to bring the narrative he wishes to tell about himself in line with a reading that, if not unproblematically, nevertheless recurrently holds out for evidence of providential design by reading divinely inspired trial into private struggle.

In fact, in the *Second Defense,* Milton clung to the idea that the English people had themselves received an education unparalleled in its divine promise: "Being better instructed and doubtless inspired by heaven, they overcame all these obstacles with such confidence that although they were indeed a multitude in numbers, yet the lofty exaltation of their minds kept them from being a mob" (YP 4.1:552). Royalists serve as a counterexample, so that Milton figures the revolution itself as a battle between rival educators: "He who teaches this right [i.e., that whatever is a king's pleasure is his right] must himself be most unrighteous, the worst of all men, for how could he become worse than by taking on the very nature which he imposes and stamps on others?" (YP 4.1:562).

MILTON'S RADICAL HUMANISM

In contrast, Milton was the conscious proponent of a system of education with a political dimension, and his last works together comprise a traditional and systematic approach to such education. This paradigm, which was his direct inheritance from the humanists of the Italian Renaissance, above all from republican Florence, was referred to then as the *studia humanitatis,* from which the term "humanism" and its diminutive contemporary form "the humanities" etymologically derive. The *studia humanitatis,* as Renaissance teachers would have understood it, comprised a set of practices that were eventually codified into an established cycle of educational programs inclusive of five parts: poetry, rhetoric, history, moral philosophy, and grammar. Not surprisingly, Milton himself published works specifically devoted to each of these genres in the last decade of his life:[45] *Accidence Commenced Grammar* (1669); *The History of Britain* (1670); *Prolusiones and Epistolae Familiares* (1674); *Paradise Regain'd, to which is added Samson Agonistes* (1671), which was hailed by Milton's great eighteenth-century editor Thomas Newton as being "full of moral and philosophical reasonings";[46] and, of course, *Paradise Lost* (1667; 2nd ed. 1674) as well as the reissue of *Poems upon Several Occasions together with a brief tractate Of Education* (1673).

The conceptual framework within which Milton received and communicated his republican ideas—namely humanism—requires a few words of explanation at this point. The emergence of English republicanism "was a consequence of the conjunction of events with the classical inheritance of humanism, and its popularity a result of the imaginative opportunities that parliamentary supremacy in the 1640s, and then a genuine republic in the 1650s, presented to educated people."[47] By the end of Milton's life, such a method of education—once on the cutting edge of educational reform—was fast becoming outmoded. Particularly with the rise of new scientific concerns, the epistemological foundation of Renaissance "humanism" had come under attack, especially for its insistent elevation of rhetoric over dialectic.[48]

Milton appropriated this (somewhat) antiquated paradigm, then, with a special appeal to the political motivations encoded in its method. The enduringly political intention of Milton's humanism makes Addison's comments—in the pages of the very newspaper in which he so beautifully defended Milton's classicism—doubly ironic; a Whig's desire to inoculate himself, and securely to partition the literary from the political, surely underlies the following aside of 1711:

> Among those Advantages which the Publick may reap from this Paper, it is not the least, that it draws Mens Minds off from the Bitterness of Party, and furnishes them with Subjects of Discourse that may be treated without Warmth or Passion. This is said to have been the first Design of those Gentlemen who set on Foot the Royal Society; and had then a very good Effect, as it turned many of the greatest Genius's of the Age to the Disquisition of natural Knowledge, who, if they had engaged in Politicks with the same Parts and Application, might have set their Country in a Flame.[49]

If the Royal Society is imagined here as having fostered endorsement for the monarchy, or as having quelled the more radical elements within the society and neutralizing them into all but passivity, then the opposite principle holds true for the social response to learning that Milton endorsed.

By way of example, we might consider in this connection between Milton's politics and humanism the inclusion of his tract *Of Education* in the second edition of his minor poetry, the *Poems upon Several Occasions* (1673). Critics have, mistakenly, supposed that this publishing event merely served a practical end, in that the gatherings of poetry needed the tract's added bulk to fill out the slender octavo volume. This act of "republication" represents the fruition of a longstanding commitment to educational reform. When *Of Education* appeared at the end of the 1673 collection, it began with a headnote that—like the more famous headnote added to "Lycidas" (first pub. 1638) for its republication in the 1645 *Poems*—historicized the reissue in a way that would have been unimaginable at its initial moments of composition and publication. When the tract appeared in 1673, the comment "Written above twenty Years since" appeared on a separate line, between the title and the text. The importance of the decision to include this extraneous and factually inexact information cannot be overstated: for *Of Education* was actually first published in June 1644, and was written closer to *thirty* years before its reissue in 1673. This published date misleadingly implies, as the headnote to the text published with the *Poems* of 1713 spells out, that *Of Education* was "Written about the Year 1650."[50] The moment in history to which the headnote alludes, then, does not coincide with the actual time of its composition, but rather the height of republican ascendancy in England. In other words, Milton, or perhaps more likely his publisher, fudges the dating to refer his readers to the period "above twenty Years since" because it had been almost exactly twenty years since the adoption of Lambert's *Instrument of Government* (1653) and Cromwell's consequent installation as Lord Protector. Therefore, "*above* twenty Years since," in 1673, puts readers in a frame of mind to consider the tract as a product of the period between the execution of Charles I (1649) and the founding of the protectorate (1653)—an event that had dashed the hopes of the more radical faction of the republican movement—thus rewriting the tract's publication history to inscribe its humanist agenda as an act of political radicalism.

Milton's educational agenda, if anything, became more assertively humanist following the Restoration. Because I have been employing the term "humanism" in a rather restricted sense, and since the term itself has often been misused in an anachronistic and inexact way—at least in relation to its origin and subsequent development in Renaissance Italy—by literary critics seeking in the twentieth century to rehabilitate Milton's achievement, a brief rehearsal of the historical meaning of the word and concept may be in order. The view of "humanism" that I attempt to counter here is the one promulgated in the vague and conflated sense of "Christian humanism," which jumbles the philosophical meaning of the term "humanism" with the historical one in a way that became common in France in the second half of the eighteenth century.[51]

The term "humanism" has definite origins that, to a large degree, limit the range of its historical reference and, consequently, determine its significance for Milton and his predecessors. As I mentioned earlier, the origin of our word for "humanism" is the Latin *studia humanitatis*.[52] The most significant classical proponent of this program of "cultural studies" or "learned pursuits," as the expression may be translated, was the republican Cicero, who used it in three orations that have direct bearing on its changing meaning. In *Pro Murena* 61, Cicero flatters his aristocratic audience: "And since my speech is to be given, not before an ignorant crowd or in some gathering of country folk, I will speak with a little more boldness of cultural pursuits [*de studiis humanitatis*] which are known and cherished by both you and me."[53] The refining function of literary study distinguishes the acculturated, equates the urban with the urbane, the literate with the literary. To know (or even to know *of*) these cultural pursuits, implies Cicero, is to cherish them for their superior humanizing influence. In his oration *Pro Caelio,* Cicero employs the term in a context that lends it a more ambiguous and, perhaps, broadly construed significance. He refers, in a brief digression, to "Titus and Gaius Coponius, who were saddened more than anyone by the death of Dio, who by his pursuit of learning and humane refinement [*doctrinae studio atque humanitatis*] as much as his hospitality were bound to him."[54]

These allusions hint at the range of meaning and the cultural cachet that the expression, and the studies to which it refers, claimed in antiquity. The most important usage for our purposes, however, occurs in the *Pro Archia* (62 B.C.E.)—an oration which had a powerful influence on Milton's Seventh Prolusion—in which Cicero clearly identifies the *studia humanitatis* with classical scholarship, fusing the connotations of its usage in the *Pro Murena* and the *Pro Caelio*. Here, Cicero defends Archias the Greek poet, an occasion that furnishes him with an opportunity to recall his own education at the Academy in Athens and to play up the association of refinement with Hellenic classicism: "But I beg of you an indulgence that is fitting in my client's case and that will not, I trust, inconvenience you: as I am speaking on behalf of a most distinguished poet and erudite man, before a court where such learned men are assembled, where the jury is so humane, where this magistrate sits on the bench, give me leave to speak somewhat of cultural and literary pursuits [*de studiis humanitatis ac litterarum*]."[55] The syntactic parallelism in the key phrase provides our clue to the practices to which Cicero refers. The study of classical texts produces a distinctly humane ethical faculty in the members of the senatorial class. Cicero's clear implication is that the jury members should regard this Greek poet as a kind of living monument and that, based on their good taste, they ought to spare someone so close to the classical tradition, which Romans know they ought to prize. When Cicero depicts the cultural milieu of Archias's childhood, he caustically suggests the relative provincialism of the capital in his simultaneous use of a passive construction and the rhetorical figure litotes: here in Rome, he says, because of the respite from civil strife, the study of the arts and disciplines of the Greeks were not neglected [*non negligebantur* (3.5)]. In times of peace, as when Marius and Catullus held the consulships (i.e., 102 B.C.E.), the study and admiration of Greek antiquity flourished. Cicero equates the study of Greek literary culture with the very business of peaceful civilization. By placing Roman culture—or that which distinguishes the acculturated member of Roman society—at one remove from present-day Rome and locating the distinguishing characteristics of learning and, indeed, ethical humanity in the remote Greek past, Cicero constructs what will become the locus classicus for the idea of belatedness inherent in republican humanism.

No humanist of the Italian Renaissance represented the pathos of this classical nostalgia more poignantly than Petrarch, whose character *Ratio* wonderfully uses the condition of the bibliophile as a metaphor for the infinite regress of ancient learning in his dialogue *De Librorum Copia:* to possess many books is "a troublesome but delightful burden and a pleasant diversion of the mind."[56] Petrarch discovered the *Pro Archia* at Liège in 1333 and copied it out in his own hand, carefully marking the passage I quoted above, which he would adapt and incorporate into his own writings. "If it is true that Italian humanists had no expression closer to 'classical scholarship' than *studia humanitatis,*" as Michael D. Reeve has recently argued, "then *Pro Archia* provided classical scholarship in the Renaissance with its charter of foundation."[57] In a famous letter to his friend Tommaso da Messina, which probably dates from the year of his discovery of the speech for Archias, Petrarch's use of the word for "human" (*humanus*) in a context where he clearly means "literary culture" (*humanitas*) diverges from Ciceronian usage: "Therefore let us be in good spirit: we do not labor in vain, nor will they labor uselessly who will be born after many epochs right up to the end of the aging world. It is rather to be feared that men will cease to exist before, by the effort of humanistic studies [*humanorum studiorum*], they break through to the most secret mysteries of truth."[58] This is precisely the sense in which Milton used the term in the autobiographical asides to his *Second Defense:* "My father destined me from boyhood for the study of humane letters [*humaniorum literarum studiis*]."[59] Neither Petrarch nor Milton, therefore, honored the philological distinction that other Renaissance humanists found in Cicero. John Veron's English edition (1552) of R. Stephanus's Latin dictionary defines *humanus* as "gentle, appertainyng vnto man, that happeneth vnto men, benygne, gracious, courteous, bounteous" and *humanitas* as "man's nature, the duetye that a manne ought vnto an other by the law of nature, bounteousnes, courtesy, the knowledge of the lyberall artes."[60]

Given the traditional humanist training Milton received at St. Paul's school in London, and the preference his *Prolusions* exhibit for this earlier educational experience over the more scholastically influenced cycle of studies at Cambridge, Milton's return to this educational philosophy toward the end of his life probably reflects his actual practice as a schoolmaster and tutor as well as his theoretical program. To the extent that Milton's own studies have been reconstructed—especially in Donald Clark's *John Milton at St. Paul's School* but also, less coherently, in H. F. Fletcher's *The Intellectual Development of John Milton*—they are available for specific comparison with the projects of the continental humanists that inspired them.[61] To this extent at least, James Holly Hanford was right in claiming that "Milton's peculiar contribution to the cause and philosophy of humanism" emerged from "a conscious and consistent endeavor to harmonize" what many saw as the "contradictory and irreconcilable motives" of Reformation and Renaissance. The mistake of those who see Milton's motives as "contradictory and irreconcilable" stems, argued Hanford, from a misinterpretation of "the character of the change in viewpoint of his later years" and a failure "to perceive that instead of passing farther from the Renaissance he had moved nearer to its central truths."[62] Among those truths, as Milton and other republicans such as Harrington would have understood them, were the lessons of the Venetian and Florentine Republics, which fostered humanistic learning as a form of responsive participation in civic life.

Hanford's special pleading ought, however, to remind us of the context in which Hanford defended Milton, during the so-called "Milton Controversy" that raged in literary circles and then classrooms through the first half of the twentieth century. ("The Milton Controversy" evokes the self-importance of some of its participants: after all, when was Milton *not* at the center of controversy?) Hanford's intervention should remind us of the politics of his adversaries in the debate over Milton's position in the canon of English literature, the politics in particular of the self-proclaimed royalist and Anglo-Catholic T. S. Eliot. Contrary to popular belief, it was often the royalists who in fact recognized the essential relationship between politics and culture. As Eliot put it in a pithy but damning essay, "Modern Education and the Classics" (1932), in which he also insists, "the hierarchy of education should be a religious hierarchy": "It is only within a particular social system that a system of education has any meaning."[63] But critics, following the important work of such scholars as Hanford and Bush, have often held the humanism of Milton's late period to signify a retreat from politics.[64] I would argue that to set the two in a false opposition is to enact a seriously anachronistic misrepresentation of the humanistic activity of the Renaissance and its afterlife in the seventeenth century. Such a concern for the propagation of dutiful yet learned and godly citizens became, if anything, more urgent as the Restoration became inevitable.[65]

EDUCATORS AND LEGISLATORS

Of course, Milton was not the only educational theorist forcefully to advance politicized programs in the Interregnum period. For royalists, the parliamentary victory and the institution of the republic made clear the need for an educational agenda that could indoctrinate the people with a counterrevolutionary ideology. "I.B., Gent.," who as "one of the most Heroick Cavaliers" chose to remain partially anonymous, published his treatise *Heroick Education* in order that, body and mind educated, the English public might "avoid that interior combat, which disturbs the peace and tranquility of our life."[66] The author's advice assumes the form of an aphoristic conduct book for teachers or "governours," and it participates in this way in a common genre that thrived throughout the Renaissance, having in the previous generation, for example, an analogue in Robert Dallington's *Aphorismes Civill and Militarie* (London, 1613), which the author rather urgently dedicated to the future King Charles I just after the death of Prince Henry. If, as "I.B." contends in *Heroick Education,* "The mind and will are absolute Monarchs and will have us observe the same circumstances and ceremony toward them," then it is logical that "the will is a Prince which commands, but is neverthelesse counseled by his servants, the Orders and Edicts are made in his name, but his servants lay the plots and projects."[67] As in the poetic manifestoes produced by royalists in exile, *Heroick Education* seeks to inculcate the willing few: "Affection is a Character which penetrates through the heart, opens the door it selfe, and makes a deep impression. 'Tis a Prince which obtains an Empire so much the more absolute, by how much the obedience is more voluntary."[68] As we shall see in the literary criticism of Davenant, Hobbes, and Dryden, these martial metaphors combat republican politics on the educational battlefield: "Those who conduct them [the young], must by their prudence, imitate the wisdom of a brave Commander, of Armies, who not willing to hazard a Battell, endeavour to ruine their enemies by cutting off all sypplyes, and provisions, dividing their forces, wearying out their souldiers by continuall alarmes, and handsomely avoiding all their dangerous attempts."[69]

A good point of comparison can be found in Harrington's *The Commonwealth of Oceana,* published in the same year as *Heroick Education,* and no less insistent upon the vital necessity of education for the polity. As Lord Archon says in "The Model of the Commonwealth of Oceana": "Now the health of a government and education of the youth being the same pulse, no wonder if it have been the constant practice of well ordered commonwealths to commit the care and feeling of it unto public magistrates; a duty that was performed in such manner by the Areopagites as is elegantly praised by Isocrates."[70] Harrington believes that schools should be erected throughout the commonwealth, and in the "twenty-sixth order" of the government he insists upon mandatory education for boys from the age of nine to fifteen.[71] Lord Archon fleshes out this order, saying that despite the fact that "some man or nation, upon equal improvement of this kind, may be lighter than some other . . . certainly education is the scale without which no man or nation can truly know his or her own weight or value."[72] A direct cultural connection exists between republican prudence and its literary manifestation, and so Harrington puts forth the university as repository of what he calls "good literature," a primary vehicle by means of which the commonwealth shall perpetuate *rem publicam* in the minds of subsequent generations: "Of this I am sure, the perfection of a commonwealth is not to be attained unto without the knowledge of ancient prudence, nor the knowledge of ancient prudence without learning, nor learning without schools of good literature; and these are such as we call universities."[73]

Although he shared Harrington's concern for educating the commonwealth, Milton nevertheless fiercely advocated the disestablishment of the universities.[74] In the ongoing debates over tithing and training for the ministry during the 1650s, Milton proposed again, as he had in the 1640s, the foundation of small local academies. Miton's friend Roger Williams, in *The Hireling Ministry None of Christs* (8 April 1652), had argued that "the churches and assemblies of the saints" are "the only schools of the prophets appointed by Christ Jesus."[75] In his own pamphlet on the subject, *Considerations Touching the Likeliest Means to Remove Hirelings* (1659), Milton concurs with Williams: "The whole gospel never sent us for ministers to the schools of Philosophie, but rather bids us beware of such *vain deceit*" (YP 7:319). The universities—the object of Milton's scorn since at least his *Elegia Prima* (1626)—propagated a trivial disputatiousness, a merely formal oratorical style without substance: "those theological disputations there held by Professors and graduates are such as tend least of all to the edification or capacitie of the people, but rather perplex and leaven pure doctrin with scholastical trash then enable any minister to the better preaching of the gospel" (YP 7:317). What, then, is required to make a man into a minister according to Milton? What sort of education ought to be provided in order to ensure the fitness of the godly? "What learning either human or divine can be necessary to a minister, may as easily and less chargeably be had in any private house" as a it may in a university—an arrangement, as we have seen, put into practice by Milton in his own home during the 1640s (YP 7:316). Therefore, the establishment of private academies, like that idealized academy described in *Of Education*, would be among the foremost uses to which the revenues saved by permanently disestablishing church education could be put:

> To erect in greater number all over the land schooles and competent libraries to those schooles, where languages and arts may be taught free together, without the needles, unprofitable and inconvenient removing to another place. So all the land would be soone better civiliz'd, and they

who taught freely at the publick cost, might have thir education given them on this condition, that therewith content, they should not gadd for preferment out of thir own countrey, but continue there thankful for what they receivd freely, bestowing it on thir countrey, without soaring above the meannes wherein they were born. (YP 7:319)

Milton persistently viewed education as the way to acculturate the nation, even to render the English people more cosmopolitan, as he writes in *Proposals of Certaine Expedients for the Preventing of a Civill War Now Feard, & the Settling of a Firme Government* (1659), proposing "the liberty to erect schooles where all arts & sciences may be taught in every citty & great towne, which may then be honoured with the name of citty whereby the land would become much more civilized" (YP 7:338). If the nation were to be "urbanized" through the institution of schools, the commonwealth would stand on the most secure foundation possible. Humanistic learning, in Milton's classical republicanism, is the fundamental condition for the existence of humane civil society: the two are mutually enabling as well as reinforcing.

History would prove, however, that the backsliding nation could not sustain the effort necessary to ensure its own freedom. In February 1660, after General Monck's army had entered London—just before 21 February 1660, when the Rump recalled the Presbyterian members to Parliament who had been excluded in Pride's Purge nearly twelve years earlier—Milton wrote *The Readie and Easie Way to Establish a Free Commonwealth*. The pamphlet was quickly printed and circulated early in the final week of February.[76] Meanwhile, hope among the republican minority sank as the population of London waited "for Monke to pull off his last hood."[77] Much to the dismay of the republican faction, the Long Parliament dissolved itself on 16 March 1660. In the weeks that followed, Milton prepared a heavily revised second edition of *The Readie and Easie Way*, which appeared in print by the first week of April. Charles II returned to England on 25 May, little more than two months after the dissolution of Parliament, and entered London in triumph on 29 May 1660.[78]

The two editions straddle the final days of the Long Parliament, and so the problem facing Milton was twofold. On the one hand, the massive insurgence of popular support for the return of a Stuart monarch ensured the futility of Milton's local aims in the pamphlet. In short, as the prospect of parliamentary rule diminished and General Monck revealed his irenic disposition toward the exiled monarch, avowed republicans fled the scene of government. Willful association with the Good Old Cause became dangerous. Even the title pages of the two editions bear witness to this phenomenon, in that, unlike the first edition, the second records neither the names nor the initials of the printer and bookseller, claiming only to have been "Printed for the Author" somewhere in London.

Moreover, pamphleteers antagonistic to Milton's cause in 1660 began to accuse him of employing aloof and grandiose Ciceronian rhetoric in the service of a disingenuous, self-interested politics. Cavalier polemicists such as Roger L'Estrange and Samuel Butler portrayed Milton's high-styled appeal for a republican meritocracy governed by a permanent legislature as an outmoded relic of 1640s and 1650s propaganda, and his idealism consequently became vulnerable to representation as the metaphorical correlative of his physical disability, his "blindness" to the imperatives of an increasingly commercial society.[79] In the first edition, the orator directs his plea to a distinctly characterized collective: "that part of the nation which consents not with them, as I perswade me of a great number, far worthier then by their means to be brought in to the same bondage, and reservd, I trust, by Divine providence to a better end; since God hath yet his remnant, and hath not yet quenched the spirit of libertie among us" (YP 7:363–4). In the same passage in the second edition, the orator less hopefully addresses "that part of the nation which consents not with them, as I perswade me of a great number, far worthier then by their means to be brought into the same bondage" (YP 7:428). The godly "remnant" and indeed the "better end" have disappeared. The logic of the metaphor proposed by the two editions neatly illustrates the assumptions underlying a hoary cliché of Milton criticism: if the second edition betrays the idealism of Milton's jeremiad by making legible a pattern of retreat, then his virtual silence after his imprisonment in the early 1660s, followed by the publication of his poetry in the late 1660s and early 1670s, reveals a circumspect (maybe even penitent) radical effecting an "inward turn" toward private devotion and quietist solidarity with fellow regicides who escaped persecution under the new regime.[80]

It is true that after the publication of the two editions of *The Readie and Easie Way*, Milton himself published nothing until the first edition of *Paradise Lost* (1667)—with the exception of a ten-year-old sonnet used as a commendatory poem for Sikes's *The Life and Death of Sir Henry Vane, Kᵗ* (1662).[81] Of course, practical necessity forced Milton not to publish during the early 1660s. It is well known that, acting on a request of the House of Commons, Charles issued a proclamation resulting in the September 1660 confiscation and burning of Milton's *First Defense* (1651 and 1658) and *Eikonoklastes* (1649) as well as John Goodwin's *The Obstructours of Justice* (1649) by the common hangman at the Sessions House in the Old Bailey.[82]

Despite the apparent contradictions and expedient revisions contained in his outline for a free commonwealth in *The Readie and Easie Way,* Milton held fast to the abstract principle of education as an exigent means for the public to reconstitute its faltering commonwealth. Characteristically, he advocated the practical implementation of his scheme to establish private academies, even when the precise connection between this plan and the governmental paradigm for which he was risking his life seemed, at best, tenuous.[83] Because "the whole freedom of man consists either in spiritual or civil libertie," the institutions of the commonwealth would require that an active citizenry understand its liberties better than the backsliding populace seemed to in April 1660 (YP 7:456). Above all, this entailed a polity aware that the very premise of their empowerment was liberty of conscience. In connection with the spiritual freedom to follow the dictates of conscience rather than established, state-sponsored forms of religion, "The other part of our freedom consists in the civil rights and advancements of every person according to his merit: the enjoyment of those never more certain, and the access to these never more open, then in a free Commonwealth" (YP 7:458). Milton's assessment, I think, implicitly guarantees a commercial benefit to society—and political advancement for the few who merit the right to govern—as a rhetorical enticement to follow his spiritual agenda.

However, as Steve Pincus has pointed out, "Milton was convinced that civic virtue, not material consideration, was the basis of political and martial power."[84] Both civil liberty and religious freedom are, ultimately, dependent upon the educational apparatus that will ensure their propagation. Milton suggests that education is the social equivalent of the circulation of blood throughout the body politic—or perhaps, as John Rogers has argued, the vital warmth thought to have infused the created universe and given all things form:[85]

They [local districts] should have heer also schools and academies at thir own choice, wherein thir children may be bred up in thir own sight to all learning and noble education not in grammar only, but in all liberal arts and exercises. This would soon spread much more knowledge and civilitie, yea religion through all the parts of the land, by communicating the natural heat of government and culture more distributively to all extreme parts, which now lie numm and neglected, would soon make the whole nation more industrious, more ingenuous at home, more potent, more honorable abroad. To this a free Commonwealth will easily assent; (nay the Parlament hath alreadie som such thing in designe)

for of all governments a Commonwealth aims most to make the people
flourishing, vertuous, noble and high spirited. (YP 7:460)

The emphasis upon locality, or a more decentralized form of judiciary and
educational authority, serves as a quasi-constitutional check against the cen-
tripetal pull of monarchy.[86] Monarchical regulation of normative modes of
civil indoctrination must be protected against at all costs, and so Milton's
aim is to set up dissenting academies not unlike those that were in fact made
necessary by the institution of the Clarendon Code a few years later.

"To make the people fittest to chuse, and the chosen fittest to govern,"
argues Milton, "will be to mend our corrupt and faulty education, to teach
the people faith not without vertue, temperance, modestie, sobrietie, parsi-
monie, justice, not to admire wealth or honour; to hate turbulence and
ambition; to place every one his privat welfare and happiness in the public
peace, libertie and safetie" (YP 7:443). But of course "the chosen" would not,
in Milton's model, be subject to the rotational model to which Harrington
remained committed. Rather, the perpetual senate would ensure, perhaps
paradoxically, the continuance of the people's fundamental liberties, above all
else their liberty of conscience. Ultimately, a little over a century after *The
Readie and Easie Way* was written, James Madison would advance a related
argument when he called, in *The Federalist* No. 10 (1787), for "the republican principle" as a protection against "pure democracy"; the "delegation of
the government" to "a small number of citizens" would ensure that "the public voice" was "pronounced by the representatives of the people" and therefore would prove "more consonant to the public good"—and less likely to
decay into the "mischiefs of faction"—"than if pronounced by the people
themselves convened for the purpose."[87] More immediately, however, "the
public peace" mandated the return of the king, which led in turn to the educational project of Milton's great poems.

POETS AS EDUCATORS: HEROISM AND EPIC FORM

How does this new emphasis on the heroism of humanistic education alter
the forms of the heroic poem, which represented heroism more directly and
self-consciously than any other literary genre in early modern culture? Traditionally held to be the highest of poetic genres, epic has always commanded
the awareness of its readers, whether critics or admirers, as an educative
medium. Homer was, according to Plato and Xenophanes, "the educator of
Hellas," and it is hardly surprising to students of antiquity that "there was no
separation between ethics and aesthetics" in ancient Greece; indeed, as

Werner Jaeger has argued, "The educational content and the artistic form of a work of art affect each other reciprocally, and in fact spring from the same root."[88] Of course, the chief objection Socrates launches against Homer, even as he awards the poet with a kind of heroic epithet, is a critique of the dangerous political influence that Homer's corrupting myths introduce into the republic. But this perceived danger also bore witness to epic's power to grant the imaginary an active political force. The political implications of epic education arise from a complex and reciprocal interchange of ideologies, in which, as Sir Henry Wotton wrote to John Donne, "men do often learn when they do teach."[89]

Whether acknowledged or, as Percy Bysshe Shelley contends, "unacknowledged legislators of the World," poets were, in the early modern period, undoubted legislators of the word.[90] Thomas Hobbes understood this potency of epic, and in his famous answer to Davenant's preface to *Gondibert* (1650/1), the philosopher manages to reinforce the idea that "the vertues you distribute there amongst so many Noble Persons, represent (in the reading) the image but of one mans vertue to my fancy, which is your own."[91] If the ennobling gesture creates a window into the psychology of the epic poet, the psychomachia is nevertheless to be conveyed in modern rationalist terms: "Time and Education begets Experience; Experience begets Memory; Memory begets Judgement and Fancy; Judgement begets the strength and structure; and fancy begets the ornaments of a Poem."[92] Hobbes promotes the rational constriction of the educated intellect, which derives its principles of composition (in a process of intellectual abstraction) from nature, as opposed to the wild and (to him) uncultivated inspiration of the puritan and republican advocates of the sublime *furor poeticus*.[93] For Hobbes, the poet ought to exemplify the same nobility of mind that poetry encourages in readers.

Davenant insists upon the political education of the princely caste as the primary aim of epic, as religion, arms, politics, and law have been made "weak by an emulous war amongst themselves: it follows next, we should introduce to strengthen those principal aids (still making the people our direct object) some collateral help; which I will safely presume to consist in Poesy."[94] Throughout the royalist theories of epic and of education during the Interregnum and after the crisis of the English republic, one finds the metaphors of "emulous" civil strife and factional warfare used to describe the displacement of political functions onto the arts. Political motivations for epic in particular appear as a displacement precisely because of the self-consciousness induced by defeat. More critically, the martial metaphors and the fractious polity do not simply mirror each other. Instead, the vehicle and tenor of such metaphors circulate by means of a cultural synergy expressive and constitutive of a new public space to be resisted, enabled, or regulated. For Davenant, the "multitude" is "that which was anciently call'd a Monster"—not unlike the gargantuan body politic as depicted in the several issues of the frontispiece to Hobbes's *Leviathan*—and its political manipulation depends upon a mimetic chain that begins with the poet's inculcation of the nobility:

> I may now believe I have usefully taken from Courts and Camps, the patterns of such as will be fit to be imitated by the most necessary Men; and the most necessary Men are those who become principal by prerogative of blood, (which is seldom unassisted with education) or by greatness of minde, which in exact definition is Vertue. The common Crowd (of whom we are hopeless) we desert, being rather to be corrected by Laws (where precept is accompanied with punishment) then to be taught by Poesie; for few have arriv'd at the skil of *Orpheus,* or at his good fortune, whom we may suppose to have met with extraordinary Grecian Beasts, when so succesfully he reclaim'd them with his Harp. Nor is it needful that Heriock Poesie should be levell'd to the reach of common Men: for if the examples it presents prevail upon their Chiefs, the delight of Imitation (which we hope we have prov'd to be as effectual to good as to evil) will rectifie by the rules which those Chiefs establish of their own lives, the lives of all that behold them; for the example of life, doth as much surpass the force of Precept, as Life doth exceed Death.[95]

Davenant takes the Aristotelian conception of mimesis to a new degree of elitism: not merely is the poet to depict those of higher station and more noble composition than the audience, but epics are to exclude the people altogether, since the orphic charming of the beastly public can be abandoned in favor of punitive laws.[96] The nobility will lead by example, and the public will follow the cavalier caste, those "most necessary men" who comprise Davenant's ideal audience.[97]

The political valence of genre theory intersected with actual poetic writing in complex and apparently contradictory ways after the Restoration, when the supporters of the republic had to accommodate their concept of poetic form to disempowerment and persecution. Milton's note on the verse of *Paradise Lost*—added to the fourth issue of the first edition (1668)—participated in a vigorous, politically charged debate about the proper form of the Heroic Poem in English, a debate that had most recently flourished in the letters of Davenant and Hobbes, though it had in fact begun during the reign of Elizabeth in an equally contentious setting. While Milton argues forcefully against rhyme, *Paradise Lost* does rhyme as a part of a broader political strategy to educate his "fit audience . . . though few." Rhyme was, according to Milton, "the Invention of a barbarous Age, to set off wretched matter and lame Meeter."[98] Most early modern histories of English versification agree about rhyme's "barbarous" origin if not effect; this is equally true among champions of unrhymed quantitative verse such as Roger Ascham and advocates of rhyme such as John Dryden, newly made Charles II's Poet Laureate in 1668. Milton's note on the verse of *Paradise Lost* is most immediately a polemical response to Dryden's *Essay of Dramatic Poesy*, which had appeared earlier in the same year. Dryden explains, "[W]hen, by the inundation of the Goths and Vandals into Italy, new languages were brought in, and barbarously mingled with the Latin, of which the Italian, Spanish, French, and ours (made out of them and the Teutonic) are dialects, a new way of poesy was practiced; new, I say, in those countries, for in all probability it was that of the conquerors in their own nations. This new way consisted in measure or number of feet, and rhyme."[99] Dryden's tale of the "conquerors in *their own* nations"—a political paradox with special resonance for the "restored" Stuart king—chronicles the invention of rhyme by the "Barbarians," who could not observe the rules of classical versification because these were not "suitable to their tongues." The invasions of the Goths and Vandals caused languages to be, as Dryden says, "barbarously mingled," in turn creating modern prosody.

The same historical fusion inaugurates the tragic shift, from republicanism centered on senatorial governance to absolutism centered on monarchical prerogative, in the writings of republican political theorists. In *Oceana*, Harrington says that the rise of Julius Caesar "extinguish[ed] liberty" by bringing about what he calls "the transition of ancient into modern prudence." Like the author of "Nostradamus's Prophesy," Harrington preferred "Venetian Libertye" to the machinations of the contemporary despotic monarchies, the "modern prudence" of which Harrington was so critical.[100] Although it was Caesar who ultimately accomplished this "transition," the concept of absolutism was, according to Harrington, "introduced by those inundations of Huns, Goths, Vandals, Lombards, Saxons which . . . deformed the whole face of the world with those ill features of government which at this time are become far worse in these western parts."[101] Depicting the "inundations" as a process of governmental miscegenation, Harrington asserts that the Roman polity was, in Dryden's phrase, "barbarously mingled," in effect producing the absolutist European monarchies.

So the historical transition from parliamentary rule to dictatorship coincides with the invention of rhyme.

After the collapse of the English Republic, a wave of rhymed propaganda dependent upon an analogy between Roman and British empires welcomed the restored monarch. In his celebratory poem of 1660, *Astraea Redux,* Dryden returns to the Roman imperial conquest of Britain as an allegory for the accession of Charles II to the throne. The rulers of the Commonwealth become the "lesser Gods" of an *Interregnum* who "owned a lawless salvage liberty, / Like that our painted ancestors so prized / Ere empire's arts their breasts had civilized."[102] Dryden characteristically equates "liberty" with the "salvage," "arts" with empire. These "arts" are of course the civilizing arts imposed by the Romans upon Britain—"arts" that Marvell had cautiously memorialized in the final lines of "An Horatian Ode": "The same arts that did gain / A pow'r must it maintain" (*Poems AM,* p. 279). Marvell's ode equivocally celebrates this "pow'r" by holding its "arts" up to critical scrutiny, whereas, for Dryden, "empire's arts" are mutually and positively reinforcing. The Romans have "civilized" the Britons by quelling the rebellion in their "breasts." Already the position Dryden would voice in *Absalom and Achitophel* (1681) was clear: "never rebel was to arts a friend" (l.873).

Military conquest, Dryden's poems contend, rhymes with pacifying cultural conquest. Thus the analogy extends to the particular form of the poem. The implicit argument Dryden makes throughout his celebration of the restored monarch finds structural, metaphoric expression in his use of rhyme: "O happy age! O times like those alone / By Fate reserved for great Augustus' throne!" (ll.320–1). The Restoration is "like" the age "reserved" for Roman imperial ascendancy, during which the "barbarians" who ultimately established the modern European monarchies were first "civilized" by Augustan imperial culture. The connotation lodged in the rhyme is that the two times are joined as a result of monarchy—the single, metonymic "throne," which they "alone" share, since both began with the collapse of republics. The remote colony of Rome has become the center of a transatlantic naval empire equipped to spread what Dryden calls the "wealthy trade" of British mercantile interests across the globe in "the joint growth of arms and arts" (ll.304, 322). It is therefore, in Dryden's conceit, poetic justice that the *pax Britannia* should complement the *pax Romana.* The *translatio imperii,* the westward translation or transferal of empire, has made rhyme indigenous to the "Imperial Arts" of the new Rome, as in Anchises's prophecy to Aeneas in Dryden's translation: "But, *Rome,* 'tis thine alone, with awful sway, / To rule Mankind; and make the World obey."[103]

So far, the histories are remarkably consistent, though interpretations of the events tend to line up like warring factions. In both republican and royalist accounts, the genealogies of the vernacular poetic traditions and of the contemporary despotic monarchies began with the "inundations" of the "barbarians." Among zealous protestant commentators, this history suggestively linked the rise of rhyme with, as the first published commentary on *Paradise Lost* put it, "the times of Monkish Ignorance," or the ascendancy of that other Rome, the Catholic Church.[104] Declaiming against rhyme's "vexation, hindrance, and constraint" in antimonarchical and anti-ecclesiastical terms, Milton concludes his preface to *Paradise Lost* with a rousing boast: "This neglect then of Rime so little is to be taken for a defect . . . that it rather is to be esteem'd an example set, the first in *English,* of ancient liberty recover'd to Heroic Poem from the troublesom and modern bondage of Rimeing." Likewise, as Milton claims in the *The Readie and Easie Way,* "the thraldom of kingship" is "a new slaverie" (YP 7:422). The "modern bondage of Rimeing," endemic to monarchic epic and romance, is the formal correlative of absolutist rule against which Milton defines his ideal of "ancient liberty."

By contrast, the "ancient liberty" of a republic is to government what blank verse is to "Heroic Poem" as a genre. "Ancient liberty" had commonly served as a rallying cry in republican political writing, from the ancient Roman historians through Machiavelli's *Discorsi,* from which Milton copied out 17 passages for his Commonplace Book (see YP 1:512). In *Eikonoklastes* (1649)—one of the official defenses of the regicide that Milton wrote at Parliament's behest—Milton urges the public to recall "how great a loss we fell into of our *ancient liberty*" by agreeing in the Triennial Act to limit how often Parliament could meet.[105] In this context, Milton appeals to the unwritten basis of the Anglo-Saxon polity before the Norman Conquest—invoking, in effect, a new history of English Common Law that was variously constructed in the period to decentralize the institutions of monarchy.[106]

The concept is crucial for understanding Milton's note on the verse. If the earliest beginnings of rhyme were to be found in the "inundations" of the barbarians, then the ascendancy of rhyming epic in England was contemporaneous with the Norman Conquest.[107] Thomas Warton, the late eighteenth-century editor and author of commentaries on Milton and Spenser, took "the Norman accession" as the ideal point of departure for his massive *History of English Poetry* because, he said, it "produced that signal change in our policy, constitution, and public manners."[108] In the opposition between "modern bondage" and "ancient liberty," Milton compresses three analogous moments of decline: the Gothic invasions of the Roman Empire, the Norman invasion of England, and the Restoration of Charles II. These phases of history and literature share a paradigmatic collapse of "ancient liberty"—the fall of a "republican" or "mixed" polity—as well as a corresponding preference for verse that rhymes. The two are symptomatic of the same intellectual decline. In the recovery of an ancient mode of poetic composition, Milton argues, the poet urges a return to the "ancient liberty" of a republic.

Political theorists from across the spectrum voiced arguments about the power of ancient literature to instigate radical political action. Harrington and Hobbes concurred about the uses of literature in ancient society, though they expressed radically different appraisals of its value. Hobbes attributes the motive that underlies such indoctrination of the populace to a pernicious, ingenuous supposition deriving ultimately from the Athenians, who "were taught, (to keep them from desire of changing their Government,) that they were Free-men, and all that lived under Monarchy were slaves." Hence, deference to the authority of the classics, Hobbes contends, has educated men at a great cost to society: "by reading of these Greek, and Latine Authors, men from their childhood have gotten a habit (under a falseshew of Liberty,) of favouring tumults, and of licentious controlling the actions of their Soveraigns; and again of controlling those controllers, with the effusion of so much blood; as I think I may truly say, there was never any thing so deerly bought, as these Western parts have bought the learning of the Greek and Latine tongues."[109] Literature unleashes the illusion that the condition of tumult is natural under a monarch. Knowing that "it is an easy thing, for men to be deceived, by the specious name of Libertie; and for want of Judgement to distinguish, mistake that for their Private Inheritance, and Birth right, which is the right of the Publique only," Hobbes reasoned that "when the same errour is confirmed by the authority of men in reputation for their writings in this subject, it is no wonder if it produce sedition, and change of Government." Ancient treatises stir up their readers, who become politically insolent because they falsely attribute authority to authors who derived their theory of government not from rational observation of "the Principles of Nature," but instead from pre-existing forms of government—in other words, from "the Practise of their own Common-wealths, which were Popular." This methodological error corresponds to the way in which modern (here, read "republican") political theorists seek justification and precedence for a system of government in books rather than in natural philosophy, just "as the Grammarians describe the Rules of Language, out of the Practise of the time; or the Rules of Poetry, out of the Poems of *Homer* and *Virgil.*"[110]

The political valence of Milton's 1668 note on rhyme was clear enough to the poem's most immediate audiences. In 1673, Richard Leigh referred to Milton as "this *Schismatick* in *Poetry* . . . nonconformable in point of

Rhyme."[111] The essence of the matter was, for Nathaniel Lee in his "To Mr. Dryden, on his Poem of Paradise" (1674?), that Milton "rudely cast what you [Dryden] could well dispose," partly because "He roughly drew on an old Fashion'd Ground, / A Chaos."[112] In "An Ode By Way of an Elegy on . . . Mr. Dryden" (June 1700), Alexander Oldys elaborates the political nature of prosody further, putting Tory praise of Dryden in a repentant Milton's mouth:

> A double share of bliss belongs to thee,
> For thy rich verse and thy firm loyalty;
> Some of my harsh and uncouth points do owe
> To thee a tuneful cadence still below.
> Thine was indeed the state of innocence,
> > Mine of offence,
> With studied treason and self-interest stained,
> Till Paradise Lost wrought Paradise Regained.[113]

The titles of Milton's epics themselves become for Oldys a trope to illustrate how Dryden's salvaging of *Paradise Lost* was its salvation. The problem remained for many eighteenth-century critics the one on which John Clarke harped in *An Essay Upon Study* (1731): "The Negligence of the Author with respect to the Smoothness of his Verse, which is sometimes scarce distinguishable from Prose."[114] The schoolmaster's objection to Milton's prosody represents a tacit rejoinder to the polemical regicide, whose prose had been republished (occasionally in rewritten form) since the end of the seventeenth century by Whigs seeking vindication for their various positions on monarchy.[115] Like twentieth-century royalist T. S. Eliot, Clarke issued his prosodic, stylistic corrective on the grounds that "the rectifying of Mistakes in the Conduct of a Poet, of *Milton's* Fame and Authority, is a Means to prevent others from being misled into an Imitation of his Faults."[116] However, royalists were not to be the only commentators on Milton's prosody in the eighteenth century. In 1786, just a decade after authoring the Declaration of Independence, Thomas Jefferson commented in his "Thoughts on English Prosody" upon the "most esteemed" form in English verse, the pentameter. For, Jefferson argues,

> it is the only one which has dignity enough to support blank verse, that is, verse without rhyme. This is attempted in no other measure. It constitutes, therefore, the most precious part of our poetry. The poet, unfettered by rhyme, is at liberty to prune his diction of those tautologies,

those feeble nothings necessary to introtrude [*sic*] on the rhyming word.
With no other trammel than that of measure he is able to condense his
thoughts and images and to leave nothing but what is truly poetical.
When enveloped in all the pomp and majesty of his subject he sometimes even throws off the restraint of the regular pause.[117]

Jefferson rhapsodizes, for one of the only times in what amounts to a rather
turgid and dry exposition of the basic principles of accentual-syllabic meter,
upon the "liberty" induced by throwing off poetic "restraint." He follows this
praise of blank verse with two quotations from *Paradise Lost:* the first is from
the invocation to the first book (1.1–10); the second is from the description
of creation and the circumscription of the universe with God's golden com-
passes (7.224–30). Jefferson looked to the start of *Paradise Lost,* together
with Milton's depiction of the universe's inception, as the exemplary
instances of poetic "liberty."

The form of the poem discloses a more profound concept of liberty
than this, however. Even on the level of poetic form, the story the poem tells
is far more complex than is sometimes realized: for the epic employs rhyme
at significant moments.[118] More integral to the design on narrative and
philosophical levels, contradiction emerges out of Milton's fundamental con-
victions about the nature of true liberty, which must, like creation itself, be
"Won from the void and formless infinite" (3.12). At the core of such liberty
as Milton fights for in his epic is the recognition that, in this world and perhaps also in heaven, time will bring out the contradictions and fractures
within any notion of freedom. In order to reconcile humanity to the
inescapable paradoxes of this condition, whether it becomes manifest in voluntary submission to God's power or involuntary repetition of the struggle
against God's authority, Milton embeds the contradictions of his political
consciousness within the myth of creation.

Chapter Four
The Inward Archives of *Paradise Lost*

In the aftermath of a revolution, more than at any other time, educational reform ought to take on the characteristics of the political scene from which it emerges: such was the considered opinion, as we have seen in the previous chapter, of philosophers and statesmen in England during the Interregnum and then once again after the Restoration. Perhaps revolutionary moments afford a special opportunity for appraising the relationship between an individual's intellectual development and social consciousness more generally. In a series of lectures delivered in the wake of the Bolshevik Revolution, Russian psychologist L. S. Vygotsky addressed the moral content of education from a social perspective. According to Vygotsky, "Criminal behavior in children does not at all point to a low overall development of the individual," but rather, contrary to expectation, "childhood offences . . . are bound up with and are quite compatible with considerable overall giftedness." Far from indicating "any sort of defect in the child's psyche," putatively antisocial behavior

> points often to a certain strength, the capacity to rebel, considerable freedom, and the capacity for powerful feelings. . . . Moral offenses not only do not point to an inability in the child for the acquisition of social skills or his incapacity for social relationships; on the contrary, very often such a child will exhibit an extraordinary degree of guile, cunning, ingenuity, true heroism, and, what is most important, the greatest devotion to a special morality of his own, whether of street thieves or pickpockets, who have their own morality, their own professional ethics, their own concept of good and evil.[1]

Sociologically speaking, such actions as adults would judge to be criminal in children arise from a conception of justice that may even manifest other valorized traits like "true heroism" in a greater degree than more conventionally accepted behavior. In any case, Vygotsky argues, adults must own up to the fact that behavior unconstrained by social conditioning will eventually conform to some system of ethics—however unconventional it might seem. An immoral act is to be differentiated from an amoral one; immoral behavior is not precisely the same as unprincipled action. To deem behavior unethical is not to deny its power as a variety of belief to which another may subscribe. Nor is it to minimize the social force of an unconventional belief system as a principle of order in part of society. Indeed, the existence of alternative moral codes can teach us important things about the way the rest of society structures its commonplace assumptions about morality. Ultimately, adherence to even a thieves' code of "professional ethics" will lead children toward "their own concept of good and evil."

What observation of children makes especially visible, according to Vygotsky, about the complex relationship between morality and education is only magnified when viewed through the lens of the Fall of Man. "The first education of man," William Kerrigan reminds us, "evokes the lived education of all men."[2] As an etiological tale of the origin of good and evil (and much else), the story of the Fall is, after all, a myth of the childhood of humanity. Like most traditional etiologies, the myth of the Fall offers an explanation for human suffering. By providing a means of reflection upon the primal loss of bliss and sanctification, the narrative itself serves as a form of compensation, however inadequate that might be. Vygotsky's language vividly recalls how Milton poses the problem of evil. As a narrative exposition of this philosophical and theological problem, *Paradise Lost* articulates its theodicy first of all as an interrogation of the formulaic norms of "true heroism" and their literary conventions, most memorably as these are distorted by Satan. Over the course of the epic, theodicy assumes the attributes of an educational problem, with the result that *Paradise Lost* confronts the complacent pieties of Milton's time with an assault on the myth of origin in its orthodox form.[3] An omnipotent and omniscient God cannot exculpate Himself by simply saying, "they themselves ordained their fall. / The first sort by their own suggestion fell, / Self-tempted, self-depraved" (3.129–31). If "man falls deceived" and "therefore shall find grace"—and God's logic stands or falls with that signal "therefore"—then the problem of evil (for human beings) must consist largely in perception, in having to see events unfold in succession without the benefit of seeing them as God does, synchronically. Viewed from an educational perspective, the problem of evil becomes, ultimately, a problem of moral perception in time.

This implies that human beings are innately gifted with a capacity to transform their consciousness by educating their minds and spirits, a process the epic represents through the ethical paradoxes upon which Milton prompts his readers to meditate.[4] The actions of Satan, Eve, and Adam lead to separate occasions for educational discourse in the epic, and yet God's effort to indoctrinate each of them is not identical to the process of angelic education and correction that they will have undergone by the end.[5] At times the two processes—the larger thematic pattern of a character's spiritual regeneration, and the immediate didactic narrative context—appear to be at odds. As a kind of narrative *discordia concors,* however, the appearance of structural discontinuity between context and theme may in retrospect have been complementary all along.[6] Because the didactic thrust of Milton's theodicy depends upon recognition of the difference between these discursive layers, the poem requires readers to develop what Jeffrey Shoulson terms "the *ethics* of interpretation." In a way that Shoulson finds analogous to midrashic creativity, Milton inculcates the kind of fine tuning in his readers that will enable them to disentangle literary art from ontology in their conception of the deity, with profound and jarring consequences for the epic's mode of representation:

> Each textual transition, change of course, or narrative shift functions to instruct the reader by temporarily undermining her or his confidence in translating landscape into character, character into concept, action into statement, and so on. The kind of theodicy produced in this heterogeneous discursive mode is predicated on a narrative didacticism that does not yield a set of theological principles so much as an act of reading that is itself an enactment of the text's theology.[7]

As a description of the poem's way of meaning, this comment explains how Milton's epic is itself a product of the tensions within scriptural interpretation. The language of education enters into the explanation of the text as a means of grounding the poem's theological project. In this regard, Shoulson is surely right to emphasize the distinction between "narrative didacticism" and "theological principles." Because development is necessarily diachronic, in experience as in narrative, one would expect the process of education to be represented by a change in Milton's characters over time. Yet when observing such a change requires our coming to terms with the transformation from a state of blessed innocence to the experience of sin and exile, we must wonder what interpretive assistance the vocabulary of educational progress might supply. It may be that memory, if not regression, is to hold the key to Adam and Eve's, and therefore humanity's, future enlightenment. Nonetheless, as we shall see, inherent in Milton's design is the possibility that the Archangel Michael's promise of a "paradise within" stands for a higher and more radically visionary form of consciousness, which becomes available to humanity only after the Fall. The question whether any such development would have been necessary or possible had humanity not fallen is hardly obviated by Raphael's prelapsarian suggestion that "perhaps" human "bodies may at last turn all to spirit, / Improved by tract of time, and winged ascend / Ethereal" (5.497–99).

Yet when rebellious transgression is regarded instead as revolution, whether in history or myth, the occasion permits the unique vantage so elegantly described by Walter Benjamin: "a conception of the present as 'the time of the now' which is shot through with chips of Messianic time." Recognizing "the sign of a Messianic cessation of happening" within the psychological experience of history, there emerges, according to Benjamin, "a revolutionary chance in the fight for the oppressed past."[8] History turns out to be a dialectical conflict between the oppressive past and the utopian possibilities of the future, but this movement of history becomes clear only with the achievement of a revolutionary "cessation of happening." Whether in this literal effort to bring about time's fruition, or in the more deeply figurative expulsion from paradise after Adam and Eve partake of the fruit itself, the seeds of beatific cessation are to be found amid the catastrophe of failed rebellion and tragic defeat.

The prophetic vision that flows into political utopias also has a strong retrospective countercurrent.[9] Meditating on the experience of exile, on the distance from humanity's lost origin in Eden, *Paradise Lost* discovers a sense of messianic potential by rehabilitating the memory of the narrator and readers alike. In this sense, the feat of memory enjoined is indeed, as Regina Schwartz has argued, an act of sacred commemoration, in which "ritual repetition becomes part of the event itself."[10] On another, more local level, Milton works back to the perception of the failed English revolution as a momentary prophetic glimpse of that promised future—a revolutionary present, as Benjamin says, "shot through with chips of Messianic time."

Paradise Lost dramatizes the narrator's confrontation with the messianic prophecies contained within and emitted by the text of Genesis in light of the discrepancy between the promised end and the present reality.[11] The poem examines the emotional and intellectual strain placed on the narrator's efforts to measure the experience of England after the return of the Stuart monarchy, by the standard of the poet's own earlier hope for "that day when thou the Eternall and shortly-expected King shalt open the Clouds to judge the severall Kingdomes of the World" and "shalt put an end to all earthly *Tyrannies,* proclaiming thy universal and milde *Monarchy* through Heaven and Earth" (*Of Reformation,* YP 1:616). For Milton the messianic prophecy, which sacred Scripture records from its beginning, exerted a continual force over history down to his own moment. The poet apprehends a prophetic depth that unifies the text of the Bible, but he is always alive to the density of historical record it lies beneath. "To the prophet," as Abraham Heschel says, "no subject is as worthy of consideration as the plight of man." The prophet attends and answers to the particularity of his present moment because, in Heschel's view, "History is where God is defied, where justice suffers defeats. God's purpose is neither clearly apparent nor translatable into rational categories of order and design. There are only moments in which it is revealed."[12] The revelation of God's just anger at human defiance becomes the substance of the prophetic utterance, so that, for the prophetic poet, the multiple layers of reference in a given proof-text together form a sacred archive of history and prophecy converging on the narrator's present. Such a perspective would have been familiar to all practitioners of typological interpretation.[13] From this vantage the Christian Bible, as Northrop Frye argues, manages to communicate a "vision of misery" that is "ironic rather than tragic." An extended historical record, the scriptural archive prefigures a simultaneous metaphoric order from the beginning: "The Genesis myth starts with what Aristotle would call the *telos,* the developed form toward which all living things grow, and the cycle of birth and death follows after."[14] This is at least in part because traces of a messianic presence are, as Jacques Derrida says, indigenous to the very concept of the archive: "The archive: if we want to know what that will have meant, we will only know in times to come. . . . A spectral messianicity is at work in the concept of the archive and ties it, like religion, like history, like science itself, to a very singular experience of the promise."[15] In *Paradise Lost,* the "promise" that gives order to the action, and structure to human history, is irreducibly textual. Both at its origin in sacred Scripture, and in its manifestation during the action of the epic poem, the prophecy, like the representation of the divine being who expresses it, tends to be represented by a discursive figuration rather than sensual data or mystical vision. As the final books of the epic show, these verbal anticipations require their recipient to undergo instruction in the proper methods of interpretation.

Belief in the presence of the messianic prophecy, or *protevangelium,* within Genesis was a cornerstone of evangelical interpretations of the Hebrew Bible. This "oracle" (10.182) foretold the coming of Christ through a "verbal sacrament" or "scripture within scripture."[16] The textual promise was the archive of "mysterious terms" (10.173) that the Reformation tradition taught readers to interpret by means of text and faith alone (*sola scriptura; sola fide*). As Dietrich Bonhoeffer, an exegete in the Lutheran tradition, lucidly explained in the introduction to his commentary on the first three chapters of Genesis, "The Church of Holy Scripture—and there is no other 'Church'—lives from the end. Therefore it reads all Holy Scripture as the book of the end, of the new, of Christ."[17] Paradoxically, the prophecy anticipated the Christian salvation myth from within the pronouncement of the curse upon humanity, in which the Lord God says to the serpent, "I will put enmity between thee and the woman, and between thy seed and her seed; it shall bruise thy head, and thou shalt bruise his heel" (Gen. 3:15, KJV). Again, Bonhoeffer's commentary is profoundly instructive: "In the destroyed world between God's curse and his promise man is tempted. He does not receive the Word of God in peace and tranquility, he becomes aware of it when the religious question is asked in the wrong way. Man does not adhere to God in peace but in enmity and conflict."[18]

Taking upon ourselves simultaneously the burden of the curse and the gift of the promise exemplified, for Bonhoeffer, the struggle by which God allowed humanity to live. Maintaining the proper interpretive attitude means becoming aware of the Word of God as a question asked "in the wrong way." The text of the curse becomes exemplary precisely because it requires interpretation in the wake of the Fall, of which the curse is the primary consequence. Milton reproduces the text of Genesis 3:15 almost verbatim in the epic (10.179–81).

After the Fall, then, the provisional status of all knowledge—enacted so aptly in Derrida's conditional clause, "if we want to know what that will have meant"—must give way to something else, a hermeneutic logic that is as ruthlessly circular as it is self-affirming. The Geneva Bible's gloss on the curse at Genesis 3:15 makes the promise explicit, yet in doing so arguably gives voice to the instability that asserting such an interpretive control implies—particularly in a sacred text which, as a consequence of the Fall it represents, articulates the origin of the human condition of exile, enmity, and suffering: "Satan shall sting Christ and his members, but not ouercome them. The Lord comforteth Adam by the promise of the blessed seede, and also punisheth the body for the sinne which the soule should haue been punished for, that the spirit hauing conceived hope of forgiuenesse, might liue by faith. 2 Cor. 14. 34." According to this version of the creation myth, the primordial falling out of grace, "man's first disobedience," ruptured the bond between the creator God and His creation and brought about a corresponding loss of interpretive transparency. This marginal gloss, which pretends to an authoritative transparency itself, actively rewrites the text as it allegorically interprets it: although God punished the bodies of Adam and Eve through the imposition of their respective forms of "labor," the "soule should haue been punished." Moreover, such access to grace as remained, from the commencement of human history on, would be intractably textual in nature—as, in the commentary quoted above, the direct appeal to the supporting text from Paul's second epistle to the Corinthians suggests. The text that Adam has to learn to interpret in *Paradise Lost* is the messianic prophecy conventionally believed by Protestants to inhere in Hebrew Scripture, and yet this text alone cannot stand for the promise deemed implicit within it. A further paradox inheres in this teaching, a task given to the Archangel Michael in the epic: faith consists in the construction of a perspicuous context within which to interpret the Hebrew text, although faith is also discovered through an interpretation of Scripture that locates the prophecy by extending this context through allusion and citation.

For readers of Milton, the prophecy is an archive present in a reconstructed vision of the past. Yet it is an archive always open to doubt because the interpretive strategy requires faith as its condition of possibility. In the world of the poem, of course, all readers' pasts (and, more problematically, the narrator's), are Adam's future. In this respect, then, the struggle for exegetical legitimacy involves coming to terms with history. "Bible commentaries," as Hegel notes, "do not so much acquaint us with the content of Scripture as with the mode of thought of their age."[19] And yet, as Lacan says in a comment on Erasmus, "The slightest alteration in the relation between man and the signifier, in this case in the procedures of exegesis, changes the whole course of history by modifying the moorings that anchor his being."[20] Taken together, these two representations of the exegetical process comprise the hermeneutic circle as it emerged in the philosophical imagination in the wake of the Protestant Reformation.[21] This conceptual vocabulary is one powerful and enduring legacy of the Reformation, a dichotomous idea about history's place in hermeneutics—on the one hand, Hegel's notion of the pervasive dialectic of history impressing itself upon all efforts at interpretation, and Lacan's idea, on the other, of the shifting linguistic "moorings" that forge history as all writing. What is at stake in gaining interpretive authority over Scripture is the power to write (sacred) history in the service of a political vision.[22]

Milton builds the "great argument" of his poem out of biblical materials that, by their very nature, contain contradiction and unyielding multiplicity (1.24). There are, for example, the two accounts in Genesis of the creation of Adam and Eve, which traditions with distinct ideological programs have sought to reconcile.[23] This chapter argues that Milton's poem of origins over time reveals the fractures in the maker's intention as a means of describing, albeit obliquely, an exemplary stance toward the materials of human memory. If these materials record the trauma of exile from God, they also paradoxically contain the seed of the salvation narrative when read aright. For the belated poet, intoning to his muse, "what in me is dark / Illumine, what is low raise and support" (1.22–23), the "great argument" can only ever arise as a function of history. Yet God will eradicate this history, unwritten in the narrative present of the epic, in the messianic future that the prophecy foretells, when Jesus shall "bring back / Through the world's wilderness long wandered man / Safe to eternal paradise of rest" (12.312–14). The poet must, therefore, continually teach—and in teaching, *learn*—to read and re-read the archive of sacred sources that contain messianic prophecy. Yet because of his chosen mode of representation, the bard must also discover the truth value of poetic traditions, just as the author must make sense of the experience of politics in his own time. In this task, the poet is no different from those who read his poem. Readers become writers of their internal myth of salvation.

INWARD ARCHIVES

As we have seen in Chapter Two, Milton derived his complex habits of appropriating Hebrew Scripture and much of his hermeneutic method from Reformation attitudes toward reading the Bible. A few more details about the relationship between these interpretive practices and the role of mnemonic techniques in historical theology will help clarify Milton's idea of the complex harmonies and dissonances of the archive as orchestrated in *Paradise Lost*. Out of the rich ferment of medieval memorial culture—against it to a degree—Luther articulated new relationships among reading, memory, and the identity of the self. The classic formulation is vividly represented in William Tyndale's 1526 English translation of Luther's preface to Romans (1522), which begins with the following sentence: "For as much as this pistle ys the principal and most excellent part of the newe testament, and most pure evangelion, that is to say gladde tydinges and that we call gospel, and also a lyghte and a waye in unto the whole scripture, I thinke it mete, that every christen man not only knowe it by roote a[n]d with oute the boke, but also exercice hym sylfe therein evermore co[n]tinually, as with the dayly bredde of the soule."[24] To know Paul's letter by rote and "with oute the boke" requires a feat of memory that most readers today would consider extraordinary, although, as Mary Carruthers has shown, such powers of recall may well have been expected of anyone who was educated in the medieval university—an expectation which continued beyond the arrival of print culture.[25] As we have seen in the discussion of Milton's recollection of Homer, Ovid, and Euripides in Chapter One, Milton himself reputedly possessed just such a memory. And he was not alone. Heinrich Bullinger reports that Huldrych Zwingli, while serving as the parish priest at Einsiedeln from 1516–18, memorized the entire Greek New Testament.[26] To "exercice hym sylfe therein evermore co[n]tinually," as Tyndale puts it, a Protestant would need to have learned the text by heart and internalized its significance. Moreover, as the Epistle to the Romans is, in Luther's powerful conception, a synecdoche of the entire New Testament, the self-scrutiny afforded by its internalization in readers will thereby provide "a lyghte and a waye in unto the whole scripture."[27]

As a matter of course, then, for Tyndale as for Luther, the internalization of the book depends upon the critical act of disencumbering the text from its bondage to traditional commentary. So that interpretation may show "a lyghte and a waye," the text must first be opened, "for it hath bene hetherto evyll darkened with glooses and wonderful dreames off sophisters, that noman cowde spye oute the entente and meaning off it, which neverthelesse of itsylfe, is a bryghte lyghte."[28] Resistance to the Catholic Church's traditions of interpretation, which have left the received text of Scripture "darkened with glooses," is in the counter-tradition of the Reformers a mark of the critical intelligence of the true believer. The method, in turn, reveals the archive of true faith to be *within* the individual reader, rather than on the page or in the church. This is why, in George Herbert's practical manual *A Priest to the Temple,* the chapter entitled "The Parson's Library" says so little about books: "The Countrey Parson's Library is a holy Life. . . . the Parson having studied, and mastered all his lusts and affections within, and the whole Army of Temptations without, hath ever so many sermons ready pen'd, as he hath victories."[29] For Herbert, as for Milton, the theology of this internal storehouse of experience yields a theory of poetic composition. Herbert wittily plays off the idea of inspiration from within in a poem commonly known today as "Jordan (II)." In the manuscript bearing emendations in his own hand, the poem is called "Invention." In the final lines, he echoes the internalized concept of the parson's library: "There is in Love a sweetnes ready pennd / Coppy out that: there needs no alteration."[30] Just as the parson's diligent study within his conscience renders external stimuli moot as sources of inspiration for sermons which arrive "ready penn'd," so the poet need not seek out external confirmation of the inner compulsion of the Holy Spirit, which delivers poems "ready pennd."

But how can poets be certain that what they "Coppy out" in fact "needs no alteration"? Herbert ironically signals this dilemma in his pun on *inventio,* the rhetorical term for the discovery of argument. The need to invent in both senses of the word—that is, to create *and* discover the resources of argumentation—led Milton to develop strategies of appropriation that, taken to their logical extreme, put him at odds with the Reformers whose writings taught him the way to construct his controversial authority.

Maintaining fidelity to sacred Scripture has always posed a special difficulty for writers seeking to appropriate the text for their own use. This vexed issue is, indeed, intrinsic to the New Testament's relationship to Hebrew Scripture. Very early in the history of Christian exegesis the problem arose: how should an interpreter maintain fidelity to the holy writings, especially when they seem contradictory? And how may interpreters gauge the sanctity of their appropriations? In his *De Doctrina Christiana,* Augustine conceived of charity as the great harmonizer of scriptural passages which seemed initially to contradict one another; the creative intellect of human beings, not to be trusted in Augustine's scheme, would be subsumed in the elucidation of obscure places in the text through the plain and open places granted by the Holy Spirit to modulate meaning.[31] Moreover, according to the systems of early medieval expositors, interpreters had to develop their sensitivity to the style of the text in order best to comprehend the rhetorical register on which God intended for the text to be read. Late Latin Father Gregory the Great, advocating a threefold method of exegesis, compared the divine word to a river that is both shallow and deep (*planus et altus*), in which a lamb may walk and an elephant may swim (*in quo et agnus ambulet, et elephas natet*).[32] One must therefore alter the profundity and creativity of one's interpretation to suit the context of the passage.

Since at least the thirteenth century, *auctoritas* had signified a scribe's moral authority as a copier and thus channel of divine intention, on the one hand, and the writer's literary creativity, style, and form, on the other.[33] The advent of Renaissance humanism, and its afterlife in the seventeenth-century schools, may justly be said to have intensified the politics of this conflict within authors, especially if, as Mary Thomas Crane has argued, "English humanists imagine a subject formed not by a narrative history of personal experience but by an assimilated store of texts that seek to forestall and replace such experience."[34] The humanistic conflict between personal narrative and the accumulated authority of a lifetime's reading animates *Paradise Lost,* though the scope of this animus enlarges to fit Milton's "vast design," as Andrew Marvell describes it in his commendatory poem "On Mr Milton's *Paradise Lost*" (l.2; *Poems AM,* p. 182).[35] Emboldened and enabled by the theological tensions believed to inhere in creativity, Milton's exegetical dilemma in *Paradise Lost* unfolds as a dramatic representation of the ways in which creative discovery and recuperative allusion clash in the effort to discern the truth "left in those written records pure, / Though not but by the Spirit understood" (12.513–14).

"SCARCE TO BE LESS THAN GODS"

To give a concrete example of how exegetical creativity nourished Milton's conception of the epic, it will be useful to look at a couple of poems from the Commonwealth period, translations of psalms which Milton undertook in August of 1653. These show Milton characteristically grappling with and modifying Scripture along thematic lines. That Milton dated them so precisely implies he meant for them to have a contemporary application. In the months before Cromwell assumed the office of Lord Protector, the Rump of the Long Parliament was dissolved, and the Barebones assembly was nominated. A motion to abolish tithes had recently been defeated, and the Leveller John Lilburne had again been arrested. A breach having formed between the Independent republicans and other parliamentarians, royalist hopes once again flourished. As when Milton translated Psalms 80–88 in April 1648—most likely responding to royalist translations that circulated just before the outbreak of the Second Civil War—the principle of selection for the 1653 translations seems to have been guided at least in part by their emphasis on political protest and outrage. Beyond that, however, specific topical application of these psalms for a political purpose cannot be established with any certainty.[36]

   In other words, in the translations of August 1653, Milton responds to the political moment obliquely. But we must recall the central importance of the metrical Psalms to church services, as well as the relationship between the formal sonic qualities of the Psalms and the ongoing debate in the period over enforcement of set forms of worship.[37] The formal variation introduced in Milton's later psalm translations, according to Mary Ann Radzinowicz, demonstrates his masterful grasp of the style of the Hebrew originals, with their tendency toward the binary structuring of figures inherent in parallelism.[38] Moreover, psalm translation allowed for considerable exploration of generic and tonal modalities.[39] Most importantly, the results of such experiments evince a personal interpretive struggle to lay claim to the archive of biblical source material in the period just before Milton began dictating *Paradise Lost*.

   Illustrating habits of thought inherent in Milton's hermeneutical approach to Scripture, the psalm translations also suggest the pedagogical direction his thought took as he shaped the plot of his epic. Milton embroiders the originals so that a clearer narrative thread stands out from the immediate lyric context. Because it is precisely by such narrative means that the educative effect of the poem extends beyond mere depictions of teaching, looking at Milton's augmentations of the Psalms will reveal how Milton finds and exploits a prophetic context within which to appropriate the Hebrew original. As in *Paradise Lost,* the assertion of prophecy opens the scriptural archive to interpretation and thus, in turn, to Milton's narrative expansion. Discovering the New Testament's anticipation within the Old Testament text and reconciling these two archives—Hebrew prophecy and Christian fulfillment—entails creating a narrative that will link the two resources.

The psalms I will discuss also share a common intertext in the Epistle to the Hebrews, where key "messianic" verses are reworked in order to show the Word of God as prefigured in Old Testament prophecies. Explaining the "general proposition of this Epistle," the Geneva Bible's gloss on Hebrews 1:1, calling Jesus a "teacher," puts the matter baldly: "The Sonne of God is in deede that Prophet or teacher, which hath actually now performed that that God after a sort and in shadowes signified by his Prophets, and hath fully opened his Fathers will to the world." Here, the presence of the Son is itself educative, in that the existence of Jesus Christ instructs readers in the meaning of the Hebrew prophecies. The complex drive to affirm the Son as Logos in Hebrews has led one modern exegete to claim that the writer of the epistle is "the theologian who, more diligently and successfully than any other of the New Testament writers, has worked at what we now describe as hermeneutics," by which he means the practice of explaining "how we may conceive the Word of God" as "being subject to historical processes and yet remaining, recognisably, God's Word."[40]

In his translation of Psalm 8 dated 14 August 1653, Milton employs diction that resounds through the epic, some of which represents a bold revision of the original. Like pieces in a mosaic, Milton's translations from the period through their shape and coloring imply the larger design of the "great argument" that will appear in *Paradise Lost.* By means of prosody and style, moreover, the poem creates sonic effects that are unprecedented in English translations, as in verse two:

> Out of the mouths of babes and sucklings thou
> Hast founded strength because of all thy foes
> To stint the enemy, and slack the avenger's brow
> That bends his rage thy providence to oppose.   (*Poems,* p. 340)

What makes this translation so Miltonic is the particular connection he draws between prophecy (figured in "babes and sucklings") and adversity (embodied in "the avenger"). The link between infancy and prophecy is reinforced throughout Scripture, Hebrew and Christian, as when Jesus rejoices in spirit and says, "I thank thee, O Father, Lord of heaven and earth, that thou hast hid these things from the wise and prudent, and hast revealed them unto babes" (Luke 10:21, KJV). But earlier English translations of Psalm 8 do not offer Milton's dramatic entwining of providence and the rage of the enemy. In fact, they make no mention of "providence" at all. Nor is there any precedent for the imagistic association between the delicacy of the prophetic infants' mouths and the relaxing of the defeated "avenger's brow." The King James Version reads simply: "Out of the mouth of babes and sucklings hast thou ordained strength because of thine enemies, that thou mightest still the enemy and the avenger." All of the vivid physicality of the opposition is abstracted out; by comparison, Milton's version is almost cinematic. And then there is the jangling musicality of the Sidneyan Psalms:

> From sucklings hath Thy honour sproong,
> Thy force hath flow'd from Babie's tongue
> Whereby Thou stop'st Thyne Enemy's prating
> Bent to revenge and ever hating.[41]

Although the Sidney version's metrical smoothness would be more conducive to singing in church services, its use of a so-called feminine rhyme (prating / hating) lowers the tone significantly. It is as if Sidney would reduce the force of the adversary's rage to chiming ridicule, where Milton makes adversity integral to the salvation narrative. Milton's voice emerges from amidst a cacophony of rattling consonants—the alliterations of "slack" and "stint," "brow" and "bends," "founded" and "foe" stand out. But Milton fully exemplifies the prophetic voice only with the improvised theological elaboration. When he adds "providence" to the end of the second verse, his diction suggests a narrative embellishment—and this looks forward to a larger framework within which to understand the conflict with the Adversary who opposes God's providential design.

　　Similarly, following the question ("what is man?") the psalm asks a parallel question ("or the son of man?"), which is given a messianic interpretation in Hebrews 2:6–7 and in the Gospels. Milton expresses his theology in the sinewy twists of his rhetoric and, again, in an augmentation of the text of verse four. "O what is man," he asks, "or of man begot / That him thou visit'st and of him art found?" Milton's embellishment is readily apparent when placed beside a flatly modern rendition of the verse: what are "mortals that you care for them?" (NRSV). Milton's "of man begot" stays close enough to the meaning of the Hebrew *ben adam* while varying it away from the formula "son of man" employed by Miles Coverdale, the King James Version, and the Geneva Version. Furthermore, the diction of Milton's verse activates a key word from the central books of *Paradise Lost*—as we shall see, the meaning of "begot" becomes a focal point of the dispute that ends in the War in Heaven—for to have been begotten rather than created was held, in the tradition of the author of the Epistle to Hebrews, to signify the ontological superiority of the Son to the Angels.[42] The theological sophistication of the parallel phrasing here raises questions about the prophecy as Milton articulates it: in what way precisely can it be said of the Son in relation to man "of him [thou] art found"? If the locution *found of him* is productively ambiguous—suggesting alternative genitive and possessive phrasings such as "found among man, belonging to man, part of man, like man"—Milton's additional phrase, "of him art found," edges the psalm closer to the representation of the begetting of the son in *Paradise Lost* by introducing a partial narrative. The tense of the participle "found," like the interpolation of "providence" in verse two, suggests a larger narrative context thrust into the present. The syntactic parallel in Milton's addition grammatically links the begetting of the son and the finding of him among humanity; the mysterious agency of the action (found by whom? when?) implicitly draws a parallel between the adversarial conflict and the providential design of history.

The details of Psalm 8 are ultimately directed toward a celebration of God's choice of humankind to rule over creation. As Milton puts it in answer to the question, "What is man?": "Scarce to be less than gods, thou mad'st his lot / With honour and with state thou hast him crowned" (*Poems,* p. 340). Despite the dominion granted humanity over the rest of the created world—the "honour" and "state" bequeathed in this symbolic coronation—the psalm neither differentiates among human beings nor stratifies them in an analogous hierarchical order. In this, the celebration of human dignity recognizes ontological difference, just as the begetting of the Son marks the categorical difference between the Son and the angels, but does not justify the presumption of monarchical authority vested in one human being over others. Coronation represented a thematic puzzle, so much so that Milton made a related coronation scene derived from the Psalms the point of origin for the War in Heaven in *Paradise Lost*. Yet the puzzlement induced by this disanalogy between ontological levels is precisely the point, in that it serves as a ward to prevent the assumption of a license for human beings to think of themselves as too godlike. To be sure, although we "can never forget the monarchism in Milton's portrayal of God and the Son," Milton was, as Nigel Smith has argued, "monarchist in heaven, republican on earth."[43]

Establishing the setting for his epic, Milton employs the tropes and formulae of the prophetic tradition, particularly as he found them in the Prophetic Psalms. Psalm 2 was among the most frequently cited Psalms in the *De Doctrina Christiana,* and Milton marked part of it in the margin of his own Bible.[44] Following the tradition of reformers like Luther and Calvin, Milton gave pride of place in the epic to the coronation poem Psalm 2, which he translated on 8 August 1653. Milton's particular interpretation—for which there is no precedent in the Hebrew original—is evident from what seems at first a casual aside in the midst of verses 6–7:

> but I saith he
> Anointed have my king (though ye rebel)
> On Sion my holy hill. A firm decree
> I will declare; the Lord to me hath said
> Thou art my Son I have begotten thee
> This day.   (*Poems,* pp. 334–35)

It is again instructive to compare the King James Version: "Yet have I set my king upon my holy hill of Zion. I will declare the decree: the Lord hath said unto me, Thou *art* my Son; this day have I begotten thee." The King James Version, as Charles Dahlberg first noted, does not include Milton's parenthetical "though ye rebel." The introduction of the parenthesis, Dahlberg observed, "shows that as early as 1653 Milton associated the idea of rebellion with the idea of elevation to kingship."[45] But precisely what form of association does Milton mean to suggest? Again marshaling the effects of an implied story, which he achieves by means of resonant diction and syntactic elaboration in Psalm 8, Milton has woven a narrative thread into the fabric of Psalm 2 that connects it to the larger Christian salvation myth. In this way, he is teaching his readers the significance of the Hebrew poem when interpreted as a prophetic revelation of Christ.

There was, of course, scriptural precedent for this revision. Reading back from the pseudo-Pauline Epistle to Hebrews (1:1–6), the subordination of the angelic host becomes the complement of the ascription of divinity to the Son. The author, according to Craig Koester, discloses the Christological significance of interlocking Hebraic texts "so that the claims about the Son's divinity could be seen as an extension" of his coronation; nonetheless, there is little to suggest "that the quotations in the middle part of the catena (1:5–12) had been understood in a messianic sense prior to the writing of

Hebrews."[46] Among the links in this chain, the author of Hebrews quotes the promise of Psalm 2:6–7 in a way that connects it to a series of selectively quoted proof-texts from the Old Testament. These extracts seek to equate Jesus' coronation with the promise of the everlasting Davidic kingship (2 Sam. 7:12–16) and the creative and immortal powers of the deity. All of this, in the second chapter of Hebrews, is given dramatic expression when the passage from Psalm 2 is woven together the quotation from Psalm 8. Through the symbolic paradox engendered by Jesus' sacrifice, Christ's eternal elevation over the angelic host is causally connected to his having been brought temporarily "lower than the angels." While the context of Psalm 8 suggests that "being made 'lower than the angels' and being 'crowned with glory and honor' are parallel . . . Hebrews takes them to be opposite. Final glory must be considered in the light of the lower status that precedes it."[47] Scarcely less than God or the angels (the Hebrew word is *elohim*), humanity is nonetheless crowned; by being lowered beneath the *elohim,* the Son redeems humanity and is therefore elevated above the angelic host.

FIRST DISOBEDIENCE

Milton transforms Psalm 2 through the commentary in his translation then applies his interpretive changes to the layers of epic action when he fills out the narrative during Raphael's account. This moment in Book 5 marks the first chronological event in the action of the epic. The proof-text, we recall, appears in the first invocation through a compressed allusion as the poet muses "or if Sion hill / Delight thee more" (1.10–11), thus proleptically linking the epic's narrative and chronological beginnings.

God the Father begins his decree surrounded by symbols of crusade and kingdom dangerously reminiscent of the "tinsel trappings" of chivalric romance, against which the narrator inveighs in the proem to Book 9 (line 36). He is surrounded, that is, by "Standards, and gonfalons" that "Stream in the air," as well as "glittering tissues" that "bear imblazed / Holy memorials" (5.589–93). We might well ask what these memorialize (future martyrdom?), since this is the earliest point in the epic action, yet Milton has warped the temporality such that we recall the limitations of our ability to comprehend the deity's logic from our perspective:

> Hear all ye angels, progeny of light,
> Thrones, dominations, princedoms, virtues, powers,
> Hear my decree, which unrevoked shall stand.
> This day I have begot whom I declare

> My only Son, and on this holy hill
> Him have anointed, whom ye now behold
> At my right hand; your head I him appoint;
> And by myself have sworn to him shall bow
> All knees in heaven, and shall confess him Lord:
> Under his great vicegerent reign abide
> United as one individual soul
> For ever happy: him who disobeys
> Me disobeys, breaks union, and that day
> Cast out from God and blessed vision, falls
> Into utter darkness, deep engulfed, his place
> Ordained without redemption, without end.   (5.600–15)

The tone of the declaration is, to say the least, provocative. As we shall see again when we turn to the education of Adam by divine instructors, the didactic potential of a divine utterance cannot be easily contained in the "process of speech" by which ontologically superior beings relate intellectual matter to beings lower in the cosmic hierarchy (7.178). In other words, God's speech gives the appearance of unintentional duplicity, of a dualistic vocation.

The very speech act itself has the effect of calling forth the Adversary, eliciting the motive for civil war in heaven. In his brilliant analysis of Book 5, Neil Forsyth has recognized that the Father's proclamation

> packs into one line around a powerful caesura the whole duality of history, and even contradicts itself: "For ever happie: him who disobeys" (5.611). The problem is there: at the very moment the Son is said to be begotten in order to make everyone happy forever, God's word also calls Satan into being, not as Lucifer, his earlier name, but as the rebel, the disobedient one. . . . Like action and reaction, God's word creates or begets both Son and Satan at the same moment.[48]

The Father proclaims the Son to have been "begotten," which seems to indicate that he has been procreated, and yet the word is supposed to mean more figuratively that the Son has been begotten in office or elevated. The matter is treated at some length in the *De Doctrina Christiana,* where, seeking to *disprove* the contention that the Son is of "the same essence as the Father," Milton argues that "nowhere in the scriptures is the Son said to be begotten except . . . in a metaphorical sense" (YP 6:210). The anointing of the messiah transforms the universe into a viceregency with a subordinate monarch governing. This occurs at the revolution of the "great year," but God, being omniscient and omnipotent, is not constrained by the limitations of temporality and therefore knows, as Milton's readers also do because he told them in Book 3, that the Son will prove to be "By merit more than birthright Son of God" (3.309).

The paradoxical relation of temporality and chronology to the narrative ordering of the epic's books conveys just this information, in the process dramatizing the selfless offering of the Son as the ultimate moral sacrifice to the highest principle of order in the universe. Applying the epic convention of beginning *in medias res,* Milton represents the typological interpretation of Hebrew prophecy as a distortion of linear narrative. As a corollary to the theological proposition offered in Christian texts such as the Epistle to Hebrews, then, Milton manipulates the temporality of his narrative argument. A further effect of this subtle theological distortion—or *clarification,* according to Christian belief—is to render the actual discourses in which God sets forth His design comparatively abstruse and legalistic. As Alexander Pope wittily claimed, "God the Father turns a School-Divine"[49] when He unpacks the future implications of the sacrificial exchange:

> because in thee
> Love hath abounded more than glory abounds,
> Therefore thy humiliation shall exalt
> With thee thy manhood also to this throne;
> Here shalt thou sit incarnate, here shalt reign
> Both God and man, Son both of God and man,
> Anointed universal king; all power
> I give thee, reign for ever, and assume
> Thy merits; under thee as head supreme
> Thrones, princedoms, powers, dominions I reduce . . .   (3.311–20)

The list of "hierarchies, of orders, and degrees" (5.591) is virtually identical in both of God's proclamations, in Books 3 and 5, a formulaic application which provides a clue that the two speeches are meant to reflect one another as a structuring principle in the epic architecture. Yet the action reveals the difference between the two contexts while relating them by means of analogous scenarios and verbal catchphrases. In Book 3 the Father complicates the coronation scene of Book 5 by proclaiming the exaltation of the Son's "manhood"—perhaps his humanity—in addition to His being. God speaks in Book 3 in the language of causality ("because," "Therefore") instead of the heavily temporal vocabulary of Book 5 ("This day," "now," "that day," "without end").

To an extent, this discrepancy may be attributed to the fact that Raphael mediates the discourse of Book 5, while God speaks directly in Book 3, though this explanation leaves the relatively explicit narrative significance unexplored. Where strictly causal explanation abounds, the elevation of the Son is persistently cast in futurity, depicted as a future consequence of the love He has shown by His offer and the humiliation He will experience when "to the cross he nails thy enemies" (12.404). In Book 5, by contrast, the elevation is depicted as a fait accompli, and the causal explanation is occluded and replaced by the flat assertion of a cosmic change to be instituted from then on.

The paradox generated by this narrative structure is worth contemplating further. The explanation of Book 3 must logically precede the apparently arbitrary move in Book 5 so that readers will grasp the sense of the Son's begetting, but the Father's effort to elucidate in Book 3 must take place later than the proclamation in Book 5 that provokes Satan's revolt—which in turn causes God in Book 3 to ask for a sacrificial remedy. The epic thus builds a complex and self-referential series of modifications and qualifications into its scenes. We cannot begin to know the meaning of one scene without the other, and in juxtaposing the two we begin to reflect upon the intentions that underlie each action in a more comprehensive light.

At times Milton articulates the enigmatic truth behind God's decrees by means of a blunt contradiction that, once unraveled, opens up a vast theological puzzle. For example, a great deal rides on the precise meaning of the word "merit" in God's two decrees from Books 3 and 5. The poem introduces the concept at crucial junctures as a means of justifying God's ways, so the virtually opposing meanings of the word sabotage efforts to reduce the causal problem of the Son's superior "merit" to a simple solution. In the passage from Book 3 quoted earlier, God grants "all power" to the Son, saying in parallel phrases to the Son, "reign for ever, and assume / Thy merits" (3.17–19). We learn from God's logical exposition in Book 3 that Christ's martyrdom is to be the model of ethical purpose in action: the Son is "by merit more than birthright Son of God" (3.390). Looking forward to Raphael's tale of the messiah's anointing, we recall that Satan had resisted the elevation of the Son, in reaction to which he rebelled. Following Romans 5:17–19, Christ's atonement for Adam's sin and the sins of humankind springs from the same source: "thy merit / Imputed shall absolve them who renounce / Their own both righteous and unrighteous deeds" (3.290–92).

To take the Son as a model of "merit" implies an ethical distinction, a sense of "merit" derived from purposeful action, and so the word is used where merit seems in opposition to birthright. In these moments, Milton employs the sense attributed to him somewhat loosely by the *OED* (def. 4a), which adduces *Paradise Lost* (3.290) as evidence that the word means "Good works viewed as entitling a person to reward from God; (also) the righteousness and sacrifice of Christ as the ground on which God grants forgiveness to sinners." But in Book 5, as we have seen, to the extent that God explains the coronation of the Son at all, it is on the basis of His having been "begotten." This implies, in the tradition of the Epistle to the Hebrews, that His elevation is a result of His ontological difference from the angels, which makes the Son's merit and birthright appear more closely united. Compounding this sense, the Messiah "by right of merit reigns" (6.43). To expose the paradox more plainly: the merit that God has used to justify the coronation of the Son is, according to this definition, the effect of an action for which it is also the sole cause—Satan's revolt and, consequently, the Fall of Man. The remedy has provoked the disease. Moreover, when Christ intervenes on behalf of the fallen yet contrite Adam and Eve, His "merit" will "perfect" or fulfill the good works of man, but His "death shall pay" for man's sinful works, which would seem to place the offer of sacrifice in opposition to an intrinsic quality of merit (11.34–36). In the epic, two competing ideas of merit coexist: the natural merit of faith, which is the entitlement of birth and election and therefore resembles grace in its unbidden effects; and the earned merit that comes from good works.[50] The effect of all this is to push us toward a deeper consideration of the nature of the Son as an example of merit that human beings may imitate, to force upon us a further questioning of how merit relates to educability. Is our merit something we can change about ourselves, or is it an essential and immutable aspect of our being?

Similarly, to trace key words, such as "begotten," through to the claim of Satan to be "self-begot," entails questioning the legitimacy of such articulations and discovering their primal meanings.[51] In this way, Milton teaches his readers to regard the claims of various agents with a skepticism attendant upon interpretation and discloses the manipulations of truth that camouflage self-interest in the language of ethical conduct. When Satan retires with Abdiel and the rebel angels to the North (perhaps glancing at Charles in Scotland), he performs his sinful *imitatio Dei* by employing the same formulaic invocation of hierarchy as Milton placed in both of God's decrees, though now evincing merely "counterfeited truth" (5.771). Satan begins his political career saying:

> Thrones, dominations, princedoms, virtues, powers,
> If these magnific titles yet remain
> Not merely titular, since by decree

> Another now hath to himself engrossed
> All power, and us eclipsed under the name
> Of king anointed . . .   (5.772–77)

And of course to ask "If" is to suggest "not"—just as the poet's deliberating "or" in the invocation to the first book implies a doubt about the foundation of his knowledge as well as the source of his identity. It is worth remembering, in connection with the figurative eclipse of the Son in this passage, that *Paradise Lost* was according to Toland almost suppressed "for imaginary Treason" by Thomas Tomkins, Charles II's Episcopal censor, because of the lines that connected solar eclipse with subversive political commentary: "dim eclipse disastrous twilight sheds / On half the nations, and with fear of change / Perplexes monarchs" (1.597–99).[52] Satan had previously, in Book 2, opened the parliament of hell "High on a throne of royal state," where he sat "exalted" as "by merit raised / To that bad eminence," with a similar formula: "Powers and dominions, deities of heaven . . ." (2.1–5, 11). With one rhetorical gesture, Satan confers upon himself the right from above to discriminate between the ranks of angels. His impropriety in this self-aggrandizing elevation is clear enough from his effort to mimic the chronologically earlier proclamations of the heavenly king—a dramatic irony that the narrator emphasizes when enjambment undercuts the notion of Satan's being "raised" by "merit." Like earthly kings who fraudulently arrogate the right of the divine king as a divine right of kings, Satan seeks to elevate himself above his equals as if he, too, were capable of parthenogenesis. Satan employs the plural "deities" as if to say that God has begun an unstoppable process of proliferating godheads.

Yet the passage contains irreducible contradiction, as when Satan seems inadvertently to admit the sameness or identity of the Father and the Son, saying, "Another now hath to himself engrossed / All power" (5.775–76). "To himself," he says, even though we have seen that it was the Father and not the Son who made the proclamation. It is a persistent quality of Satan's rhetoric that he refers to the instability of the entire discursive register within which he proclaims his own moral imperative as a self-willing agent. As William Walwyn said in a Leveller pamphlet of 1649, "Satan's chief agents" are themselves "made up of Contradictions. . . . In a word, observe them well, and you shall see Christ and Belial, God and Mammon, in one and the same person."[53] Satan speaks so insistently of his intentions that one cannot help but question them. In Satan's diction, Milton has interwoven an irremediable conditionality, a kind of endemic subjunctive mood; we recall, in reading Satanic grandiloquence, that he is the type of all doubters, and that his first word in the epic is "if" (1.84). God is arguably at his most satanic when the omniscient deity, however improbably, removes himself from responsibility for the Fall in the dyspeptic outburst: "if I foreknew, / Foreknowledge had no influence on their fault, / Which had no less proved certain unforeknown" (3.117–19). Moreover, in Satan's chronologically earliest example of oratory, at his "royal seat/ High on a hill," in which he has questioned "If these magnific titles yet remain / Not merely titular," the Adversary further asks: "But what if better counsels might erect / Our minds" (5.77–74, 786–87)? "If" is a satanic word, in that it riddles his speeches and operates as a synecdoche for his enterprise. It is hardly surprising that his questioning of the stability of public rhetoric should hinge upon his own duplicitous nature, which he assumes immediately following the first chronological moment depicted in the epic: "So spake the omnipotent, and with his words / All seemed well pleased, all seemed, but were not all" (5.616–17). This effect of Satan's is particularly apt, not least because, "Wonderfully," we may say with George Steiner, "the Satan in *Job* suggests the figure of the critic. He is acidly intimate with the Deity as critics too often are with artists. His role may have been seminal: Satan may have provoked God into creating."[54]

As his name implies, Satan is both inwardly and outwardly divided; *ha satan* signifies adversity wherever it appears in the Hebrew Bible, as in Job or at Numbers 22:22, where the term refers to an adversary angel sent, on account of God's wrath being kindled, to oppose the path of Balaam.[55] When the narrator interjects a comment, following Satan's first speech in Book 1, Milton's tactical deployment of caesurae reproduces the sense of internal division: "So spake the apostate angel, though in pain, / Vaunting aloud, but racked with deep despair" (1.125–26). In these lines, the choppiness of the verse serves to undercut the heroic boast; the Homeric "Vaunting aloud" is diminished as it is surrounded by suffering rather than doing, loss instead of victory. So Satan is both inwardly divided and outwardly divisive.

Just as Satan willfully manipulates the notion of the public good for self-serving ends, so he adduces the language of resistance to tyranny to advance his own tyrannical bid for power. Feeling himself to have been "eclipsed" by the Son, who according to the devil masquerades "under the name / Of king anointed," Satan employs the incendiary rhetoric of the revolution: "what if better counsels might erect / Our minds and teach us to cast off this yoke?" (5.776–77, 785–86) When Satan claims to "teach" his fellow angels that their freedom will be born in resisting the tyranny of heaven, Milton teaches his readers to decode the rhetorical duplicity of tyrants. Only by recognizing the diabolical contradictions in this political speech can we come to understand the discrepancy between legitimate merit and illegitimate ambition. In exposing the first disobedience of Satan as a calculated political act founded upon lies and deception, Milton undermines the conceptual justification for disobedience to God even as he inculcates the skepticism necessary to resist tyrants who arrogate God's logic as their own.

"THE TYRANT'S PLEA"

As the angelic choir sings God's praise after creation, the heavenly spheres ring like church bells. By Milton's inverted logic, to emphasize the uncere-monious rhymes and even the ritualistic iconography of heaven is to contrast the Church of England's crude institutional hierarchy. And yet, at the very moment of creation—before the song in celebration of "the imperial throne / Of godhead" is finished—the angelic choir accidentally suggests that, until the end of time, God's plan will suffer a cosmic flaw. The angels ask what they mistakenly think is a rhetorical question: "Who can impair thee, mighty king, or bound / Thy empire" (7.585–86, 608–9)? The answer is Satan, who will "impair" the deity and "bound" at least this much of His empire. When He creates humanity, God introduces the idea of His earthly empire changing hands—Adam and Eve are to exercise dominion over the rest of creation. Having foreseen the Fall of Adam, however, God relin-quishes the concept of empire that governed the freshly created universe. Milton undermines the imperial idea by exposing it as an evil ambition when Satan transfers the world to the dominion of Sin and Death.[56] Obfuscation of motive in the transfer of empire may be said to serve as a trope for the unrecoverable origins of the created world. The conceptual justification of imperial expansion changes its valence as creation, "The addition of [God's] empire" (7.555), falls into the hands of Satan.

Satan's despotic pretension becomes clearest after he perversely opposes genuine merit, slippery as that concept is, and enlivens its fraudulent double, as seen in Satan's "sense of injured merit" and the "monument / Of merit" constructed by Sin and Death (1.98; 10.258–59). We witness the way Satan frames his ambition as an ethical achievement when the narrator shows us Satan's tight control over apparently open debate; what we see as the parlia-mentary council of hell turns out to have been arranged beforehand by Satan and Beelzebub and is thus the outcome of political manipulation: "Thus Beelzebub / Pleaded his devilish counsel first devised / By Satan, and in part proposed" (2.378–80). In this passage, Milton is making a central political point about the nature of consent in government, affirming the distinction between the public good and public reason—also referred to in the period as "necessity," or "reason of state." Satan becomes a figure very much like Sulla—the object of Milton's scorn in the epigraph added to the second edition of *The Readie and Easie Way*, an adaptation of Juvenal, who makes Sulla the embodiment of ambition: "I too have given advice to Sylla, now let me give it to the people [*et nos / Consilium dedimus Syllae, demus populo nunc*]."[57] If Satan exhibits classic attributes of a tyrant, then he is rhetorically even more like Emperor Tiberius, whose diction, according to Tacitus, "by habit or by nature, was always indirect and obscure, even when he had no wish to obscure his thoughts"; and who, in Tacitus's withering account of the emperor's rhetorical manipulation, "organized the state, not by instituting a monarchy or a dictatorship, but by creating the title of First Citizen [*principis nominee constitutam rem publicam*]."[58] Tiberius's kind of equivocation—which has a clear analogue in Charles's use of the "Jesuitical slight," Milton's term for rhetorical duplicity in *Eikonoklastes* (1649, 2nd ed. 1650; YP 3:526)—comes so naturally to Satan that he perpetuates his deception even in soliloquy.

Milton scorns the calculated ambiguity of this false niceness of diction as a tool of political coercion, for instance when Satan finesses the difference between "Beseeching or besieging" God as he tries to persuade the angels to join his rebellion (5.869). Milton also shows us this aspect of the devil—in his attempt to rationalize "conquering this New World"—to undermine Satan's claim that "public reason" or reason of state "compels" him (4.389; 391).[59] He acts, of course, on behalf of no public *good*. Satan always sheds responsibility for his evil deeds, presenting the illusion that he has no choice, whereas it is precisely the allowance of his freedom of choice that has enabled his rebellion.[60] Satan's claim finds its corollary in the dense nexus of rhymes connecting his putative rationale with tyranny and the Tree of Life, a symbol of all that will be lost in the effort to analogize human with divine power:

> So spake the fiend, and with *necessity,*
> The tyrant's *plea,* excused his devilish deeds.
> Then from his lofty stand on that high *tree*
> Down he alights . . .   (4.393–6; my italics)

In *Paradise Lost*, rhyme's conspicuous appearance triggers our recognition of the dangers of mellifluous rhetoric—the "tyrant's plea" couched in the seductive rhetoric of political "necessity." In Satan's appeal to "public reason just" as a rationale for his pursuit of "Honour and empire with revenge enlarged" (4.389–90), the devil shows himself to be, as Marvell put it in *The First*

Anniversary, "mad with reason, so miscalled, of state" (l. 111; *Poems AM,* p. 291).[61]

Like Alcibiades in Thucydides' history of *The Peloponnesian War*—especially when Alcibiades advocates the disastrous Sicilian expedition—Milton's Satan continually tries to persuade the other angels, Eve, and even himself, of the necessity for preemptive and expansive conquest. "Nor is it in our power," says Alcibiades in Hobbes's translation, "to be our own carvers how much we will have subject to us; but considering the case we are in, it is as necessary for us to seek to subdue those that are not under our dominion, as to keep so those that are; lest if others be not subject to us, we fall in danger of being subjected unto them."[62] Alcibiades's logic resonates with Beelzebub's proposal for "Some advantageous act" against humanity in Book 2, as it does with Sin's suggestion that she and Death "try / Adventurous work," and a similar line of reasoning is implicit when Satan complains that Adam and Eve have advanced "Into our room of bliss" (2.363; 10.254–55; 4.359). Certainly such examples of immoral sophistry underpin the simile that precedes Satan's impassioned praise of the Tree of Knowledge to Eve:

> As when of old some orator renowned
> In Athens or free Rome, where eloquence
> Flourished, since mute, to some great cause addressed,
> Stood in himself collected, while each part,
> Motion, each act won audience ere the tongue,
> Sometimes in height began, as no delay
> Of preface brooking through his zeal of right.
> So standing, moving, or to height upgrown
> The tempter all impassioned thus began.   (9.670–78)

Satan actually believes that he acts under political compulsion—in expedient redress of an unfair imbalance in cosmic power. As the type of all future tyrants, Satan's special pleading will resurface in Michael's critical commentary on the decay of "Rational liberty" with the rise of Nimrod and the tower of Babel:

>   know withal,
> Since thy original lapse, true liberty
> Is lost, which always with right reason dwells
> Twinned, and from her hath no dividual being:
> Reason in man obscured, or not obeyed,
> Immediately inordinate desires

> And upstart passions catch the government
> From reason, and to servitude reduce
> Man till then free.   (12.82–90)

The "government" of the passions, according to the psychology of the passage, confers political freedom upon the agent, but indulgence and intemperance render the transgressive agent an enslaved subject. Reason may have been "obscured" by the Fall, but, owing to preventable human short-comings like the lack of virtuous self-discipline, it will fail to be "obeyed." Inordinate and upstart, the irrational chaos of desire will "catch the government" off-guard, as when Macro in Ben Jonson's *Sejanus* explains how to thrive in government: "Men's fortune there is virtue; reason their will; / Their licence law; and their observance, skill."[63] The polity's "outward freedom" will be "undeservedly" enthralled, since, as Michael laments, "tyranny must be, / Though to the tyrant thereby no excuse" (12.95–6). On the other hand, just as the Father had commanded at the elevation of the Son that the angels "confess him Lord: / Under his vicegerent reign abide / United as one individual soul" (5.608–10), so right reason "hath no dividual being" apart from "true liberty." Willful subordination to God is therefore seen as liberty's condition of possibility, whereas the immoderate satanic desire of the appetite overthrows the powers of ratiocination that consent to be governed by the deity.

By this principle, the "government" of the passions does not imply that they are stamped out altogether, only that they need to be moderated, like unruly subjects, by a temperate and prudent ruler and by obedience to the law. By associating Satan with the tyrants of antiquity, Milton reveals how much is at stake historically in the effort to discipline the will of the public— a message he had tried to drive home to the backsliding English populace on the eve of the Restoration. The characteristics of life under a tyranny remain the same, and as we witness the effects of the triumph of will over reason throughout the epic, we see the political implications of libertinism. To this end, when the poet implores Urania to "drive far off the barbarous dissonance / Of Bacchus and his revelers" (7.32–33), Milton clearly alludes to the contemporary tyranny of Cavalier drinking culture and its political counterpart in the court of Charles II. The echo of *The Readie and Easie Way* is unmistakable: "Let our zealous backsliders forethink now with themselves, how thir necks [are] yok'd with these tigers of Bacchus" (YP 7:452). Drunk with the expectation of her newfound power, Eve eats the forbidden fruit and is likewise "heightened as with wine, jocund and boon" (9.793). Wine and the human will, in the moral writings of Petrus Berchorius and others, were seen as synonymous, particularly as each signified the loss of rationality and the burning of desire.[64] Demonstrating the inextricable link between libidinal irrationality and the lust for political power, Milton trains his readers to exercise a political sensitivity that will prevent them, as individuals and as citizens of a commonwealth, from being ruled by their passions. Thin and illusory as the rhetoric that couches it, the leadership of Satan the demagogue is the political equivalent of his overpowering will to rule heaven. In the failure of Satan to master his own appetite, Milton foreshadows the enduring consequences of the tyranny that, in Michael's ominous words, "must be" (12.95).

"WHAT MEANT THAT CAUTION JOINED"?

As we have seen, the character of Satan provides a means for Milton to exploit the didactic potential to refine moral discriminations and to sharpen the perception of distinctions in political rhetoric. Yet, time and again, we are left to wonder if it is an intrinsic feature of divine instruction to introduce the idea of disobedience. After all, God the Father at the elevation of the Son threatens punishment for an act of disobedience—which only God can foresee. The provocation is lodged in the ostensible effort at its prevention. An identical ethical problem is present when the logic of temporality makes Raphael the conduit by which Adam first imagines sin; there is again an aura of inadvertency surrounding the introduction of the concept of disobedience, as there had been during God's anointing decree. Raphael's propaedeutic tale of the War in Heaven and of Creation commences in response to the suggestion of disobedience. Another way of putting this would be to say that, in *Paradise Lost,* the notion of rebellion everywhere spawns a narrative reaction.

Arriving in Eden, the "Divine instructor" tells Adam how human "bodies may at last turn all to spirit, / Improved by tract of time" (5.546, 497–98),

> If ye be found obedient, and retain
> Unalterably firm his love entire
> Whose progeny you are. Meanwhile enjoy
> Your fill what happiness this happy state
> Can comprehend, incapable of more.   (5.501–5)

Having ordered Raphael to "advise [man] of his happy state, / Happiest in his power left free to will, / Left to his own free will," God had set up the encounter so that Adam would understand the consequence of disobedience, "Lest willfully transgressing he pretend / Surprisal, unadmonished, unfore-warned" (5.234–36, 243–44). What, we might ask, are the deity's motives for delegating such a tremendous responsibility? God's assumption that the angel will be an effective teacher proves to be deeply problematic. This is unquestionably so unless we misunderstand—and Raphael likewise miscon-strues—just what it is that God has sent him to teach. In the event, it might almost be said that Raphael has come to Eden to run Adam through the machinations of a fallible intellect.

Some confusion about the content of the lesson is natural, since God's laconic instructions to the angel are not explicit about the best way to teach Adam the meaning of transgression: "such discourse bring on / As may advise him of his happy state," and so on (5.234–35). How precisely is Adam to beware "deceit and lies" when he may not be able to discern "Hypocrisy, the only evil that walks / Invisible, except to God alone, / By his permissive will" (5.243; 3.683–85)? In response to Raphael's instruction, Adam shows he has learned how human beings should contemplate "sensible things," very much as Milton had described in *Of Education* (YP 2:368). Adam has grasped the proper method for comprehending sensory data, but the angel's moral teaching has failed where the mechanical method for understanding has prevailed. For in the next breath, Adam insinuates that Raphael has pro-duced the conundrum which God sent the angel to prevent:

> O favourable spirit, propitious guest,
> Well hast thou taught the way that might direct
> Our knowledge, and the scale of nature set
> From centre to circumference, whereon
> In contemplation of created things
> By steps we may ascend to God. But say,
> What meant that caution joined, *If ye be found*
> *Obedient?* Can we want obedience then
> To him, or possibly his love desert
> Who formed us from the dust, and placed us here
> Full to the utmost measure of what bliss
> Human desires can seek or apprehend?   (5.507–18)

The speech shows Adam's growing confusion over the two kinds of "knowledge" acquired through scientific inquiry and moral questioning—one of which, he learns, is sanctioned and the other forbidden. At times in human experience, moral and scientific knowledge mingle, as when nature's beauty "instructs" Adam and Eve to be generous and hospitable upon Raphael's arrival (5.320). The confusion goes deeper, however, as a result of Raphael's instruction. The idea that Adam might "want obedience"—perhaps hinting through a pun that he does not "want" to be obedient at all—and that human desires may surpass what he can "apprehend" at this moment seems first to occur to Adam in response to Raphael's caution. That satanic "if" keeps cropping up as an invitation to transgression. To be sure, we may wonder how much Adam can know of any "utmost measure" when his experience has remained unvaryingly blissful. Likewise, the threat of mortality can hardly be effective to beings who do not possess an ability to imagine death—"what e'er death is," says Adam (4.425). Is it too much to suggest that Raphael has just created in Adam the possibility of falling by telling him that angels have already fallen? This warning was supposed to "advise him of his happy state," where perhaps the only definition possible would be by negation. The promise of higher or lower forms of existence for humanity introduces the instability of the status quo and registers as uncertainty and confusion. The "bright consummate flower" promised in Raphael's grand speech about ontological upward mobility for humankind has occasioned the planting, instead of Raphael's intended piety, of a seed of doubt.

Thus Milton introduces the very structure of theodicy implicitly in these remarks that preface Raphael's cautionary tale. The suggestion of disobedience triggers the recognition of the existence of evil; doubt spreads, intensifying as the need for justification of God's ways; and instruction follows, in the form of the exemplary narrative. God's logic here spurs Adam on toward recognition of the problem of evil, a problem Adam had known of but not fully realized. Perversely, God's response to the disorientation of a human being in the face of inscrutable providence smacks of the Stoics' paradoxical denial of theodicy. As Seneca says in his moral essay *On Providence,* "It is not possible that any evil can befall a good man," even though "Disaster is virtue's opportunity" (*calamitas virtutis occasio est*).[65]

As we have noticed in discussing the relationship between God's decrees in Books 3 and 5, Milton foregrounds the problem of how narration relates to chronology.[66] In the beginning of Book 5, Eve tells of her dream, and Satan is her "guide" (5.35–94). When a new narrative enters into the poem, Satan is there goading on the plot. In this respect there is, as Neil Forsyth says, a certain "likeness of Satan" in the structure of "the poem itself." If the entire action hinges on his transgressions, then it is no exaggeration to claim that Satan's role is to be "the one who motivates the plot, who drives the story into motion."[67] The salvific plot, in this view, requires the sacrifice of not one, but two beings. Even at this level, the providential design, reaffirmed by the interpolated commentary of the narrator, emerges first as one of Satan's musings:

> If then his providence
> Out of our evil seek to bring forth good,
> Our labor must be to pervert that end,
> And out of good still to find means of evil;
> Which oft-times may succeed, so as perhaps
> Shall grieve him, if I fail not . . .   (1.162–67)

Satan plots confidently within what begins as a delusive syllogistic framework, moving from "If then" to "if I." Satan asserts that he possesses free will, even as his rhetoric hedges his agency in, his doubt posing as narrative suspense ("may succeed"; "as perhaps"; "if I fail not"). Satanic plotting thus begets the confirmation of that providential logic which the fiend has set out to deny.

The heavy alliterations in the narrator's subsequent comment point ahead to God's alliterations in the anointing of the Son, where, says the Father, I "on this holy hill / Him have anointed, whom ye now behold / At my right hand; your head I him appoint" (5.604–6). More in the manner of a discomfiting parity than a simple parody, Milton forges a sonic bridge between these two inaugural passages. The narrator interrupts himself to remark, as if bestirred by wisdom's sudden emergence (or Athena's allegorical double in Sin's birth):

> So stretched out huge in length the arch-fiend lay
> Chained on the burning lake, nor ever thence
> Had risen or heaved his head, but that the will
> And high permission of all-ruling heaven
> Left him at large to his own dark designs,
> That with reiterated crimes he might
> Heap on himself damnation, while he sought
> Evil to others, and enraged might see
> How all his malice served but to bring forth
> Infinite goodness . . .   (1.209–18)

The narrator's imprecation answers to the reiterative quality of satanic consciousness. The alliterative "dark designs" are a sad pastiche of the open vista brought forth in "Infinite goodness," just as "Heap on himself" and "heaved his head" deflate the image of the holy hill on which the Son becomes the "head" of the universe. The elevation of the Son is preceded in the narrative (but followed in time) by Satan literally raising his head. The inversion spelled out by the narrative voice bends the verse back on itself in an imaginative example of unintended consequences: the narrator's irresistible urge to pun satanically on "at large." Satan is "at large" because, for now, his assumed shape compares to that of Leviathan, while, at the same time, he is "at large" as a result of God's permitting him to rise from the lake. At the end of Book 1, the infectious pun has spread, such that the narrator deploys a verbal analogue for the vertiginous shift in perspective when the devils "to smallest forms / Reduced their shapes immense, and were at large" (1.789–90). This variety of Miltonic wordplay, so ably recuperated by Christopher Ricks, opens up the tonality of the poetry to greater scrutiny, if only because it invites consideration as a calculated "lapse" that Milton would attribute to his narrator.[68]

At the very moment in which the narrator seeks to enforce dogma, the tone of the poetry subtly undermines the doctrinaire application of its meaning by identifying the narrator with a rhetorical characteristic that the poem associates elsewhere with Satan. Again Milton deepens the pun by extending it through the architectonics of the epic: the phrase eerily resurfaces later when Adam attempts to demonstrate that he has learned the most important lesson Raphael has to teach him, saying,

> apt the mind or fancy is to rove
> Unchecked, and of her roving is no end;
> Till warned, or by experience taught, she learn,
> That not to know *at large* of things remote
> From use, obscure and subtle, but to know
> That which before us lies in daily life,
> Is the prime wisdom. . . .   (8.188–94; my italics)

Adam's dogmatic musings ironically promote "wandering thoughts," suggesting his identity with the pilot who mistakes Leviathan for an island. His pun, like the narrator's puns in the first book of the epic, is spatial and perspectival, employing the figurative language of antithesis—things small because "remote" need not be known up close or "at large" because they lack utility. Does Adam know the aptitude of his own "mind or fancy," terms that are curiously equivalent in his formulation, like *warning* and *experience?* As when the Ghost, finding Hamlet "apt," prompts the latent fantasy of vengeance that already inhabits Hamlet's "prophetic soul," Adam betrays his natural cast of mind when he speaks axiomatically.

Raphael courteously but nervously reminds Adam that God has established boundaries around moral knowledge and that crossing these and perhaps other barriers to godhead symbolizes apostasy. If Raphael ultimately fails as a pedagogue, it is not for lack of trying. To counteract Adam's wandering and naturally rebellious fancy, Raphael frequently offers reminders of his presence as narrator. Repetitions of narrative markers intrude in order to ensure that the mediation of the divine instructor's storytelling stays constantly in view. This aspect of reported discourse in the epic serves to keep a certain distance between the author and the text. Taken structurally, the narrative becomes pedagogical. But as in the epic voice's interjections, narration provides not so much a corrective medium catechistically scolding readers, as an oblique medium through which Milton explores the theological perplexities that beset signification. We are, of course, at two removes at least from the events depicted when the narrator recounts Raphael's tale, and at an even greater remove when we are forced to rely upon Raphael's memory of the speeches of God, Satan, or Abdiel. Milton endows Raphael with self-consciousness about this narrative function and the intrinsic difficulty it presents for his educational task. The element of surprise, so crucial to the reader-response paradigm, assumes inattentiveness on the part of readers as much as it presumes an early moment in the first reading of the poem—after several books, is anyone still "surprised"?[69] The evidence of early readers such as Jonathan Richardson (father and son) has been adduced in support of the idea that the Miltonic voice magisterially upbraids the reader, whereas the following rhapsodic description conveys almost the opposite notion, that Milton gives his readers too much credit:

> a Reader of Milton must be Always upon Duty; he is Surrounded with Sense, it rises in every Line, every Word is to the Purpose; There are no Lazy Intervals, All has been Consider'd, and Demands, and Merits Observation. . . . he Expresses himself So Concisley, Employs Words So Sparingly, that whoever will Possess His Ideas must Dig for them, and Oftentimes pretty far below the Surface. if This is call'd Obscurity let it be remembered 'tis Such a One as is Complaisant to the Reader, not Mistrusting his Ability, Care, Diligence, or Candidness of his Temper . . . if a Good Writer is not Understood 'tis because his Reader is Unacquainted with, or Incapable of the Subject, or will not Submit to the Duty of a Reader, which is to Attend Carefully to what he Reads [sic].[70]

Richardson places the burden entirely upon "the Reader," who must "Submit to the Duty" of attending "Carefully to what he Reads": the presumption, common enough in the period, is that there is a meaning which inheres in the text and that can be excavated, "that whoever will Possess His Ideas must Dig for them." Unearthing the intention that underlies the vagaries of obscure diction entails a hermeneutic process best compared to interpretation of Scripture.[71] The comparison is instructive in its qualification of what Richardson means by "edification," and it also hints at the danger associated with textual interpretation gone awry. Narrative induces an immediate awareness of the distance between the intention of the writer and the discourse to be interpreted, just as an interpreter's explanation is the product of a dialectical interaction with his or her understanding of the text.[72]

Implicitly, the form of Raphael's narrative exposes the poem's regressive points of origin as a pedagogical device. Throughout the poem, Milton inserts reminders and qualifications that call attention to the difficulty and the presumption of his own "Sad task and hard" (5.564). Narrative mediators such as Raphael and Michael function pedagogically in that, through their failure to teach at key moments, they demonstrate a more profoundly edifying truth beyond the reach of superficial didacticism. Although he has been instructed by God to tell the tale of Satan's fall, Raphael still wavers in his concern for the propriety of explaining what the poet terms, in the invocation to Book 3, "things invisible to mortal sight" (3.55). Even before the Fall, Raphael worries about the unintended consequences and unforeseen effects of human language upon his lesson when he converts the divine truth into his tale. Angels receive "intuitive" information most often, which differs "but in degree" from human linguistic faculties (5.487–90). But the fear of overstepping an unspoken boundary by translating from intuitive to discursive reason suddenly becomes palpable when the discursive register shifts from expository to narrative modes:

> how shall I relate
> To human sense the invisible exploits
> Of warring spirits; how without remorse
> The ruin of so many glorious once
> And perfect while they stood; how last unfold
> The secrets of another world, perhaps
> Not lawful to reveal?   (5.564–70)

The basic premise of accommodation, or "likening spiritual to corporal forms" (5.573), cannot inoculate even an angelic narrator against the dangers that attend evoking the deity and equating the two books of nature and of God. Raphael's use of anaphora, a common trope of biblical rhetoric, suggests the problem of accommodation, even as it looks forward to the appearance of sacred Scripture as God's solution to the problem of communication with fallen humanity.[73]

Divine instruction requires that the boundaries which separate the levels of the cosmic hierarchy be breached without the loss of proper decorum. If conversation with a being lower on the ontological ladder entails the sophistication—even the confounding—of the discursive register on which the interaction is to transpire, then angelic or divine teaching will saturate the verse with polysemous diction and rhetorical mutivalence. The doctrine of accommodation—which provides a means for explaining the appearance of the divine word in human systems of signification—cannot fully account for the way a poetic utterance acquires its multiplicity in Raphael's speech. But the angel introduces this representational quandry into the unfallen world as a problem associated with expressing intentions in an educative discourse. From Lucifer-Satan's first speech onward, the language of education ironically forms the primary rationale for disobedience—the need to test and to learn by experience. Even the good angels cannot quite figure out how to reconcile properly the disparate ontological status of humankind to the larger providential order. After all, like the narrator of the epic in his proclamation of his theodicy, Raphael too wants to "inquire / Gladly into the ways of God with man" (8.226).

Subtle poetic effects are instrumental to Milton's pedagogy and lead to startling questions about the nature of the scenes in which they occur. In Raphael's colloquy with Adam, when he tells his epic tale of arms and the greater man, who is learning from whom? At the end of the lesson, the offering of mutual congratulations by Adam, the narrator of the epic, and even the archangel, can only function as dramatic irony, given what every reader knows about the coming Fall. Adam thanks Raphael for conveying "Intelligence of heaven" (8.181), but not before his belated response calls into question the success of his teacher's didactic approach. Milton depicts the instability of the angel's message as an almost magical property of the verse:

> The angel ended, and in Adam's ear
> So charming left his voice, that he awhile
> Thought him still speaking, still stood fixt to hear.   (8.1–3)

This does not instill confidence. Adam may think himself "cleared of doubt," but moral matters will become far more ambiguous before long, which implies that the doubt he facilely dispenses with has been the very thing keeping him pure until now (8.179). The incantation of the angelic bard has failed to convey a proper appreciation of the seriousness of the situation in which tempted humanity is about to find itself. The rhyme of "ear" and "hear" jingles, the poetry thus sounding an alarm to warn that ancient liberty is at risk.

Human forays into didactic speech also expose cracks in the foundation of knowledge, even before the arrival of Raphael. For example, Eve's dream occasions an exchange where we are invited to witness Adam's self-righteous disquisition on the nature of evil, of which he has apparently no more experience than he has, so far, of death. When Adam, reiterating the church fathers' punning Latin, *unde malum,* says, "nor can I like / This uncouth dream, of evil sprung I fear; / Yet evil whence?"—an unfallen being, we recall, is already inquiring about the origins of evil, something he cannot understand.[74] Still, Adam feels confident enough to lecture Eve ponderously on the topic of "Reason as chief" among the faculties—clearly fancying himself as Reason and Eve as Fancy personified, since "She forms imaginations, airy shapes" (5.102–5). His limited knowledge, experience, and imagination mitigate his assertions, and so his speculations beg the question when he speaks gnomically: "Evil into the mind of god or man / May come and go, so unapproved, and leave / No spot or blame behind: which gives me hope" (5.117–19). The two halves of that last line heavily qualify what follows. Adam's hope—that what Eve dreamt she never will consent to do—is simply self-deluding because he speaks either from some very strange assumptions about the mind of God, or he has already encountered evil in such a way that he may no longer be aware of its manifestation within himself. The lines suggest that Adam believes he knows what God thinks or is capable of thinking, and also assumes he comprehends *Eve* because he recognizes *evil.*

The "Intelligence of heaven" God wishes to bestow upon created man necessitates an ontological and representational coup of sorts, a logic which can only be articulated by opening a vertiginous perspective on what it means to "know to know no more" (8.181; 4.775). The ironies of this situation are nowhere more evident than when Adam reports his request to God for a mate. Adam requites Raphael's tale and satisfies the archangel's curiosity through an explanation perilously resonant with Satan's inquiry into origins: "For man to tell how human life began / Is hard; for who himself beginning knew?" (8.250–51).

DIVINE MAIEUTICS

In Book 8 of *Paradise Lost,* Adam reports that in his first speech-act, he could already "feel that I am happier than I know" (8.282). Human consciousness begins with this curious disjunction, with the first man's intuition of the discrepancy between his perception and his capacity to conceive reality. The ironic disparity is essential to Milton's design, no less than his God's. For the ethical dilemma that deepens Adam's self-sacrifice for Eve is born with him in that distinction between what he feels and what he knows. Insufficient as his tragic choice may seem, it will in the fullness of time be answered by Christ's sacrifice for love. And, as Michael promises, the fallen Adam may still "possess / A paradise within . . . happier far" (12.586–87). In Adam's first words, Milton ironically telescopes the whole human drama of sin and salvation.

Human consciousness is born with the observation of an anthropomorphic detail: "all things smiled," says Adam (8.265). The strangeness of the analogy relates to the immeasurable distance between a human being who can, with "sudden apprehension," grasp the substance of another creature and speak that being's essence, and a fallen desire to tailor perception so that it fits a fallible understanding (8.354). Unaccommodated man no longer can expect unmediated access to the higher registers of ontology. From the start, no answer awaits the first man's immediate queries about his own nature and origin, but sleep comes over him quickly: "Pensive I sat me down" (8.287). Adam believes that he is "passing to my former state / Insensible" until "suddenly stood at my head a dream" (8.290–92). Adam first becomes sensible of his own precognitive state in such a way as to allow a prelapsarian taste of mortality. The phenomenology of the dream state also forecasts the theophany that is about to follow. In man's first visit with his maker, the movement toward consciousness out of "the dream" that "lively shadowed" the encounter with the deity warps chronology in order to convey the paradoxes of a priority that is ontological as well as, in the moment of experience that he seeks to represent, phenomenological. In other words, as Adam relates to the sociable spirit Raphael, the dream creates an "inward apparition" that he says "gently moved / My fancy to believe I yet had being, / And lived"—which of course Adam has and does (8.293–95).

The effect of all of this is to enfold Adam's narration in a series of perceptual confusions that dramatize the jarring experience of theophany. The dreamlike quality of Adam's description serves to create a conspicuous buffer between human representation of the theophany and the actual deity that appeared. As the dream becomes manifest reality, God admonishes Adam not to eat the fruit—as if, to compensate for answering the prototype of all prayer, God needed to set up the rules and limitations of divine and human interaction. What follows is the naming of the animals in an act of division and classification, after which Adam asks for a mate.

The foregoing summary cursorily overlooks the rich details of the poetic language in order to lay bare a critical point about the structure of the interaction. In the first theophany represented in *Paradise Lost,* the rhetorical mode changes from admonition, to division and classification, and ultimately to dialogue proper. Adam's request for "Collateral love, and dearest amity" (8.426) engenders God's discursive ascent from injunction to dialectic, which in turn arouses the rational faculty, the "image of God" in unfallen Adam, by allowing Adam to realize, and then actualize, an "other self."

God decides to test Adam before granting his wish. In the process, Milton depicts what must be the most significant educational scenario in the epic, since it is here that humankind reaches its first perfection, and it is also here that Adam first learns. God created Eve, as the gloss on Genesis 2:22 in the Geneva Bible says, "Signifying that mankind was perfite, when the woman was created, which before was like an vnperfite building." God tests Adam by creating a situation in which the discrepancy in their knowledge allows Adam to realize the concept of rational love and formulate a way of expressing it. To this end, then, God plays the role of a Socratic interlocutor with Adam. In an important sense, both God and Socrates induce the same effect in the mind of the person on the receiving end of their "irony."[75] Milton depicts the theophany of Book 8 as an extraordinary, yet recognizable, form of Socratic education—a divine maieutics. Before Adam literally gives birth to Eve, he first gives birth to the *idea* of Eve in his dialogue with God. What God is teaching Adam is crucially and inextricably linked to the *way* God is teaching him.

I have referred to this process as "Socratic" with the thought in mind of the specific description of "method" in Plato's dialogues. The dialectical content of the theophany in Book 8 of *Paradise Lost* is aptly paired with a dialogic structure, and the most relevant paradigm for this remained what Socrates calls, in the *Theaetetus,* his art of maieutics, or "midwifery."[76] The metaphor has a special relevance in this context, and a deeper and more consequential irony, especially when we consider that God actually *is* playing midwife to the first human birth, and that, as by the odd inversion of the philosopher, it is a man who is giving birth instead of a woman. It is not enough, however, to recognize the aptness of the metaphorical borrowing; nor is it enough to suggest, with Irene Samuel, that the subject of the discourse, the rationality of ideal love, evokes passages in praise of the philosophical ascent in *The Symposium.*[77] The depth of Milton's reading of Plato has gone, I think, largely unnoted.[78] This is especially unfortunate given the centrality of pedagogy to the epic, and given the importance of dialogue to Milton's educational design, as Barbara Lewalski has observed: "God himself takes on the role of educator as he engages in Socratic dialogue with his Son about humankind's fall and redemption (3.80–343) and with Adam over his request for a mate (8.357–451). Adam and Eve's dialogues with each other involve them in an ongoing process of self-education about themselves and their world. The Miltonic Bard educates his readers by exercising them in rigorous judgment, imaginative apprehension, and choice."[79] Some rehearsal of the fundamentals of Platonic education may, therefore, be in order, so that the instruments Milton employs in the scene where God educates Adam will become more evident.

There are several passages from the dialogues that will help elucidate the "method" I am attributing to Plato (who was in fact the creator of the word *methodos*).[80] In the *Sophist*, Plato differentiates between sophistry, or the rhetorical education then in vogue in Athens, and Socratic dialectic. As a preliminary to the more central discussion of the relation between being and not-being—also of relevance in the context of Adam's tale—the Eleatic Stranger acts out a refutation of the implicit connection between Socrates's method and the so-called art of the sophists. Like Socrates in the *Gorgias*, the Eleatic Stranger will reveal rhetoric to be a mere *eidolon*, "an insubstantial image of a part of politics" (463d).[81] In the *Sophist*, the elenchic refutation first involves an extended daiaretical paradigm—a division and classification of the two kinds of arts, creative and acquisitive, into their proper subsets. Then the Stranger goes about differentiating mere rhetorical training— sophists being "merchants of the learnings of the soul" (231d)—from dialectical education, "the greatest and most authoritative of purifications" (229a-230e).[82]

First, the Stranger purges education of its primitive sense (as mere admonition), "an old-fashioned and paternal kind, which fathers used to apply specially on their sons" (229e); as the Stranger says, with special significance, for our purposes, in relation to God's ultimately ineffective admonition to Adam: "With a lot of effort the admonitory species of education accomplishes little" (230b). The *Sophist* moves through the various stages of dialectical argumentation in the Socratic method: elenchus (short answers refuting a thesis believed to be true by the interlocutor); daiaresis (division and classification producing an analytical paradigm of relations); and, less directly and effectively in the *Sophist*, maieusis (realization or birthing of ideas).

The exposition of the concept lies elsewhere in the Platonic corpus. In the *Phaedrus*, Socrates explains the relations between dialectic and the need for multifarious investigation (e.g., 273e). There Socrates also famously combines speeches about love and an extended discussion of the differences between speech and writing, in which Socrates prefers speech as a means of begetting legitimate thought in the mind of the listener (276a-277a). Contrary to the art of rhetoric, Socrates argues, the "art of dialectic" provides the key to human happiness: "Such discourse makes the seed forever immortal and renders the man who has it as happy as any human being can be" (277a).[83]

For Plato, immortality is itself the process of birthing, or, as Diotima puts it, according to the speech delivered by Socrates in *The Symposium,* "begetting in beauty, in respect to both the body and the soul" (206b).[84] The definition of love, or Eros, is the desire to possess the good for itself forever (206a). If the object of love is to possess the good *forever,* and that object must be recognized in the soul of a mortal, then immortality can only be achieved in reproduction—the compensation for mortality, both in body and in soul. Socrates explains that beauty impregnates the soul, which occurs when the particular body of a beautiful person is observed, and this is the first step up the ladder of love (210a). A philosopher is not made by another philosopher: a philosopher is impregnated in the observation of beauty, as Adam will be in his realization of the beauty of "rational delight": "There are those . . . who are still more fertile in their souls than in their bodies with what it pertains to soul to conceive and bear" (209a).

The role of the philosopher, who in this case corresponds to Milton's God, is to induce awareness on the part of the impregnated soul, to allow the neophyte to realize that he is pregnant. The philosopher, like a midwife, helps the impregnated to realize that he is pregnant with ideas. The philosopher asks questions that show the interlocutor that he's expecting, and thus the "midwife" helps the person give birth to the immortal, which is the Idea of Beauty itself (210e-212a). Beauty is the immortal Form that gets reproduced by the lover in love, which, in *Paradise Lost,* correlates the image of God with the rationality Adam expresses in seeking "Collateral love."

The most extended articulation of the Socratic method is in Plato's *Theaetetus,* where Socrates refers to "my art of midwifery," which "midwifes men and not women" and "examines their souls in giving birth and not their bodies" (150b).[85] According to Socrates, "whoever associate with me undergo this same thing as women in giving birth do. They suffer labor-pains and are filled with perplexity for nights and days far more than women are, and my art is capable of arousing this kind of labor pain and putting it to rest" (151a-b). Teaching, in this scheme, does not involve demonstrative exposition or explicit logical proof on the part of the teacher. To teach, as Lewis Campbell says in his commentary on this passage, "is not to put something into the mind but to evolve something out of it, or to turn the mind from darkness to light."[86] This is precisely how Milton's God teaches Adam. God allows him to evolve, bodily *and* spiritually, by creating a context in which Adam learns by recollection—recalling, that is, the nature of the divine image with which he has been endowed. [87]

Implicitly Milton follows St. Augustine in this scene. The doctrine of anamnesis was reclaimed for Christianity most influentially in the *Confessions,* where the idea of learning as recollection is connected to an allegorical reading of the creation of Eve. For Augustine, learning means piercing through the realm of accidents, or "insubstantial" events, in order to gather up scattered recognitions of the eternal within the temporal: "The process of learning is simply this: by thinking we, as it were, gather together ideas which memory contains in a dispersed and disordered way, and by concentrating our attention we arrange them in order as if ready to hand, stored in the very memory where previously they lay hidden, scattered, and neglected."[88] As we have seen, in the evangelical interpretation of Scripture, the archive of messianic prophecy is always already present within the text of the curse in Genesis or the coronation in Psalm 2. Faith is the instrumental power by which the spirit awakens this dormant repository of knowledge and allows the intellect to collate and reassemble the fragments retained in memory. This accounts for the psychology, but not the theology, of anamnesis. Augustine laments that he is "scattered in times whose order I do not understand" (11.29.39), though God's "vision of occurrences in time is not conditioned." Recollecting the divine origin of human consciousness and thus extricating the mind and spirit from superficial, temporal perception, the rational light becomes, according to Augustine's later formulation in *De Trinitate,* "the indwelling Teacher."[89]

The analogy extends much further. For Augustine, the exercise of reason entails recognition of the likeness between human intelligence and God's image. This likeness allows humanity to assert dominion over the animals, just as reason constructs a coherent context within which to subordinate action to prudent moral reflection. The rational mind surrounds all such deliberation with the memory of the origin of human authority in the divine likeness:

> We see the face of the earth adorned with earthly creatures and humanity, in your image and likeness, put in authority over all irrational animals by your image and likeness, that is by the power of reason and intelligence. And as in his soul there is one element which deliberates and aspires to domination, and another element which is submissive and obedient, so in the bodily realm woman is made for man. In mental

power she has an equal capacity for rational intelligence, but by the sex
of her body she is submissive to the masculine sex. This is analogous to
the way in which the impulse for action is subordinate to the rational
mind's prudent concern that the act is right. (13.33.47)

Women have "an equal capacity for rational intelligence," though the gen-
ders are not equal, according to Augustine's misogynist logic, because of
Adam's physical priority. Thus Adam was created first and Eve was "made
for" him. The political sense of gender relations has been determined for
Augustine by this second account in Genesis. But the salient point for the
theory of learning by recollection is that both men and women remember
the nature of their relative authority, which is exercised in prudent action
and derives from their ability to recognize likeness to God. In early modern
England, Francis Bacon's *Advancement of Learning* rehearsed this connection
between hierarchy of authority and learning as remembering. According to
Bacon, King James was the best example "of Plato's opinion, that all knowledge is but remembrance, and that the mind of man by nature knoweth all
things, and hath but her own native and original notions (which by the
strangeness and darkness of this tabernacle of the body are sequestered) again
revived and restored."[90]

In Book 8 of *Paradise Lost,* Adam's tale of his request for a mate operates
according to just this logic. Adam learns by recognizing his likeness to his
maker, though God also enjoins him not to forget their immeasurable distance.
In giving birth to Eve, Adam provides the answer to the question Fulke Greville
had asked in *A Treatie of Humane Learning:* "Who those characteristicall *Ideas* /
Conceiues, which Science of the Godhead be?"[91] In order to produce the right
circumstances to evolve love out of the mind and body of Adam, God alters the
effect of his omniscience and plays the role of the Socratic educator.

Unlike Raphael—or, perhaps, Socrates—God has all the answers. The
profession of ignorance, the disavowal of knowledge or foreknowledge,
becomes therefore the special condition for God's test. In this, God's posture
is not altogether different from the whirlwind of questions that answers Job's
lament, though that theophany, of course, reflects a postlapsarian condition
that differs as radically as can be from the friendly interaction between God
and newly created man. The rhetorical questions in the Book of Job, as Maimonides explains, ultimately expose the condition of *fallen* humanity in
order to mark and preserve the distinction between creatural and divine
senses of providence.[92]

Adam, relating his tale to the archangel, expresses an awareness of the
"presumptuous" nature of his own request (8.367). And this is surely part of

God's lesson—to draw a line sharply between man and his maker, to induce a perception of the difference as well as the similarity between them. God facetiously asks, "What call'st thou solitude?" and goes on to claim that the animals "reason not contemptibly," so that Adam has an opportunity to assert his need for "All rational delight" and to differentiate between the special, ontological superiority of humankind and the lower status of the beasts (8.391). Adam implores, "Hast thou not made me here thy substitute, / And these inferior far beneath me set?" and God responds in kind with a further illustration of the "infinite descents" that separate the creator from the created (8. 381–82, 410). God reasserts the distinction between the heavenly and the earthly orders because the logic underlying the admonition not to eat of the forbidden tree needs some elaboration and analogical illustration.

To teach the first and most important lesson that humanity will ever learn, God dissembles. In the lucid retrospect of narrative, Adam articulates an awareness of the difference between what God knew and what God said. So Adam structures his tale around an awareness of this difference, which also allows him to recognize his likeness to God by means of the human dominion over the animals, precisely in the way that Augustine described: "with these [the animals] / Find pastime, and bear rule; thy realm is large. / So spake the universal Lord, and seemed / So ordering" (8.374–77). God "seemed" to Adam to be saying one thing—"ordering" is a playful pun, since God, like Adam, performs speech-acts for which there is no correlative in postlapsarian language, at once commanding and accomplishing the placement of everything in its proper order. But, as Adam is about to learn, God was all the while inducing a gradual awareness of something quite other than the explicit "order" of the admonition not to eat the fruit, a consciousness not available on the epistemological level of naming by "sudden apprehension":

> Thus far to try thee, Adam, I was pleased,
> And find thee knowing not of beasts alone,
> Which thou hast rightly named, but of thy self,
> Expressing well the spirit within thee free,
> My image, not imparted to the brute,
> Whose fellowship therefore unmeet for thee
> Good reason was thou freely shouldst dislike,
> And be so minded still; I, ere thou spak'st,
> Knew it not good for man to be alone,
> And no such company as then thou sawst
> Intended thee, for trial only brought,
> To see how thou couldst judge of fit and meet . . .   (8.437–48)

God describes His intention in withholding from Adam His understanding that Adam had need of what God, echoing Aristotle's term for friendship, *heteros autos,* calls "thy other self" (8.450). God allows Adam to exercise "the spirit within thee free / My image" so that, charged with the rational, benevolent, and sanctioned task of future propagation, Adam begins to conceive his beloved.

So far Adam has encountered the experiential grounds for faith and hope, but he awaits the opportunity to discover charity, a necessarily social virtue. Adam relays his understanding:

> But man by number is to manifest
> His single imperfection, and beget
> Like of his like, his image multiplied,
> In unity defective, which requires
> Collateral love, and dearest amity.   (8.422–26)

Alone in mysterious seclusion, God is according to Adam's paradoxical phrase "Best with thyself accompanied," though for solitary man neither such plenitude nor such "secrecy" can exist (8.428). The need for "solace of his defects" causes an "emboldened" Adam to pursue conceptual begetting just before he, in fact, begets Eve (8.419, 434). God thus leads Adam toward cognizance of his likeness and unlikeness to the deity. The analysis and identification appear to have emerged from Adam's own cognition, but it is in fact the divine spark (the *synteresis*) within Adam that ignites his mimetic desire to create. Adam speaks of his *inability* to humanize the beasts, yet he does so in terms of God's having "deified" him through their colloquy, whether "union or communion" (8.431). Adam's first thought of Eve, in the moment just before he asks God for a mate, emerges as a shock of "apprehension" in the other sense, when the sudden awareness of a lack accompanies the freeing up of his "emboldened" and even presumptuous tongue: "I found not what methought I wanted still" (8.355). "By withholding Eve," as Marshall Grossman says, "God insures that Adam first conceives her as absent, as what he wants."[93] Thus the scene is proleptic, anticipating already the irruption of loss, absence, and lack that Adam will face as he decides to fall with Eve. The symmetry is striking. "With thee / Certain my resolution is to die" (9.906f): not only will Adam's certitude and commitment to obey God die as he chooses to become mortal, but his "resolution" (from the Latin, *resolvere*) or the very possibility of his "untying," "releasing," or "loosening" from Eve will die as he acknowledges his bond to her.

The Socratic education Adam undergoes in Book 8 of *Paradise Lost* has its tragic counterpart. For this, Milton could easily have found a precedent in the Book of Genesis itself. After the Fall, Adam and Eve hide themselves from God out of shame for their nakedness: "And the Lord God called unto Adam, and said unto him, Where art thou? And he said, I heard thy voice in the garden, and I was afraid, because I was naked; and I hid myself. And he said, Who told thee that thou wast naked? Hast thou eaten of the tree, whereof I commanded thee that thou shouldest not eat?" (Gen. 3:9–11, KJV). This, the pendant scene to the theophany in day six of the creation story, may have suggested to Milton the interrogative "trial" that prefaces the creation of Eve. At this moment, there is no question that the omniscient deity knows what Adam has done and seeks to teach erring humanity the meaning of its apostasy. God obviously knows where Adam is, and so provokes Adam to reveal his shame through the attempt to hide his nakedness. As E. J. Speiser notes, God speaks to Adam "as a father would to his child," which is especially appropriate because the Yahwist "has thus evoked . . . the childhood of mankind itself."[94]

Moreover, God is not content to leave this mode of instruction there; God insists on the recognition, so significant for Christian interpretations of the episode, that Adam has tasted disobedience because of a failure of his own conscience. As Luther puts it:

> The words "Where are you?" are words of the Law. God directs them to the conscience. Although all things are plain and known before God (Heb. 4:13), He is speaking according to our way of thinking; for He sees us considering how we may withdraw from His sight. . . . He wants to show Adam that though he had hidden, he was not hidden from God, and that when he avoided God, he did not escape God.

The point, for Luther, is that Adam "hears from the Lord his very thoughts"—that is to say, his own thoughts. "But while he is reflecting on these thoughts," Luther continues, "he is forced to accuse himself, and within him he hears his conscience convicting him of a lie and charging him with sin."[95] One obvious consequence of the divine accommodation to fallen human thought is that, allowing a deepening awareness of the inevitable judgment that must follow, God provokes the consideration of accountability in Adam. In *Paradise Lost,* the matter is not as straightforward as it is in Luther's comment, for Adam deliberates prior to his eventual acceptance of guilt, in fact requiring Eve to become heroically humble before he does; that is, she falls repentant at his feet, which is the first step the couple takes toward contrition and prayer (10.909–13).[96] Never before the Fall did Adam invoke heaven as if in a lament or curse:

> O heaven! In evil strait this day I stand
> Before my judge, either to undergo
> Myself the total crime, or to accuse
> My other self, the partner of my life . . .   (10.125–28)

The second theophany, therefore, forms the tragic counterpart to the first dialogue between God and man. Indeed, just before pronouncing the curses, God relates the Fall to a fatal disruption of the sociability between Adam and God. The "Presence divine" now attributes a loss of pleasure to Adam's defection, God recalling in his own experience of "solitude" the same lack of companionship that led Adam to plead for Eve:

> Where art thou Adam, wont with joy to meet
> My coming seen far off? I miss thee here,
> Not pleased, thus entertained with solitude,
> Where obvious duty erewhile appeared unsought:
> Or come I less conspicuous, or what change
> Absents thee, or what chance detains?   (10.104–7)

God does not "come . . . less conspicuous," except insofar as he wants to provoke in Adam an acute realization of "what change / Absents" him from his creator. Although we know from God's subsequent battery of questions that Adam "oft hast heard" the divine voice (10.119), the only point of reference in the epic is the previous dialogue of Book 8. It may be that the postlapsarian moment of God's rhetorical questioning, attested to in chapter 3 of Genesis, provided Milton with the template for the Socratic lack of divine disclosure in Book 8, in which case the structural principle in effect would be retrospective. We may, in passing, recall how this pattern is integral to the epic as a whole. After all, we see Satan in action before we see God, and we often witness the satanic effort at parity first—which means this effort cannot properly be parody until we later see the divine model that Satan imitates. Moreover, this is the structure of a fallen reader's experience—in which our experience belies the syntax so that the order of our perceptions is best conveyed first as loss, then as remembrance of what we have lost—lost . . . paradise, rather than paradise . . . lost.[97] The title itself in this way reorders our pedestrian perceptions and allows an internal reorientation toward the historical narrative rather than the self's circumscribed experience of exile. The awareness that in the instance of the curse, as in the generative love that begets Eve, God conveys his message of rational love by means of "holy irony," is central to the patterning of Milton's ultimate pedagogue.[98] Recognizing this providential design in the divine maieutics, Adam first gives birth to the very form of beauty.

Whereas the hidden nature of God's intent had previously disclosed Adam's proximity to God, the same technique now becomes an ironic means to communicate Adam's dissimilarity as a result of his apostasy. The Son's tragic use of dramatic irony teaches Adam how *unlike* God he became in his effort to analogize the human and the divine. Transgressing the one Law, the first covenant between God and humankind, the image of God in Adam has suffered the same change as the rest of fallen nature, as when Eve ate the fruit and "Earth felt the wound." God's irony induces an awareness of the pain of loss, where it had, in the dialogue that led to the creation of Eve, bodied forth pleasure as wholly rational love.

THE SWORD AND THE WORD

God's rhetorical questions to Adam in Book 10 show Milton reforming the ironic or Socratic structure of Adam's first education. After the fatal calamity, learning by recollection means taking cognizance of human alienation from God, this melancholy task replacing at first the memory of unfallen man's intimacy with his creator. Milton therefore builds a structural homology into the educational method by which Michael instructs Adam: just as the narrator interjects interpretive commentary in the midst of the epic action, so Michael repeatedly alerts Adam to his misinterpretations before guiding him toward the truth. But parity in the local method of corrective instruction does not consistently extend to similar tones of voice in Michael's interjections and those of the narrator. In insisting upon the *difference* between the voices of the epic's various pedagogues—and in claiming that the *discrepancy* between the narrator's occasionally hectoring voice and the poetry's contextual meaning forms one of Milton's key educational methods—I contend that Milton's overall intention to educate his readers is grounded in the critical wisdom of the humanist tradition, a "Rational liberty" hard won (12.82).[99] Much as the cultivation of learned and virtuous attention had proved to be the goal of humanist argument in the political tracts during the Civil War and Interregnum, Milton in the final books of the epic shows how interpreting the consequences of the Fall is a strenuous act of the critical intellect, demonstrating in the faltering perceptions of Adam and the patient instruction of Michael a model of the internal operations of the spirit when trained upon ethical action and redemption in Christ.

The education of Adam, ultimately an exercise in biblical hermeneutics, is supposed to lead Adam to the recognition of God's providential design, to make legible the "mysterious terms" in which God inscribes history (10.173). In the pedagogy of the final two books, Milton differentiates between pre- and postlapsarian modes of representation in a way that is commensurate with Adam's fallen abilities, but it is not surprising that Adam nevertheless has some difficulty comprehending the implications of his disobedience. Milton reveals the distortions that infuse human consciousness after the Fall in the encounter between Adam and Michael, the "heavenly instructor" sent by God to teach what He has foretold, "the final victory of his Son" over Sin and Death, "and the renewing of all things" (11.418; 10.Arg, p. 539). The fallenness of Adam only compounds a problem of communication that has already interfered, when Raphael tries to warn and instruct him before the Fall. It is now up to Adam's last angelic "teacher" Michael to accomplish the educational transformation that will allow Adam and Eve and their progeny to engraft themselves in their redeemer (11.450). As the Son, presenting the prayers of Adam and Eve to the Father, says in an analogy so simple it is hard to grasp: "with me / All my redeemed may dwell in joy and bliss, / Made one with me as I with thee am one" (11.42–44).

In that breathless last line, Milton requires us to perform analogical operations that are likely to elude our ability to conceptualize the meaning of the unity expressed through the similitude "as I with thee am one." At each point in fallen Adam's education, the work of the intellect is to stretch the memory back so that a future union with Christ will be recognizable. In each individual lesson, the archangel will remind Adam of the internal archive of past experience by which he can catch inspired glimpses of what future unity in Christ will mean for humankind. God tells Michael:

> If patiently thy bidding they obey,
> Dismiss them not disconsolate; reveal
> To Adam what shall come in future days,
> As I shall thee enlighten, intermix
> My cov'nant in the woman's seed renewed . . .   (11.112–16)

Michael is to communicate the subsequent history of the human race to Adam "As" God "shall . . . enlighten" him. The intermixing, which seems for a moment's hesitation at the line break to be the method of man's enlightenment, is ultimately reserved for "My cov'nant in the woman's seed renewed," but the implication is also conveyed imagistically, since the intermingling of god and humanity in "the woman's seed" will produce the new covenant. Moreover, because the adjective "renewed" can modify either the "woman's seed" or the "cov'nant," God's syntax here follows a paradigm of calculated ambiguity that shadows the verse increasingly after the Fall.

Although, as we have seen, the shift from intuitive to discursive logic shrouds the language of Raphael's teachings with distortion and inadvertent duality, God sets Michael the task of introducing to human awareness a suspended and doubtful grammar that requires retrospective faith in order to resolve itself in the fallen mind. In the hermeneutic mode that Michael teaches Adam, analogy must give way to actuality, and the accommodation of the divine intention to its scriptural traces must be shown to be a strikingly accurate proportional representation. The ratio at the heart of the doctrine of accommodation, as Milton proposes, is to be taken quite seriously.[100] As Milton had written in the *Animadversions* (1641): "Wee shall adhere close to the Scriptures of God which hee hath left us as the just and adequate measure of truth, fitted, and proportion'd to the dilligent study, memory, and use of every faithfull man, whose every part consenting and making up the harmonious *Symmetry* of compleat instruction, is able to set out to us a perfect man of God" (YP 1:700). Such adherence is, however, fraught with the complexities of the grammar through which God conveys His word.[101] As Milton says in the *De Doctrina Christiana,* "one often has to take into account the anomalies of syntax, as, for example, when a relative does not refer to its immediate antecedent but to the principal word in the sentence, although it is not so near to it" (YP 6:582–83). In this exegetical precept, Milton provides a clue for interpreting his practice in the epic as well. Milton continued to adhere to the Analogy of Faith as the ultimate adjudicating factor in scriptural interpretation, a conviction about the nature of postlapsarian consciousness that the epic allows us to experience along with Adam in the lesson taught by Michael. The "Protestant bias" of Milton's thought, as H. R. MacCallum contends, "consistently caused him to emphasize the inward and spiritual nature of the antitype" and "the apprehension of the letter through faith and charity."[102] The core reliance upon faith as an inner compulsion affects our interpretation of the sense encoded in the grammar and rhetoric of history. Yet the historical sentence under construction in the final two books of the epic is not only exile, "the sad sentence rigorously urged" (11.109), but also the one fated to end "at the world's great period" (12.467).[103]

Embedded in a resilient textual archive, the prophecy is already placed at one remove from the deity when Michael instructs Adam in its meaning. In the event, Michael will through repetition and mnemonic assistance teach Adam to interpret the covenant in its connection to God's promise to Abram (12.147–51), the giving of the Ten Commandments (12.232–35), and the everlasting Davidic throne (12.325–28). Along with Adam and Eve, readers of the epic have already heard the substance of the great argument in the Son's pronouncement of the curse on the enemy:

> Between thee and the woman I will put
> Enmity, and between thine and her seed;
> Her seed shall bruise thy head, thou bruise his heel.   (10.179–81)

The narrator immediately interprets "this oracle" typologically and proclaims it "verified / When Jesus son of Mary second Eve / Saw Satan fall like lightning down from heaven . . ." (10.182–84). Christ's resurrection is quickly interpreted as his victory over Satan, "Whom he shall tread at last under our feet; / Even he who now foretold his fatal bruise" (10.190–91). At this very moment in the action, as Jason Rosenblatt has argued, the *protevangelium* "devalues peremptorily the literal Torah as authoritative source of the law and history, turning it into the Old Testament" and constricting it to typological prefiguration for the duration of the epic.[104] The common source for this interpretation of the curse was Romans 16:20; Milton here echoes the diction of the Geneva Version: "The God of peace shall treade Satan vnder your feete shortly." Over the course of Michael's instruction, Adam must learn to interpret the messianic prophecy in the way that the narrator does.[105]

As the archangel descends, Milton reminds us of the pedagogical force of these interjections into the narrative, as if to say that with the Fall, the need for a new kind of didacticism, more like that of the epic narrator, is now required. Adam observes the "double object in our sight"—the "mute signs in nature" which portend violence, expulsion, and enmity—the "bird of Jove" stooping to hunt "Two birds of gayest plume" (11.185–201). One "further change" symbolically hinted at in this emblematic tableau as awaiting Adam's discovery is the idea of duplicity, like the "two twins cleaving together" in *Areopagitica* (YP 2:514). The vagueness of Adam's perception emphasizes his degraded sensitivity to the supernatural when he mistakes the angel's descent for a natural phenomenon "with something heavenly fraught" (11.207). The narrator then obtrudes, encoding the theological significance in the postponed syntactic resolution:

> He erred not, for by this the heavenly bands
> Down from a sky of jasper lighted now
> In Paradise, and on a hill made alt,
> A glorious apparition, had not doubt
> And carnal fear that day dimmed Adam's eye.   (11.208–12)

The verb mood does not resolve until the final clause, a revisionary syntactic structure that underscores the allusion to last things in the apocalyptic "sky of jasper" (Rev. 4:3, noted by Fowler, p. 609). More immediately, this qualification may serve as a reminder of the similarity between the diminished capacity of fallen Adam and the metaphysical perplexities endemic to the world Adam will leave his progeny. It is possible to regard the syntax of the sentence as conditional throughout—retrospectively reformed by the addition of the last clause. In this reading, it would mean something like "Adam would not have erred if doubt and carnal fear had not dimmed his eye, for the apparition descended," instead of the more indicative phrasing, "Adam was not wrong, because there was a glorious apparition, if only he could have seen it without the doubt induced by his carnal fear." Either way the clarity that Adam had taken for granted before the Fall has become double vision, creating doubt, and Milton has embodied this realization in the syntax of the description. Our linguistic perception tracks Adam's interpretation of the visible scene. Just as the need for empirical verification had underpinned the sinful act itself, so the duplicitous intent evinced by our first parents manifests itself as an inability to cling to the evidence of things not seen.

Using inadequate experience, rather than faith, as the criterion for interpretation had been Eve's downfall: "For good unknown, sure is not had, or had / And yet unknown is as not had at all," she rationalizes just before falling (9.756–57). Eve falls prey to Satan's deception, though Milton, following St. Paul (1 Tim. 2:14), allows that Adam elects to fall "Against his better knowledge, not deceived" (9.998). "Let none henceforth," says Adam after the Fall, as he renews his protracted and self-serving accusation of Eve, "seek needless cause to approve / The faith they owe; when earnestly they seek / Such proof, conclude, they then begin to fall" (9.1140). In the desire to found moral knowledge upon experience, a form of idolatry arises; drawn down into the state of fallen nature, Adam and Eve become idolatrous as a sign of their apostasy. For Milton, as for Luther, apostasy is instigated by credulously weighing alternative sources of pedagogical authority to God's, as Eve "casts aside the Word of God and offers her whole self to Satan as his pupil."[106] The Fall enacts a contest between pedagogues in which the satanic schoolmaster teaches self-possession, pursuit of "side-long" self-interest by "tract oblique" (9.510), and literalistic interpretation of freedom.

Satan's habitual literalism leads to his conveniently self-serving exegesis of the *protevangelium*. "A world who would not purchase with a bruise?" he asks, which is sensible enough if the curse is reduced to bare physicality (10.500). Following a pattern established early in the first book, Milton structures the action so that we see Satan literally misinterpreting the prophecy that Adam must learn to comprehend figuratively. In this way, Satan inverts theodicy, wondering why God created human beings and gave them Paradise, and his questioning dovetails with an emphasis on experience as the most valued teacher. Mental reliance on experience, shown throughout the epic to be a most fallible guide, engenders the satanic insistence, often repeated, upon "proof." It must be conceded that even obedient saints resort to the category: "by experience taught we know how good" God is, Abdiel says (5.826). Whereas Satan inverts the theodical structure by deriving a need for empirical evidence from theological doubt, however, theodicy operates in precisely the opposite direction, moving from the experience of suffering toward an attempt at resolving doubt through the rational explanation of the ways of God. Precisely this paradoxical countermovement to empirical experience informs the defense of God's justice that Leibniz mounts in the *Theodicy* (1710): "It is true that one may imagine possible worlds without unhappiness . . . but these same worlds again would be very inferior in goodness. I cannot show you this in detail. For can I know and can I present infinities to you and compare them together?"[107] As is suggested by the antithesis in the title of John Hick's classic modern treatment of "soul-making theodicy," *Evil and the God of Love,* the lived experience of evil makes necessary a defense of the idea of divine benevolence.[108] *Paradise Lost* also manages to imply the ambiguity that would result if we reversed the terms of Hick's antithesis: The God of Love and Evil. If evil brings forth good, according to the providential plot—as in the description, "Knowledge of good bought dear by knowing ill" (4.222)—then it is perhaps also true that, from the perspective of created creatures, good brings forth evil.

The cosmic struggle is, at any rate, intelligible to human beings only backwards, which leads to Lactantius's important but—as Milton realized long before writing the epic—inadequate formulation: "Why does God permit evil? So that the account can stand correct with goodness. For the good is made known, is made clear, and is exercised by evil. As Lactantius says, Book 5. chapter 7, that reason and intelligence may have the opportunity to exercise themselves by choosing the things that are good, by fleeing from the things that are evil. lactan de ira dei. chapter 13. however much these things fail to satisfy" (YP 1:363). When Milton entered these thoughts in his Commonplace Book, he added the comment to the end of the passage that acknowledges how (intellectually) unsatisfying such blatant rationalization is. As an emotional response to the conceptual shortcoming of simple justice, these remarks help us to understand the relative effects of Milton's God and Milton's Satan upon generations of readers, from Dryden to Blake to students today. As we have seen in the discussion of free will in Chapter

One, justifications of God's ways tend toward a rectification of the soul by making evil instrumental to salvation. This permission of uncertainty and doubt allows for a profound and genuine assertion of faith, a greater good that would not have been possible without the element of free will and choice. In this sense, the Son's decision to sacrifice Himself for humanity springs from the free will granted to all beings and serves as a model choice of obedience.

Milton's great argument requires that readers witness an evolving process of argumentation that is indirect, multifarious, and open to challenge on political, spiritual, and experiential grounds. This, I submit, is how *Paradise Lost* responds to the dissatisfaction Milton himself found in Lactantius's solution to the problem of evil. Milton's theodicy is rhetorical before it is logical and therefore defies, even thwarts, the effort to reduce it to a propositional form. This is why Adam needs above all, as Michael tells him, "to learn / True patience" (11.360–61), so that he may "believe, and be confirmed" in his faith (11.355). Calling to mind a pendant scene of instruction, Michael commences with an allusion to the birth of Eve and thus to the Socratic method by which God taught Adam to conceive rational love: Eve will sleep "while thou to foresight wak'st, / As once thou slepst, while she to life was formed" (11.369–69). Michael instructs Adam in the meaning of his having been granted time before death (11.255–57); tells Adam what he will teach him and what he will need to learn (11.355–66); and places three drops from the well of life on Adam's eyes, which pierce "Even to the inmost seat of mental sight" (11.418).

To accomplish the transformation of his understanding and to bring about a consciousness of charity as the means to imitate the paragon of virtue, the Son of God, Michael teaches Adam through trial and error to interpret history faithfully, as a sacred text. Adam, as Michael tells him, must understand what he sees in the most "mysterious terms" (10.173):

> So law appears imperfect, and but given
> With a purpose to resign them in full time
> Up to a better covenant, disciplined
> From shadowy types to truth, from flesh to spirit,
> From imposition of strict laws, to free
> Acceptance of large grace, from servile fear
> To filial, works of law to works of faith.   (12.300–06)

Learning patience means learning the meaning of the Passion, moving from "shadowy types to truth," comprehending "the fullness of time" (Gal. 4:4).

In typical Reformist fashion, Milton filters his Pauline text through a stricture against the doctrine of works (encoded as "works of law") in favor of the
"Acceptance of large grace" (described as "works of faith"). The Law appears
imperfect owing to Adam's transgression against the first law of God, and
therefore, in St. Paul's account of the bondage of the spirit in Romans 7, the
Law was given: to increase sin. Spiritually, says Paul, "I delight in the law of
God after the inward man: But I see another law in my members, warring
against the law of my mind, and brining me into captivity to the law of sin
which is in my members" (Rom. 7:22–23, KJV). Because Michael guides
him through the consequences of his apostasy, the implication for "*the olde
man*" Adam is essential so that he may gain greater knowledge of himself and
thereby aspire to become the first "inward man" rectified by the Son, "one
greater man" (see the Geneva gloss). Condensing several verses from the
Epistle to the Romans (esp. 2:20–23), Luther in Tyndale's English unites the
comprehension of the Law with the development of charity, the central tenet
of the new covenant, in a way that illuminates Michael's speech on typology
in *Paradise Lost:* "Thou teachest another ma[n], but teachest not thy sylfe, ye
thou wotest not what thou teachest, for thou vndersto[n]dest not the lawe
aright, how that it can not be fulfylled and sastified, but with inwarde love
and affectio[n], so greatly it can not be fulfilled with outeward dedes and
werkes only."[109] Tyndale captures the sense of increasing interiority that Milton grants the hermeneutic task at the heart of Adam's education.

Adam's understanding takes a turn from primitive animism, to espousal of
the doctrine of works, to avowal of idolatry that explicitly alludes to Cain's
response after he is cursed in the primal episode of postlapsarian idolatry: "as
from [God's] face I shall be hid" (11.316; cf. Gen. 4:14). In the debate with Eve
that leads to their first show of contrition, Adam recalls the promise spoken at
the curse. Responding to Eve's suggestion that they commit suicide, Adam does
not yet understand its figural dimension. As when Adam chooses to fall with
Eve, mention of self-slaughter again activates the most profound resonances of
Christ's self-sacrifice, the true paradigm of charitable human action:

>   let us seek
> Some safer resolution, which methinks
> I have in view, calling to mind with heed
> Part of our sentence, that thy seed shall bruise
> The serpent's head . . .   (10.1028–32)

Adam's recollection of the promise marks the intellectual shift toward regeneration, but Milton demonstrates the pervasive infection of literalism when

Adam glosses the prophecy in the satanic manner: "to crush his head / Would be revenge indeed" (9.1035–36). Adam's facile optimism, here as so often during his subsequent tutelage by Michael, betrays an overconfident reading of the prophecy, which neglects the tragic suffering for which he is responsible. Through all its iterations in the last two books of the epic, we watch as the prophecy becomes ever more intractably *textual*—even though it precedes, in the temporality of the epic action, its future scriptural embodiment—which transforms the promise into an object urgently awaiting interpretation.

As becomes increasingly evident through Michael's lesson, Adam usually thinks he grasps the text rather on the model of his former, prelapsarian gift of "sudden apprehension" than on the new, strenuous model of Christian liberty in fallen nature (8.354). Thus Michael, correcting Adam's interpretive error, must help him shed his inflexible understanding of the "their fight / As of a duel, or the local wounds / Of head or heel: not therefore joins the Son / Manhood to Godhead . . ." (12.387–90). The imagery of repairing, regaining, and restoring imbues Milton's writings on the education of the spirit, and so Michael likewise directs Adam's awareness away from literal and outward senses of meaning toward inward healing and reformation: humanity must in the present reality that follows the first disobedience suffer "death's wound: / Which he, who comes thy saviour, shall recure, / Not by destroying Satan, but his works / In thee and in thy seed . . ." (12.392–95). Hence his constant misunderstanding, which Milton underscores by drawing out the elaborate irony of his self-assertions: "O prophet of glad tidings, finisher / Of utmost hope! Now clear I understand / What oft my steadiest thoughts have searched in vain . . ." (12.375–77). Adam persists relentlessly in his narrow interpretation of what Michael puts before him: "Needs must the serpent now his capital bruise / Expect with mortal pain: say where and when / Their fight, what stroke shall bruise the victor's heel" (12.382–85). Recapitulating the misplaced physical heroism of ancient martial epic, Adam reveals the limitation of his fallen intellect by applying the wrong standard of interpretation, much as Satan had done in the early books of the epic.

Adam's realization about the spiritual nature of the Son's victory over Satan is therefore analogous to the gradual recognition—encouraged by Milton in his readers—of the limitations of the epic genre's violent heroism. Christ's new heroism demands articulation in a new conceptual vocabulary. To represent "the better fortitude / Of patience and heroic martyrdom" (9.31–32), Michael must insist upon suffering rather than combat as the medium for spiritual victory over Satan. Spiritual heroism thus undermines the tendency in epic since Homer "to nourish that sanguinary madness in mankind, which has continually made the earth a theatre of carnage."[110]

Michael tells obstinate Adam over and over to watch for the spiritual significance of what was "obscurely then foretold" (12.543).

In response, Milton endows Adam with a tendency toward what might be termed *ironic theodicy*, since such a reaction falsely bears witness to redemption without acknowledging the enormity of its cost. Whereas Adam spins out, in the manner of the narrative interjections in Book 1, the facile implications of an ironic theodicy—

> Oh goodness infinite, goodness immense!
> That all this good of evil shall produce,
> And evil turn to good; more wonderful
> Than that which by creation first brought forth
> Light out of darkness!   (12.469–73)

—Milton roundly denounces the unqualified optimism of such expressions of untested faith:

> Full of doubt I stand,
> Whether I should repent me now of sin
> By me done and occasioned, or rejoice
> Much more, that much more good thereof shall spring . . . (12.473–76)

Michael therefore inevitably returns to the "mortal taste" of martyrdom, the suffering of Christians down through the ages, as a remedy for Adam's hasty oversimplifications. Adam's form of theodicy is precisely the one that has led thinkers such as Emmanuel Levinas to be dismissive of theodical reasoning as an ethical lapse derived from an inattention to the Other: "The justification of the neighbour's pain is certainly," Levinas argues, "the source of all immorality." In this view, theodicy itself is a temptation to diminish the suffering of others for social utility, "the grand idea necessary to the inner peace of souls in our distressed world. It is called upon to make sufferings here below comprehensible."[111]

EDUCATION AND THE "PARADISE WITHIN"

Although Adam's angelic pedagogues have served "to render man inexcusable" for his fall (5.Arg, p. 281), Milton's God designs the tragic expulsion from paradise to represent the enigmatic comfort of the regenerate soul, "the peace of God, which passeth all understanding" (Phil. 4:7, KJV). In preparation for exile, Michael teaches Adam to see that God by means of the Holy Spirit will arm him "against such cruelties / With inward consolations recompensed" (12.494–95). Yet, against Adam's difficulty countenancing the ever-deepening wound of human suffering and loss, Milton reveals a glimpse of the self-transcendence of the blessed. In the memory of such loss begins the responsibility to create within ourselves the conditions for true theodicy in the recognition that the tragedy contains the seed of salvation. In this sense, at least, Louis Martz is right when he says that "the action moves from the world we know toward the inward light by which man is enabled to see a Paradise that lies within the center of the poem and within the center of the mind and memory."[112] It is, nevertheless, important that Milton does not *depict* this feat of memory that the poem describes. That this final lesson should be, in effect, lost on Adam until the last moment in paradise is crucial to the epic's pedagogical design, for only through time will the full acknowledgment of suffering lead to a radical inwardness.[113] Such inward attention, Milton suggests, may initiate a transformation of fallen humanity's predicament, a new politics born of the highest ethical conduct and manifest in the deepest compassion and love for fellow human beings. A renewed polity, sprung from a new commitment to spiritual education, begins as a development fundamentally within individuals "happier far" for their loss, and this development may then radiate outward to society (12.587).

Despite his erring, Adam finally attains a serviceable understanding of Michael's teachings. Even though he is not yet able to perform unfailingly the paradisal hermeneutics required after the expulsion, Adam repeats the moral of the long human story dutifully:

> Henceforth I learn that to obey is best,
> And love with fear the only God, to walk
> As in his presence, ever to observe
> His providence, and on him sole depend,
> Merciful over all his works, with good
> Still overcoming evil, and by small
> Accomplishing great things, by things deemed weak
> Subverting worldly strong, and worldly wise
> By simply meek . . .   (12.561–69)

Inculcated in his faith, Adam has at last worked out the basic pattern of virtuous living that begins in obedience to God and thereby unlocks the paradoxical force to subvert worldly power. "Taught this by his example whom I now / Acknowledge my redeemer ever blest" (12.572–73), Adam stands prepared to observe God's providence and receive Michael's final consolation. Concluding his tutelage of Adam, Michael describes the possibility of redemption much in the way that Milton, in his earlier *Art of Logic,* had explained the reciprocity of descriptive language: "just as definition can be argued by the thing defined . . . so also description can in turn be argued from the thing described" (YP 8:315). Milton's example of logically consistent attributes from the treatise applies in this case especially well; as he says, *"man is a mortal animal, capable of being instructed"* (YP 8:315).

Never relinquishing the pedagogical method by which he intends to enlighten Adam, Michael replies to the man's humility:

> This having learned, thou hast attained the sum
> Of wisdom; hope no higher, though all the stars
> Thou knewst by name, and all the ethereal powers,
> All secrets of the deep, all nature's works,
> Or works of God in heaven, air, earth, or sea,
> And all the riches of this world enjoyedst,
> And all the rule, one empire; only add
> Deeds to thy knowledge answerable, add faith,
> Add virtue, patience, temperance, add love,
> By name to come called charity, the soul
> Of all the rest: then wilt thou not be loath
> To leave this Paradise, but shalt possess
> A paradise within thee, happier far.   (12.575–87)

As befits his pedagogical strategy throughout the epic, Milton gives the last word of the lesson to the angelic teacher, not his pupil, with the stipulation of an onward promise that remains enigmatic, accessible to Adam only "With meditation on the happy end" (12.605). Milton seasons Michael's exhortation with further ironies, as in the rhetorical stretch that begins with *"only* add"—as if what follows would be the simplest task of the human will—and ends with a syntactic bridge to the inward paradise that looks ahead both logically and temporally, *then.*

Yet Milton implies that there remains within human time both a causality of and plausibility for the inner sanctum of paradisal redemption. We recall that Milton effects the unity of educative pursuits in the social and political realms of human experience precisely through the critical and ethical intellect in the famous sentence from *Of Education:* "The end then of learning is to repair the ruins of our first parents by regaining to know God aright, and out of that knowledge to love him, to imitate him, to be like him, as we may the neerest by possessing our souls of true vertue, which being united to the heavenly grace of faith makes up the highest perfection" (YP 2:366–67). Insofar as it is within their receptive capacity to unite with heavenly grace, human beings may achieve "the highest perfection." The template of Christ's behavior is within Adam, just as Jesus proclaims in the Gospel of Luke: "behold, the kingdom of God is within you" (17:21, KJV). In postlapsarian futurity, Adam and his descendants must remember this not merely by the kind of trial and error that has led him through Michael's lesson, but by the awakened sense of Christ as the creative principle of the universe, that which will teach humankind how to possess "our souls of true vertue." Learning how to be, in Miltonic education, means remembering what is already within the human mind and spirit through the mediation of the messiah. In the accretion of consciousness by means of "Deeds to thy knowledge answerable," the reinvention of paradise occurs within each individual human being, and so "the ruins of our first parents" may be repaired by means of ethical and compassionate action, "charity, the soul / Of all the rest" (12.81, 84–85).

In these key passages from the epic and *Of Education,* Milton refers to the enlightened recognition on the part of the human as the individual's *possessing* paradise and virtue. Repairing the ruins of our first parents begins with their re-pairing. By owning the ethical obligation to act charitably—for which the actions of the Son of God provide the ultimate model, according to Milton—each human being undergoes an inspired transformation, a rebuilding of paradise inside human consciousness that promises a more compassionate political world for all. Milton's radical inwardness therefore projects a politics that I would argue is not quietist but revolutionary.[114] The hermeneutics of paradise with which Michael ends his lesson and Milton concludes *Paradise Lost* evinces a special logic that is destined to appear circular if one stands outside of belief. To find the "paradise within," Milton implies, we must comprehend the hermeneutic circle. Internalizing the archive of human loss as recorded in sacred Scripture, he urges us, as he had from the divorce tracts on, to use our understanding of Christ Himself as the interpretive principle, the wholeness of history that we must employ to grasp the significance of each part.

The goal of education is to be like God, Milton says in *Of Education,* but this is bound to prove a confusing injunction when we perceive the Son as the Word embodied, and therefore as the archive itself through which we may gain access to the deity. For Milton, education is the illumination of this archive of human experience, and Christ serves as the ultimate figure for the learning that we must persistently relearn through memory. Failure of memory becomes a metaphor for our inability to conceive of the whole simultaneously, as in the allegory of Truth's injured body with which this book began, and therefore we experience the memory of our connection to God, in the wake of the Fall, as the dismembered totality. For Milton, learning becomes the attempt to recover wholeness, to restore integrity. We imitate the messiah in seeking education without end, since at the end of all is learning.

The stark shift when Adam and Eve reach "the subjected plain" necessarily counteracts the cheerfulness of Adam's acceptance of Michael's dogma:

> In either hand the hastening angel caught
> Our lingering parents, and to the eastern gate
> Led them direct, and down the cliff as fast
> To the subjected plain; then disappeared.   (12.637–40)

Adam has indeed been "greatly instructed," as he maintains (12.557). Without yet grasping his own culpability, however, Adam cannot comprehend the depth of his humanity. The sons and daughters of Adam and Eve will be left to locate the paradise within, but their consolation will henceforth be strenuously achieved, a rational liberty that emerges as the end of learning which "Our lingering parents" have only just begun (12.638).

Coda

Perhaps it is true, as Aristotle claims at the start of the *Metaphysics,* that by nature all human beings desire to know. Aristotle held that, in general, "it is a sign of the man who knows and of the man who does not know, that the former can teach, and therefore we think art more truly knowledge than experience is; for artists can teach, and men of mere experience cannot."[1] The artist in this conception is a person whose rational faculty has deduced universal principles from a class of particular experiences, but experience itself does not yield universal judgment. If a longing drives the pursuit of knowledge, and reasonably manifests itself in the ability to teach, the same desire does not necessarily produce wisdom, and this realization formed a critical distinction within and throughout Milton's works.

Others more proximate to Milton's era and episteme meaningfully clung to a similar distinction. The mind, according to Montaigne, is a perpetual motion machine, and ambiguity is our nourishment. As a consequence, thought is naturally, in one sense, without end: "There's more adoe to enterpret interpretation, than to interpret things: and more bookes upon bookes, then upon any other subject. We do but enter-glose ourselves."[2] Of this charge all literary critics are to some extent invariably guilty; yet it is equally true that knowledge endures in the memory and therefore as a reconstruction enabled by the interpreting of interpretations. Thus Francis Bacon plotted the trajectory of studies toward the fashioning of a universal wit: "Reading makes a full man; conference a ready man; and writing an exact man."[3] It is natural that "most men fail in one or another of the ends proposed," Samuel Johnson confessed in an essay on intellectual life that begins by misquoting Bacon's axiom; "it is, however, reasonable to have perfection in our eye; that we may always advance towards it, though we know it never can be reached."[4] But knowledge, as Sir Thomas Browne remarked, "is made by oblivion; and to purchase a clear and warrantable body of Truth, we must forget and part with much we know."[5] Learning is equally the product of remembrance and forgetting, and it is within this push-and-pull that the motion, whether it is deemed advancement, preservation, or regression, inheres.

Likewise, Milton construes the end of learning as an act of recuperation, an effort to reconstruct an edenic mentality or a "paradise within." His educational project is, as I have sought to show, spiritual as well as rational— two parallel pursuits whose vanishing point lies in Milton's ethical insistence upon charity. But the indirectness of Milton's educational theory, when taken beyond practical pedagogy, has at times caused it to be greatly misunderstood.[6] Probably the passage most responsible for the tendency of critics to diminish Milton's view of human beings' educative potential—upon which Milton insisted throughout his writings—is the famous disavowal of classical learning by Jesus in *Paradise Regained*. But as I have endeavored to show throughout this book, disavowal is one of Milton's favorite ways of promoting the opposite of that which he has claimed. Heuristically considered, disavowal is only the challenging gesture that prompts further reflection:

> Think not but that I know these things, or think
> I know them not; not therefore am I short
> Of knowing what I ought: he who receives
> Light from above, from the fountain of light,
> No other doctrine needs, though granted true. . . .   (*PR* 4.286–90)

The odd internal rhyme of "not" and "ought" draws our attention to the chiseled epigrammatic quality of Jesus' sentence. Its symmetry and balance are set against the bias toward classical culture that Satan introduces in his temptation. Christ's judgment need not mean what it seems to say, for Jesus *has* studied pagan culture enough to insist that it is derivative of Hebraic knowledge, and He tells Satan not to think that He has not learned what He needs to know.[7] Euhemerism, as we have seen in the chapter devoted to the divorce tracts, provided the most widespread commonplaces about the relation between things pagan and things Christian; in fact, Christians throughout the Renaissance were constantly triangulating pagan and Christian with Hebraic, so that the Christian interpretation could be seen as the true original of which all mythology formed a mere shadow.

Of course, in *Paradise Regained*, the Son of God is in the process of discovering that He has a very different relationship to the "Light from above" than the rest of us. The temptation of Athens, we do well to recall, depends upon the lure of knowledge not adequately tempered by a properly spiritual end. It is also, like the other temptations, carefully meted out in classically perfected verse; the disavowal of Athens was published in a volume that included *Samson Agonistes* with its neoclassically informed preface. Therefore we need not share the agony over this passage so eloquently expressed by Douglas Bush: "It is painful indeed to watch Milton turn and rend some main roots of his being, but we must try to understand him."[8] Milton puts words in Jesus' mouth that echo Ecclesiastes 12:12: "Of making many books there is no end; and much study is a weariness of the flesh." Jesus warns,

> However many books
> Wise men have said are wearisome; who reads
> Incessantly, and to his reading brings not
> A spirit and judgment equal or superior,
> (And what he brings, what needs he elsewhere seek)
> Uncertain and unsettled still remains,
> Deep-versed in books and shallow in himself,
> Crude or intoxicate, collecting toys,
> And trifles for choice matters, worth a sponge;
> As children gathering pebbles on the shore. (*PR* 4.321–330)

Milton opposed this potential for shallowness in his readers throughout his writings; nowhere does he encourage idle learning, or intellectualism divorced from the ethical commitment to virtuous living. To read *Paradise Regained* as an endorsement of anti-intellectual attitudes, however, is crudely to misrepresent the rhetorical environment, the context, the artfulness of Jesus' strategies for destabilizing and vanquishing Satan's ploys.

A further point about the brief epic requires clarification. By the eighteenth century, the innovative publisher Jacob Tonson had arrived at what was to be the most successful formula for marketing the volume of 1671, *Paradise Regain'd . . . To which is Added Samson Agonistes*. Tonson's strategy was to sell the book as an essential work of moral education in the humanist tradition. Beginning with the fifth edition (London, 1713), publishers of the volume began to bundle these late works together with the minor poems and with Milton's tract *Of Education*. This combination was issued 27 times during the eighteenth century, passing gradually out of favor only when the addition of Thomas Newton's annotations from 1752 created a more readily marketable edition. Clearly this was the "minor poems" volume to accompany prestigious editions of *Paradise Lost* for readers who wanted the poetical works of Milton. The minor poems were offered as a "supplement"—but the educational treatise was carried over along with them from the 1673 publication of *The Poems upon Several Occasions.* Publishers only separated the tract from the shorter poems when the variorum commentary became popular in the editions by Newton and Todd. Readers throughout the eighteenth century were therefore encouraged not only to read the poems as a fulfillment of the educational project advocated in the brief tractate, but also to read the tractate as a gloss of sorts on the poems, including *Paradise Regained.* Yet even this reception history will not exhaust interpretation of the disavowal of learning that so troubles readers of what is probably the last poem Milton wrote.

Nor should it. Throughout this book I have argued that the "end" of learning for Milton comprises both the aim and limitation of reason. Milton characteristically finds ways to ask those questions that, according to a more orthodox conception of the human capacity for curiosity, simply ought not to be asked. However, as Hans Blumenberg maintains, "The questions that cannot be asked confront reason with its impotence more pitilessly than those that do not need to be asked."[9] Milton is most characteristically drawn to precisely these questions—questions regarded by Blumenberg as epoch-making in the way they reoccupy theoretical positions that were established by an earlier worldview. The problems, instead of the proposed solutions to those problems, are what survive in this model of intellectual continuity.

Consideration of the period to which Milton belongs has always been endemic to the field of Milton studies.[10] Is he a belated interloper in the emerging early modern world, a holdout for a nostalgically beheld but ultimately fictitious Renaissance ideal? Or is he more forward-looking, his commitments legible as proleptic signs pointing toward increased liberty for the political subject? As I have just formulated the problem, no useful answer would seem to be forthcoming. The contradictions in his thought, as well as the continuities, teach us much about the culture of which he was a part. In his poetry, as much as his prose, Milton taught his readers to respect the God-given abilities made possible by human reason, but he also reminded us that every effort at understanding must finally give way to devotion.

Notes

NOTES TO THE INTRODUCTION

1. Nathan Tarcov, *Locke's Education for Liberty* (Chicago: University of Chicago Press, 1984).
2. This of course depends entirely upon how one defines "virtue," a question radically reframed for modern political thought by Machiavelli, especially in *The Prince*. For a concise account of the traditional view in Plato and Aristotle, against which Machiavelli's treatment of the relation between knowledge and virtue should be measured, see Werner Jaeger, *Paedeia: The Ideals of Greek Culture*, trans. Gilbert Highet, 3 vols. (New York: Oxford University Press, 1943–45), esp. 2:235, 2:239, 3:227–28, 3:341n93.
3. Thomas Hobbes, "A Review and Conclusion," *Leviathan*, ed. Richard Tuck, rev. ed. (Cambridge: Cambridge University Press, 1996), p. 491.
4. John Amos Comenius, *The Great Didactic* (1657), trans. M. W. Keatinge, 2nd ed. (1910; reprint New York: Russell and Russell, 1967), p. 56.
5. Jean Piaget, "The Significance of John Amos Comenius at the Present Time," *John Amos Comenius on Education*, ed. Lawrence A. Cremin (New York: Teachers College Press, 1967), pp. 1–31 (at 9). For more on Comenius's influence upon seventeenth-century English thinkers, see Robert Fitzgibbon Young, *Comenius in England* (London: Oxford University Press, 1932).
6. My account of allegory in this and the following paragraphs is indebted to Victoria Kahn, "Allegory and the Sublime in *Paradise Lost*," in *Milton*, ed. Annabel Patterson (London: Longman, 1992), pp. 127–52; Gordon Teskey, "Allegory," in *The Spenser Encyclopedia*, ed. A. C. Hamilton et al. (Toronto: University of Toronto Press, 1990), pp. 16–22; idem, *Allegory and Violence* (Ithaca, NY: Cornell University Press, 1996), esp. pp. 70–72; and Catherine Gimelli Martin, *The Ruins of Allegory: "Paradise Lost" and the Metamorphosis of Epic Convention* (Durham, NC: Duke University Press, 1998).
7. C. S. Lewis, *The Allegory of Love: A Study in Medieval Tradition* (1936; reprint London: Oxford University Press, 1953), p. 52.

8. The standard scholarly account remains Henri de Lubac, *Exégèse médiévale: les quatre sens de l'écriture,* 4 vols. (Paris: Aubier, 1959–64). For a helpful explanation of the impact of medieval hermeneutics on Reformation thought, see Alister E. McGrath, *The Intellectual Origins of the European Reformation,* 2nd ed. (Oxford: Blackwell, 2004), pp. 148–66.

9. For Milton's recollections of the *Moralia,* see, e.g., *Prolusion 7* (YP 1:303), the Nativity Ode ll.173ff., and the preface to *Samson Agonistes* (*Poems,* p. 355). For other possible sources and analogues, see Douglas Bush, *Mythology and the Renaissance Tradition in English Poetry* (Minneapolis: University of Minnesota Press, 1937), p. 269n52.

10. Plutarch, "Isis and Osiris," 351–52, *Moralia,* ed. and trans. Frank Cole Babbitt, 14 vols., LCL (Cambridge, Mass.: Harvard University Press, 1927–1936), 5:9.

11. Plutarch, *Moralia,* 5:47 and 87.

12. Jacques Lacan, "The Signification of the Phallus," *Écrits: A Selection,* trans. Alan Sheridan (New York: W. W. Norton, 1977), p. 288, articulates the concept of the phallus as the symbol of the signifier and the association of the castration complex with aporias inherent in signification: the phallus "can play its role only when veiled, that is to say, as itself a sign of the latency with which any signifiable is struck, when it is raised (*aufgehoben*) to the function of signifier. The phallus is the signifier of this *Aufhebung* itself, which it inaugurates (initiates) by its disappearance. That is why the demon of Αιδως (*Scham,* shame) arises at the very moment when, in the ancient mysteries, the phallus is unveiled." Mikkel Borch-Jacobsen, *Lacan: The Absolute Master* (Stanford: Stanford University Press, 1992), pp. 210–11, elucidates this key passage: "the phallus is itself the ultimate veil of absence . . . it is *the* signifier of desire—that is, in Lacan's terms 'the signifier of the signified,' 'for it is the signifier intended to designate as a whole the effects of the signified.'" Slavoj Zizek, *Looking Awry: An Introduction to Jacques Lacan through Popular Culture* (Cambridge, Mass.: MIT Press, 1991), p. 91, explicates the uncanny effect of the "phallic stage" of signification thus: "Nothing is what it seems to be, everything is to be interpreted, everything is supposed to possess some supplementary meaning. The ground of the established, familiar signification opens up; we find ourselves in a realm of total ambiguity, but this very lack propels us to produce ever new 'hidden meanings': it is a driving force of endless compulsion. The oscillation between lack and surplus meaning constitutes the proper dimension of subjectivity."

13. Bessel A. van der Kolk and Onno van der Hart, "The Intrusive Past: The Flexibility of Memory and the Engraving of Trauma," in *Trauma: Explorations in Memory,* ed. Cathy Caruth (Baltimore: Johns Hopkins University Press, 1995), pp. 158–82 (at 176).

14. Hans-Georg Gadamer, *Truth and Method,* 2nd ed., trans. Joel Weinsheimer and Donald Marshall (New York: Continuum, 1994), p. 295.

15. See Christopher Grose, *Milton and the Sense of Tradition* (New Haven: Yale University Press, 1988).

16. Gadamer, *Truth and Method*, p. 277.

17. Deborah Kuller Shuger, *The Renaissance Bible: Scholarship, Sacrifice, and Subjectivity* (Berkeley: University of California Press, 1994), p. 9.

18. T. S. Eliot, "Tradition and the Individual Talent," *Selected Essays* (New York: Harcourt Brace Jovanovich, 1950), p. 4.

19. Augustine, *On Christian Doctrine*, trans. D. W. Robertson Jr. (Indianapolis: Bobbs-Merrill, 1958), Books 1 and 2, lays out the theory of signification against which I define Milton, although, as I show in Chapter Two, Milton retained key hermeneutic strategies that derive from Augustine's exegetical practices.

20. In this assertion, I believe I am in agreement with Victoria Silver, *Imperfect Sense: The Predicament of Milton's Irony* (Princeton: Princeton University Press, 2001). Silver allies Milton with an alternative tradition of "formative dissenters" in that Milton "requires an effort to grasp the position and motive behind a species of expression which invites, even insists, upon the acknowledgment of its eccentricity, indecorum, and sheer difficulty" (p. 193). If Milton's representational technique is, as Silver argues, an "antipathetic medium of transfigured understanding," then it is clear that his "virtuosic use of convention . . . tends rather to efface what he actually does with it" (pp. 192–94). Silver analogizes a dazzling array of Reformation theologians and antifoundationalist philosophers to show "the speaker's recounting—that is, the operation of grace upon his speech—as somehow elucidating but not remedying his situation" (p. 196). This Silver sees as a way to address indirectly questions of God's justice or injustice. Less probably, Silver pictures Milton "having his speaker impersonate himself" by revising his own writings, thus distancing the speaker's presumption from himself (p. 195). While I concur with the description of "a methodically intransparent expression" in Milton's major writings, I find that I differ with Silver's interpretation of Milton's inheritance from Reformation theology (p. 285).

21. Richard Rorty, *Philosophy and the Mirror of Nature* (Princeton: Princeton University Press, 1979), pp. 5–6, 357–65.

22. Gerald L. Bruns, *Hermeneutics Ancient and Modern* (New Haven: Yale University Press, 1992), p. 9.

23. This concern with the boundaries of periods, in theory much maligned in literary and cultural studies, has remained a recalcitrant feature of the field, both in the syllabus and the historical narratives of surveys. Periodization is less the problem here than the sense of historical rupture deemed intrinsic to modernity, which calls into question both the principle of selection in a critical study such as this one and its relevance. For a useful précis of the New Historicist attitude toward historiography, principles of selection, and

exemplarity in evidence and argumentation, see Catherine Gallagher and Stephen Greenblatt, *Practicing New Historicism* (Chicago: University of Chicago Press, 2000), pp. 1–74.

24. Stephen Toulmin, *Cosmopolis: The Hidden Agenda of Modernity* (1990; Chicago: University of Chicago Press, 1992).

25. Quentin Skinner, *Reason and Rhetoric in the Philosophy of Hobbes* (Cambridge: Cambridge University Press, 1996). On the relationship between logic and rhetoric in *Leviathan,* see Robert E. Stillman, "Hobbes's *Leviathan:* Monsters, Metaphors, and Magic," *ELH* 62 (1995): 791–819.

26. For an explanation of this distinction, see Lisa Jardine, "Humanist Logic," in *The Cambridge History of Renaissance Philosophy,* ed. Charles B. Schmitt and Quentin Skinner (Cambridge: Cambridge University Press, 1988), pp. 173–98. For a long view of the debate between rhetoric and philosophy, see Brian Vickers, *In Defence of Rhetoric* (Oxford: Clarendon Press, 1988), pp. 148–213.

27. Donald L. Clark, *John Milton at St. Paul's School* (New York: Columbia University Press, 1948).

28. Milton's quotation from Dante is especially inspired, and the fuller context is revealing. Charles Martel explains his natural political philosophy to the pilgrim: "And if the world there below would give heed to the foundation which Nature lays, and followed it, it would have its people good. But you wrest to religion one born to gird on the sword, and you make a king of one that is fit for sermons; so that your right track is off the road." *The Divine Comedy,* trans. Charles S. Singleton, 6 vols. (Princeton: Princeton University Press, 1975), 5:93 with commentary further located at 6:152–60.

29. Aristotle, *Nichomachean Ethics,* 1180b, trans. and ed. Roger Crisp (Cambridge: Cambridge University Press, 2000), p. 202.

30. Erasmus, *De pueris statim ac liberaliter instituendis;* Richard Sherry, trans., *A Treatise of Schemes and Tropes* (1550), in *English Humanism: Wyatt to Cowley,* ed. Joanna Martindale (London: Croom Helm, 1985), p. 54. The text goes on to ask: "What is a greater inconvenience than beasts, that be without reason, to know and remember their duty to their young, man, which is divided from brute beasts by prerogative of reason, not to know what he oweth to nature, what to virtue and what to God?" (p. 57). For Milton, the theological distinction becomes less meaningful, which renders the harshness of the natural metaphors of acculturation correspondingly less abrasive.

31. Sir Thomas Elyot, *The Boke Named the Gouernour* (1531), ed. Henry Herbert Stephen Croft, 2 vols. (London: Kegan Paul, 1883), 1:38. Compare Castiglione, *The Book of the Courtier,* trans. Sir Thomas Hoby, ed. Virginia Cox (London: Everyman, 1994), p. 71: "maisters shoulde consider the nature of their scolers, and taking it for their guide, direct and prompt them in the way that their witt and natural inclination moveth them unto."

32. Roger Ascham, *The Schoolmaster (1570)*, ed. Lawrence V. Ryan (Charlottesville: University Press of Virginia), p. 35.

33. On the politics of the English humanists, see Fritz Caspari, *Humanism and the Social Order in Tudor England* (Chicago: University of Chicago Press, 1954). For a critique of the nationalism of Milton's project, see Gauri Viswanathan, "Milton and Education," in *Milton and the Imperial Vision*, ed. Balachandra Rajan and Elizabeth Sauer (Pittsburgh: Duquesne University Press, 1999), pp. 273–93.

34. Stephen Jay Gould, "Father Athanasius on the Isthmus of a Middle State: Understanding Kircher's Paleontology," in *Athanasius Kircher: The Last Man Who Knew Everything*, ed. Paula Findlin (New York: Routledge, 2004), pp. 207–37, suggested to me the nature of the problem with approaching Milton from the perspective of the historian of education. The histories of education, like those of paleontology critiqued by Gould, tend to minimize if not devalue altogether the contribution to intellectual history by a figure like Milton because of their implicitly evolutionary view of progress. This view, in turn, leads to a reductive streamlining of the thought of such a figure, which dwindles to a systematic paradigm for which the thinker becomes representative. In the case of Milton, the coexistence of several competing philosophies of education often proves to be incompatible with his biography or with an anachronistic and limiting idea of his religious views. For an insightful refutation of the standard line on "puritans," which shows the multifarious ways that Protestants could ask questions that might seem preempted by their faith, see John Morgan, *Godly Learning: Puritan Attitudes toward Reason, Learning, and Education, 1560–1640* (Cambridge: Cambridge University Press, 1986).

35. For more information on their project, see *Samuel Hartlib and Universal Reformation*, ed. Mark Greengrass, Michael Leslie, and Timothy Raylor (Cambridge: Cambridge University Press, 1994).

36. For the debate on the Comenian reformers, see Foster Watson, *The English Grammar Schools to 1660* (Cambridge: Cambridge University Press, 1908). Watson's views are ably critiqued by Ernest Sirluck in his introduction in YP 2:185ff. A serviceable, if brief, comparison between Milton and earlier educational theorists—which is finally more balanced than the judgment Sirluck offers—can be found in O. M. Ainsworth, *Milton on Education* (New Haven: Yale University Press, 1928), pp. 1–47. Ainsworth details Milton's connections to the mainstream of traditional humanist thought in his introduction and then gives copious selections from Milton's writings to illustrate the effect of the theory more broadly on his thought.

37. See Timothy Raylor, "New Light on Milton and Hartlib," *Milton Quarterly* 27 (1993): 19–31.

38. For the Comenian perspective, see chapter 25 of *The Great Didactic*, pp. 231–48.

39. Francis Bacon, *The Advancement of Learning* (1605), in *The Oxford Authors: Francis Bacon,* ed. Brian Vickers (Oxford: Oxford University Press, 1996), p. 123.

40. Bacon, *Advancement,* p. 125.

41. Bacon, *Advancement,* p. 146.

42. Bacon, *Advancement,* p. 124; on the principle of segregation, see p. 168: "But it must be remembered . . . that in probation of the dignity of knowledge or learning I did in the beginning separate divine testimony from human." It is perhaps worth comparing, in this context, the reservations expressed in Howard Schultz, *Milton and Forbidden Knowledge* (New York: MLA, 1955).

43. See Vickers, ed., *The Oxford Authors: Francis Bacon,* pp. 584–85, 608–9. These analyses were prepared by W. A. Wright for his edition of *The Advancement of Learning,* 2nd ed. (Oxford: Clarendon Press, 1873).

44. William G. Riggs, "Poetry and Method in Milton's *Of Education,*" *Studies in Philology* 89 (1992): 445–69, shows how the transcendental force of poetry dislodges and contradicts the apparently systematic method of education in the tract.

45. Bacon, *Advancement,* p. 173.

46. B. Rajan, "'Simple, Sensuous and Passionate,'" *Review of English Studies* 21 (1945): 289–301, rightly stresses the superiority of poetry over rhetoric in Milton's educational scheme, in which preference of course Milton differs from thinkers such as Bacon and Cicero, with whom he agreed in many other respects. For more on Milton and Bacon, see Sirluck's introduction to YP 2: 204–5, 215.

47. Bacon, *Advancement,* p. 165.

48. Emmanuel Levinas, "Peace and Proximity," *Basic Philosophical Writings,* ed. Adriaan T. Peperzak, Simon Critchley, and Robert Bernasconi (Bloomington: Indiana University Press, 1996), p. 169.

49. Martin Dzelzainis, "Milton's Classical Republicanism," in *Milton and Republicanism,* ed. David Armitage, Armand Himy, and Quentin Skinner (Cambridge: Cambridge University Press, 1995), p. 11.

50. See *The Tenure of Kings and Magistrates,* YP 3:199ff.

51. Louis Althusser, "Ideology and Ideological State Apparatuses (Notes toward an Investigation)," *Lenin and Philosophy,* trans. Ben Brewster (New York: Monthly Review Press, 1971), pp. 127–86, attacks modern schools as instruments of specifically capitalist ideology. His emphasis upon education as one of the primary sites in which the subject is interpellated or "hailed" by the state is structurally useful for a discussion of Milton's overt ideological definition of education, even if the specific contextual application of Althusser's structure is irrelevant.

52. Quentin Skinner, *Liberty before Liberalism* (Cambridge: Cambridge University Press, 1998), p. 19.

53. John Rawls, *Justice as Fairness: A Restatement,* ed. Erin Kelly (Cambridge, Mass.: Harvard University Press, 2001), pp. 56–57.

54. Fish, *Surprised by Sin: The Reader in "Paradise Lost,"* 2nd ed. (Cambridge, Mass.: Harvard University Press, 1997), p. 341.

55. See Mary Ann Radzinowicz, "The Politics of *Paradise Lost,*" in *Politics of Discourse: The Literature and History of Seventeenth-Century England,* ed. Kevin Sharpe and Steven N. Zwicker (Berkeley: University of California Press, 1987), reprinted in *John Milton,* ed. Annabel Patterson (London: Longman, 1992), pp. 120–41, quotations at pp. 122–23, 140n8. For a complementary view of Milton's humanism, see also Joan S. Bennett, *Reviving Liberty: Radical Christian Humanism in Milton's Great Poems* (Cambridge, Mass.: Harvard University Press, 1989), pp. 1–32.

56. Barbara K. Lewalski, *The Life of John Milton* (Oxford: Blackwell, 2000), p. 460.

57. Fish, *Surprised by Sin,* p. 1 (emphasis added).

58. For a judicious and thoroughgoing critique of the assumptions that govern the reader response model, with a detailed history of literary-critical paradigms in their reliance upon or resistance to intentionality, see David Scott Kastan, *Shakespeare After Theory* (New York and London: Routledge, 1999), pp. 23–70.

59. Fish, *Surprised by Sin,* pp. 130, 4, 9, 44, 70 and ix–lxix. The model of catechism brings to mind what may remain Fish's most convincing and useful book, *The Living Temple: George Herbert and Catechizing* (Berkeley: University of California Press, 1978), in which the model of determinism in theology seems possibly more apt. Michael Allen, "Divine Instruction: *Of Education* and the Pedagogy of Raphael, Michael, and the Father," *Milton Quarterly* 26 (1992): 113–21, perpetuates the opinion that Milton's educational model is "catechetical" (120n1). But compare the learned and devastating critique launched in A. D. Nuttall, "Everything is over before it begins," Review of *How Milton Works,* by Stanley Fish, *London Review of Books,* 21 June 2001, 19–21.

60. For an excellent summary of the problems associated with reader response theory, see the trenchant criticism by Thomas N. Corns in his review of Sharon Achinstein, *Milton and the Revolutionary Reader, Modern Philology* 94 (1997): 530: "While Achinstein historicizes the reader as a developing and shaping presence, she neither adduces evidence for the distribution or reception of specific texts nor identifies who read them and why. Of course such an investigation would be difficult and calls for skills rather different from those of a literary critic, but until it is done, 'the reader,' revolutionary or otherwise, is an ahistorical abstraction." For an example of just this kind of historical work, see the learned journal articles Nicholas von Maltzahn has published in recent years: "Laureate, Republican, Calvinist: an Early Response to *Paradise Lost,*" *Milton Studies* 29 (1992): 181–98; "Wood,

Allam, and the Oxford Milton," *Milton Studies* 31 (1994): 155–77; and "The First Reception of *Paradise Lost* (1667)," *Review of English Studies,* new series, Vol. 47, No. 188 (1996): 479–99.

61. John P. Rumrich, *Milton Unbound: Controversy and Reinterpretation* (Cambridge: Cambridge University Press, 1996), pp. 28, 149, 37. See further p. 45.

62. Theodor Adorno, *Minima Moralia,* trans. E. F. N. Jephcott (London: Verso, 1974), p. 74.

63. Ludwig Wittgenstein, *The Blue and Brown Books,* 2nd ed. (New York: Harper and Row, 1960), p. 27.

NOTES TO CHAPTER ONE

1. Ben Jonson, *Timber: or, Discoveries,* under the topic *Autodidaktos,* in [*Works*], ed. C. H. Herford and Percy and Evelyn Simpson, 11 vols. (Oxford: Clarendon Press, 1925–52), 8:563.

2. Stanley Fish, *Is There a Text in This Class? The Authority of Interpretive Communities* (Cambridge, Mass.: Harvard University Press, 1980). Roger Chartier, *The Order of Books,* trans. Lydia G. Cochrane (Stanford: Stanford University Press, 1994), chap. 1.

3. Plato, *Symposium,* 177a, trans. R. E. Allen (New Haven: Yale University Press, 1991), p. 116. The irony is even further complicated by the narrative situation: Plato is telling us that Apollodorus reports Aristodamus recalling Eryximachus citing Euripides. Moreover, the remainder of the line, not quoted by Eryximachus, looks forward to Diotima's configuration (208e-209b) of education as reproduction: "Mine is not the tale; my mother taught me" (quoted in Allen's note on 177a). On the relations between education, the transmission of knowledge, and the problematic of textual tradition as intellectual property as seen by Renaissance readers of the *Symposium,* see Kathy Eden, "Friends and Lovers in the *Symposium:* Plato on Tradition," *Friends Hold All Things in Common: Tradition, Intellectual Property, and the Adages of Erasmus* (New Haven: Yale University Press, 2001), chap. 2. Since Milton made several specific references to the *Symposium* throughout the divorce controversy, we may be sure he had the text in mind in the period under discussion in this chapter. See, for example, YP 2:252, 522, 589.

4. My thinking about this crucial distinction in Milton's thought has profited most immediately from related remarks made by William Kerrigan concerning the place of "argument" and "proposition" in Milton's works, particularly the general assessments of "Milton's Place in Intellectual History," in *The Cambridge Companion to Milton,* 2nd ed., ed. Dennis Danielson (Cambridge: Cambridge University Press, 1999), pp. 253–66 and *The Prophetic Milton* (Charlottesville: University of Virginia Press, 1974), pp. 6–7, as well

as the more specific treatments of the philosophical use of contradiction in *The Sacred Complex: On the Psychogenesis of "Paradise Lost"* (Cambridge, Mass.: Harvard University Press, 1983), *passim*. Dayton Haskin, *Milton's Burden of Interpretation* (Philadelphia: University of Pennsylvania Press, 1994), has had a formative influence on my understanding of the shift in Milton's conception of biblical hermeneutics in the 1640s.

5. Milton's copy of *Euripidis Tragoediae*, ed. Paulus Stephanus, 2 vols. (Geneva, 1602) is now housed in the Bodleian Library, shelfmark don. d. 27, 28. When citing the marginalia, I have provided where possible the translations found in the Columbia Milton (CM), though for the sake of future researchers I provide citations to the volume and page number of *ET* in the text, for reasons that should become clear.

6. The Columbia Milton does not differentiate between the states of Milton's hand and offers only a select transcription of the marginalia. First-hand paleographic analysis makes the distinction between the two states of Milton's handwriting more evident than mere verbal description can. Nevertheless, the most apparent distinguishing features that differentiate earlier from later markings are as follows: the size of the inscription (the later writing being almost invariably larger); the quality of the ink employed and how it has faded over time (the later tends to be lighter in color, more sepia tone showing); the particular features of the lettering, in particular the lower case letter "e" (Milton prefers the Greek epsilon "ε" in the earlier, an Italian "e" in the later) and of the non-verbal supralinear and marginal markings "*" (earlier) "x" (later). The argument from paleographic evidence for dating the two states of Milton's handwriting, based on comparison between Milton's hand in the Trinity Manuscript and the Commonplace Book, was made by Helen Darbishire, "The Chronology of Milton's Handwriting," *The Library*, 4th ser., Vol. 14 (1933): 229–35, a refinement and corroboration of the suggestions made earlier by James Holly Hanford, "The Chronology of Milton's Private Studies," *PMLA* 36 (1921), reprinted in *John Milton, Poet and Humanist* (Cleveland: Western Reserve University Press, 1966), pp. 75–125. It is, however, important to keep the limited quantity of evidence in perspective. Peter Beal, *Index of English Literary Manuscripts, Volume II: 1635–1700, Part 2: Lee-Wycherly* (London: Mansel, 1993), pp. 78–81, argues that the provenance of only seven annotated books from Milton's library can be proven genuine "by virtue of the presence of his authentic signature, inscription or annotations" (79). See also John T. Shawcross, *John Milton: The Self and the World* (Lexington: University of Kentucky Press, 1993), pp. 282–84, for further useful information on Milton's handwriting as an aid to dating his reading.

7. Samuel Johnson, *Lives of the English Poets*, ed. G. B. Hill, 3 vols. (Oxford: Clarendon Press Press, 1905), 1:154.

8. *Euripidis Quae Extant Omnia: Tragoediae nempe XX . . .* , ed. Joshua Barnes (Cambridge, 1694). According to the index, Milton is only credited with

one emendation, an omission to improve the meter at *Phoenissae* 962 (sig. V2ʳ). Two modern accounts of Milton's Euripides marginalia provide critical points of departure for any examination of the books, Maurice Kelley and Samuel D. Atkins, "Milton's Annotations of Euripides," *JEGP* 60 (1961): 680–87; and John K. Hale, "Milton's Euripides Marginalia: Their Significance for Milton Studies," *Milton Studies* 27 (1991): 23–35. Kelley and Atkins helpfully compare Milton's "some 560 annotations" with Bentley's emendations to Horace, remarking that although Bentley "offered over 700 conjectures to the text . . . only one or two have found general acceptance" (p. 686n27, p. 687). For an evaluation of Barnes's use of Milton's marginalia, see Hale, "Milton's Euripides Marginalia," p. 25.

9. William H. Sherman, *John Dee: The Politics of Reading and Writing in the English Renaissance* (Amherst: University of Massachusetts Press, 1995), p. 89.

10. Anthony Grafton, *Commerce with the Classics: Ancient Books and Renaissance Readers* (Ann Arbor: University of Michigan Press, 1997), p. 153.

11. Stephen Orgel, "Margins of Truth," in *The Renaissance Text: Theory, Editing, Textuality,* ed. Andrew Murphy (Manchester: Manchester University Press, 2000), p. 107.

12. William Riley Parker, *Milton: A Biography,* 2ⁿᵈ ed., ed. Gordon Campbell, 2 vols. (Oxford: Clarendon Press Press, 1996), 1:186; cf. 2:836.

13. Parker, *Milton,* 1:248.

14. Parker, *Milton,* 1:286, 299; J. Milton French, ed., *The Life Records of John Milton,* 5 vols. (New Brunswick: Rutgers University Press, 1949–58), 2:128. Edward Phillips, "The Life of Mr. John Milton" (1694), in *The Early Lives of Milton,* ed. Helen Darbishire (London: Constable, 1932), p. 68.

15. Parker, 2:882, 837, 922–25.

16. Phillips, "Life," pp. 67, 66.

17. Quoted in Parker, *Milton,* 1:312. For persuasive evidence of a more complex and longstanding relationship between Milton and Hartlib than biographers have often supposed, see Timothy Raylor, "New Light on Milton and Hartlib," *Milton Quarterly* 27 (1993): 19–31. For more general appraisals of the impact of their intellectual relations see Barbara K. Lewalski, "Milton and the Hartlib Circle: Educational Projects and Epic *Paideia,*" in *Literary Milton: Text, Pretext, Context,* ed. Diana Treviño Benet and Michael Lieb (Pittsburgh: Duquesne University Press, 1994), pp. 202–19; and Nigel Smith, "*Areopagitica:* Voicing Contexts, 1643–5" in *Politics, Poetics, and Hermeneutics in Milton's Prose,* ed. David Loewenstein and James Grantham Turner (Cambridge: Cambridge University Press, 1990), pp. 105–7ff.

18. Phillips, "Life," p. 60. For a discussion of Milton's Latin curriculum in the context of his teaching environment, see Richard J. DuRocher, *Milton Among the Romans: The Pedagogy and Influence of Milton's Latin Curriculum* (Pittsburgh: Duquesne University Press, 2001), esp. pp. 1–18, 171–75.

19. Milton's philological achievement has been the subject of an astute study by John K. Hale, *Milton's Languages* (Cambridge: Cambridge University Press, 1997), esp. pp. 74–80.

20. See Steven Zwicker, "Reading the Margins: Politics and the Habits of Appropriation," in *Refiguring Revolutions: Aesthetics and Politics from the English Revolution to the Romantic Revolution,* ed. Kevin Sharpe and Steven N. Zwicker (Berkeley: University of California Press, 1998), pp. 101–15.

21. See for example *Euripides: Hippolytos,* ed. W. S. Barrett (Oxford: Clarendon Press, 1964), pp. 134, 349; *Euripidis fabulae,* ed. James Diggle, 2 vols. (Oxford: Clarendon Press, 1981–84), 1:251; and Euripides, [*Works*], ed. and trans. David Kovacs, LCL, 5 vols. (Cambridge, Mass.: Harvard University Press, 1994–2002), 2:220–221.

22. On the hermeneutic tradition of accommodation and its origins in ancient rhetorical practice, see Kathy Eden, *Hermeneutics and the Rhetorical Tradition: Chapters in the Ancient Legacy and its Humanist Reception* (New Haven: Yale University Press, 1997), pp. 1–19.

23. *Hippolytus,* trans. David Grene, in *The Complete Greek Tragedies,* ed. David Grene and Richmond Lattimore, 4 vols. (Chicago: University of Chicago Press, 1959), vol. 3.

24. Hence we may observe the continuity between Hippolytus and Pentheus, the self-destructive moralizer of Euripides' later masterpiece, *The Bacchae.* Milton's emendation may have come to mind because of the prominence accorded to *epaggellein* and its cognates in later Greek, especially the New Testament, where *epaggelia* and *epaggellomai* are used to signify announcement or promise. See *A Greek-English Lexicon of the New Testament and Other Early Christian Literature,* ed. Walter Bauer (5th ed., 1958), trans. W.F. Arndt et al., 2nd ed. (Chicago: University of Chicago Press, 1979), svv.

25. Milton also cites books referred to in the printed commentaries accompanying his text (cf. Kelley and Atkins, 684). Although (post-1638) Milton refers to Scaliger's Manilius for the work's authority on a particular question of astronomy, the reference nonetheless shows that he had read and considered one of the editions (1579, 1600, and, posthumously, 1655). Scaliger's Manilius would have provided Milton with an exemplary model of textual criticism, since "Scaliger began by trying to correct the text" and ended up devising an "exegetical method" that "turned out to be one of his most original creations." See Anthony Grafton, *Joseph Scaliger: A Study in the History of Classical Scholarship,* 2 vols. (Oxford: Clarendon Press, 1983–93), 1:180–226, esp. 186, 192 (quoted above), 207–8 (on Euripides). For an estimation of the importance of the *Astronomica* to Milton's tutorial and writing, see DuRocher, *Milton Among the Romans,* pp. 98–129.

26. Milton's copy of Aratus, *Phainomena kai diosaemia,* ed. Guillaume Morel (Paris, 1559) is held in the British Library Department of Printed Books, shelfmark C.60.L.7 (at p. 1).

27. Maurice Kelley and Samuel D. Atkins, "Milton's Annotations of Aratus," *PMLA* 70 (1955): 1098–99, 1102.
28. Phillips, "Life," p. 60.
29. The relative scarcity of copies makes this almost certain. Aratus was not published in England until the Oxford edition of 1672. Consultation of union catalogues has turned up twelve continental editions in Greek, other than that read by Milton, available prior to the Oxford edition.
30. Along with other quotations Paul made before the Areopagus (Acts 17), this verse became one of the most eagerly proffered means of articulating Christianity's relation to pagan classics. See, for example, St. Augustine, *City of God*, 8.10, trans. Henry Bettenson (Harmondsworth: Penguin, 1972), p. 312. In the English Renaissance, apologists for poetry such as Thomas Lodge alluded to the passage to counter "that shamelesse GOSSON": "let the Apostle preach at Athens, he disdaineth not of Aratus authoritie" (*Elizabethan Critical Essays*, ed. G. G. Smith, 2 vols. [Oxford: Oxford University Press, 1904], 1:71; cf. Sidney, *Apology*, 1:191).
31. The sources for this story are admittedly sketchy. As Dr. Johnson tells it, "The books in which his daughter, who used to read to him, represented him as most delighting, after Homer, which he could almost repeat, were Ovid's *Metamorphoses* and Euripides" (*Lives*, 1:154). A composite of earlier biographies, the story draws upon John Toland, "The Life of John Milton" (1698), in *Early Lives*, p. 179, for the bit about Homer, though Johnson may have come across relevant details in one of Newton's editions. In addition to recycling the remark about Milton's knowledge of Homer from Toland, Newton says of Deborah Milton, "As she had been often called upon to read Homer and Ovid's Metamorphosis to her father, she could have repeated a considerable number of verses from the beginning of both of these poets, as Mr. Ward, Professor of Rhetoric in Gresham College, relates upon his own knowledge: and another Gentleman has informed me, that he has heard her repeat several verses likewise out of Euripides." See *The Poetical Works of John Milton*, ed. Thomas Newton, 5th ed., 3 vols (London, 1761), 1:lxix, lxxvi.
32. See Stephen B. Dobranski, *Milton, Authorship, and the Book Trade* (Cambridge: Cambridge University Press, 1999), pp. 106–8. The most immediate context for Milton's tract was the response by Presbyterians to the first edition of *The Doctrine and Discipline of Divorce* (1643), which appeared exactly one month after the Westminster Assembly had begun to meet. Milton was condemned by orthodox critics such as Herbert Palmer, William Prynne, and Ephraim Pagitt, among others, including the anonymous author of *An Answer to a Book, Intituled, The Doctrine and Discipline of Divorce*. See Arthur E. Barker, *Milton and the Puritan Dilemma, 1641–1660* (Toronto: University of Toronto Press, 1942), pp. 63–97; and William Riley Parker, *Milton's Contemporary Reputation* (Columbus: Ohio State University

Press, 1940), pp. 73–75ff. For an account of the way the tract appropriates the discourses in play in its context as a central technique of its effort to persuade the Erastians in Parliament not to support the Order, see Smith, "*Areopagitica:* Voicing Contexts, 1643–5," pp. 103–22.

33. *Poems,* p. 355. Carey notes that, although the maxim is actually from Menander's *Thaïs,* not Euripides, "the fragment in which it survives is found in editions of both Euripides and Menander."

34. The scriptural passage in question is Ecclesiastes 12:7 by way of Job 34:14–15 (KJV). The interpretive strategy I attribute here to Milton may be, it is true, a subtle variation on the instruction *spoliabitis Aegyptum.* The Church Fathers referred to God's command that the Israelites plunder the Egyptians (Exodus 3:22, 11:2, 12:35) as a way of justifying the incorporation of the pagan liberal arts into Christian teaching. Pagan "precepts concerning morals" and "even some truths concerning the worship of one God" were, according to Augustine, "their gold and silver, which they did not institute themselves but dug up from certain mines of divine Providence." (*On Christian Doctrine,* trans. D. W. Robertson, Jr., Library of Liberal Arts 80 [Indianapolis: Bobbs-Merrill, 1958], 2.40). By the first half of the twelfth century—according to E. R. Curtius, *European Literature and the Latin Middle Ages,* trans. Willard R. Trask (Princeton: Princeton University Press, 1953), pp. 466–67—Conrad of Hirsau had broadened interpretation of the passage so that "by the gold and silver of Egypt is meant *litteratura saecularis.*" For a history of the *spoliatio Aegyptiorum* from Patristic origins to the Renaissance, see Eden, *Friends Hold All Things in Common,* pp. 8–32.

35. Quoted and reproduced in photographic facsimile in David Norbrook, *Writing the English Republic: Poetry, Rhetoric and Politcs, 1627–1660* (Cambridge: Cambridge University Press, 1999), p. 128.

36. See John K. Hale, "*Areopagitica's* Euripidean Motto," *Milton Quarterly* 25 (1991): 25–27, responding to David Davies and Paul Dowling, "'Shrewd books, with dangerous Frontispieces': *Areopagitica's* Motto," *Milton Quarterly* 20 (1986): 33–37. It is a telling irony that modern critics, fixated on the question of Milton's fidelity to the Greek original, have often missed the tract's other "vigorously productive" appropriations. On Milton's purposeful modifications of source material, see Christopher Grose, "Trying all Things in the *Areopagitica,*" *Milton and the Sense of Tradition* (New Haven: Yale University Press, 1988), pp. 85–103.

37. Milton's exordium, like the rest of the speech, employs the conventions of classical oratory, particularly in its emphasis on the ethos of speaker and audience. The conventional *captatio benevolentiae* is described, among other places, in the *Rhetorica ad Herennium,* 1.4.7–1.5.8, trans. H. Caplan, LCL (Cambridge, Mass.: Harvard University Press, 1954), pp. 12–17. Cf. Brian Vickers, *In Defence of Rhetoric* (Oxford: Clarendon Press, 1988), p. 69.

38. Philip Melanchthon, "Oration On Occasion of the Funeral of Doctor Martin Luther," *Orations on Philosophy and Education,* trans. Christine F. Salazar, ed. Sachiko Kusakawa (Cambridge: Cambridge University Press, 1999), p. 257.

39. Erasmus, *De Libero Arbitrio,* in *Luther and Erasmus: Free Will and Salvation,* trans. and ed. E. Gordon Rupp and Philip S. Watson, Library of Christian Classics (Philadelphia: Westminster Press, 1969), p. 49.

40. Stanley Fish, "Driving from the Letter: Truth and Indeterminacy in Milton's *Areopagitica,*" in *Re-membering Milton,* ed. Mary Nyquist and Margaret W. Ferguson (New York: Methuen, 1987), pp. 234–54, esp. 236 = *How Milton Works* (Cambridge, Mass.: Harvard University Press, 2001), pp. 187–214, esp. 190–91.

41. See Donne, *Devotions upon Emergent Occasions,* 9th Expostulation, ed. Anthony Raspa (Montreal: Queen's-McGill University Press, 1975), p. 49; and Browne, *Religio Medici,* 1.16, *The Major Works,* ed. C. A. Patrides (Harmondsworth: Penguin, 1977), pp. 78–81. Both Donne and Browne remark upon the expression of the divine image in the Book of Nature as well as the Book of God, which would by Fish's standard equate their thought, too, with idolatry. Logically, any creation within Nature—anything created as a secondary function of God's creation—may bear the image of an order that is beyond human conception, even when it derives most immediately from a human mind. This is the point of Vaughan's modification of the commonplace in "The Book," where God's "knowing, glorious spirit" is invoked in the final stanza: "Give him amongst thy works a place, / Who in them loved and sought thy face" (*The Complete Poems,* ed. Alan Rudrum [Harmondsworth: Penguin, 1976], p. 310).

42. See Haskin, *Milton's Burden of Interpretation,* chap. 3.

43. Maimonides, *The Guide of the Perplexed,* trans. Shlomo Pines, 2 vols. (Chicago: University of Chicago Press, 1963), 1:23; cf. 2:235 (premises 1–3). See also Milton's refutation by superior knowledge of the context from which Salmasius quotes Maimonides, *First Defense* (YP 4.1:354; CM 7:102). Leo Strauss, *Persecution and the Art of Writing* (Glencoe, Ill.: Free Press, 1952), pp. 23, 192n, offers a valuable context for juxtaposing the two.

44. John Pearson, *An exposition of the Creed* (1659), 3rd ed. (London, 1669), pp. 115–17, interprets Genesis 1:26 in relation to John 1:1–3, bringing Paul's epistles (esp. Col. 3:10 and Eph. 4:23) to bear: "The apostle chargeth us to be *renewed in the spirit of our mind, and to put on the new man, which after God is created in righteousness and true holiness; and which is renewed in knowledge, after the image of him that created him.*" This "renovation," which as Pearson notes "is called by Paul a 'metamorphosis'" (Rom. 12:2), consists in "a translation from a worse unto a better condition by way of reformation; by which those which have lost the image of God, in which the first

man was created, are restored to the image of the same God again, by a real change, though not substantial, wrought within them." In this, Pearson like Milton differs from Calvin, *Institutes of the Christian Religion*, 1.15, trans. Henry Beveridge (1845; reprint. Grand Rapids: Eerdman's, 1995), p. 165: "as the image of God constitutes the entire excellence of human nature, as it shone in Adam before his fall, but was afterward vitiated and almost destroyed, nothing remaining but a ruin, confused, mutilated, and tainted with impurity, so it is now partly seen in the elect, in so far as they are regenerated by the Spirit." Calvin seeks to debunk Augustine, *City of God*, 11.26, in particular to eradicate the Trinitarian emphasis on the faculties of the intellect.

45. Cf. Aristotle, *Prior Analytics*, 68b; *Posterior Analytics*, 71a-72b, 99b-100b; *Nicomachean Ethics*, 1139b.

46. Thomas Aquinas, *Summa contra Gentiles*, 3.25, *Selected Writings*, trans. Ralph McInerny (Harmondsworth: Penguin, 1998), p. 264.

47. For the most notable example, see the magisterial study by Brian Stock, *Augustine the Reader: Meditation, Self-Knowledge, and the Ethics of Interpretation* (Cambridge, Mass.: Harvard University Press, 1996).

48. *Pseudodoxia Epidemica*, 1.5, *The Major Works*, ed. Patrides, p.185.

49. Robert Greville, Lord Brooke, *A Discourse opening the Nature of that Episcopacy which is Exercised in England* (1641), 2nd ed. (London, 1642), p. 13. For Greville's debt to the Smectymnuans, see Barker, *Milton and the Puritan Dilemma*, pp. 54, 56.

50. Greville, *Discourse*, pp. 26, 25, 31.

51. Greville, *Discourse*, p. 13. And see Robert Greville, *The Nature of Truth, its Union and Unity with the Soule, which is one in its essence, faculties, acts; one with truth* (London, 1640).

52. Plato, *Republic*, 505d; *Gorgias*, 467a ff., 499e, *Protagoras*, 358b-d. Compare Marcus Aurelius, *Meditations*, 4.3. For an incisive critique of the commonplace expression of the Socratic paradox, see the commentary in *Ion, Hippias Minor, Laches, Protagoras*, trans. R. E. Allen (New Haven: Yale University Press, 1996), pp. 159–61.

53. On the interrelation between knowledge and virtue, see Plato, *Meno*, 87c-89a; *Phaedo*, 69a-c; *Protagoras*, 351b-360e. My discussion of Milton's epistemology is greatly indebted to Edward W. Tayler, *Milton's Poetry: Its Development in Time* (Pittsburgh: Duquesne University Press, 1979), esp. pp. 185–213, 261n15, 262n26; and "Milton's Grim Laughter and Second Choices," in *Poetry and Epistemology: Turning Points in the History of Poetic Knowledge: Papers from the International Poetry Symposium, Eichstätt, 1983*, ed. Roland Hagenbüchle and Laura Skandera (Regensburg: Verlag Friedrich Pustet, 1986), pp. 72–93.

54. The concept of substance disclosed in this passage maintains its central structural importance in Milton's thought throughout his writings, at least

through the completion of the epic. See John Peter Rumrich, "Milton's Concept of Substance," *ELN* 19 (1982): 218–33.

55. Browne, *Christian Morals,* 3.15, *The Major Works,* ed. Patrides, p. 461.

56. *Luther and Erasmus: Free Will and Salvation,* ed. and trans. Rupp and Watson, pp. 73, 48, 50. In *Areopagitica*'s insistence that choice present a moral dilemma to the reasonable will of a human being, Milton approaches Kant's proposition that "all theodicy should truly be an *interpretation* of nature insofar as God announces his will through it" ("On the Miscarriage of All Philosophical Trials in Theodicy," *Religion within the Boundaries of Mere Reason and Other Writings,* ed. and trans. Allen Wood and George di Giovanni [Cambridge: Cambridge University Press, 1998], pp. 17–30, at 24). Although we cannot sincerely claim to comprehend God's will, we must nevertheless be able to aspire to what Kant considers a Jobean "negative wisdom," knowing to know no more (p. 23). This is especially true "if this dismissal . . . is a pronouncement of the same reason through which we form our concept of God—necessarily and prior to all experience—as a moral and wise being. For through our reason God then becomes himself the interpreter of his will as announced through his creation" (p. 24). When, as Abdiel says, "God and Nature bid the same," both freedom and omniscience prevail (*PL* 6.176).

57. Irenaeus, *Against Heresies,* 4.37, in *Ante-Nicene Fathers, Vol. 1: The Apostolic Fathers, Justin Martyr, Irenaeus,* ed. Alexander Roberts and James Donaldson, rev. A. C. Coxe (1885; reprint Peabody, Mass.: Hendrickson, 1994), p. 520. Free will, as Irenaeus goes on to say, ensures that education ascends to devotion: "having been rationally taught to love God, we may continue in His perfect love: for God has displayed long-suffering in the case of man's apostasy; while man has been instructed by means of it." For a useful survey of thought about the "trilemma," see Mark Larrimore, ed., *The Problem of Evil: A Reader* (Oxford and Malden, Mass.: Blackwell, 2001), esp. pp. xviii-xxiv, xxix.

58. C. S. Lewis, *A Preface to Paradise Lost* (London: Oxford University Press, 1942), p. 7. The sense of good and evil will always be in this world mutually dependent and reciprocally defining, like the two twins conjoined and sundered by the polar meanings embedded in the pun "cleaving." As Victoria Silver, *Imperfect Sense: The Predicament of Milton's Irony* (Princeton: Princeton University Press, 2001), has persuasively argued, "what Milton suggests is that we apprehend the one in the other, by an interpretive sense of their distinction which requires good and evil to be reciprocally present" (p. 96). Therefore, "In Milton's theodicy, when the true and false, good and evil, are not understood to be practically contingent meanings but instead separate and exclusive, we peremptorily render ourselves incapable of recognizing any of these values" (p. 101).

59. Tayler, *Milton's Poetry,* p. 194.

60. While the most commonly cited reference to the Cadmus episode—or to the analogous moment in Jason's story—is Ovid, *Metamorphoses,* 3.103 and 7.102 (*vipereos dentes*), the fullest collection of materials pertaining to Cadmus is to be found in Apollodorus, *The Library,* trans. J. G. Frazer, 2 vols., LCL (Cambridge, Mass.: Harvard University Press, 1921), 3.1.1, 3.4.1–2, 3.5.2, 3.5.4.

NOTES TO CHAPTER TWO

1. *Tracts Relating to the Jews, 1608–1724,* British Library shelfmark 482.b.3 (1–21). See also the bound collection assembled by Francis Hargrave, *Tracts Concerning the Jews, etc. 1752–53,* British Library shelfmark 1123.c.30 (1–7).
2. For a lively discussion of Milton's views on toleration, see Elizabeth Sauer, "Religious Toleration and Imperial Intolerance," in *Milton and the Imperial Vision,* ed. Balachandra Rajan and Elizabeth Sauer (Pittsburgh: Duquesne University Press, 1999), pp. 214–30.
3. See Jeffrey S. Shoulson, *Milton and the Rabbis* (New York: Columbia University Press, 2001), p. 63; and, further, the stimulating discussion of parallels between pagan and Jewish antiquity in Milton's thought, pp. 80–89.
4. E. A. Speiser, "Introduction," *Genesis,* The Anchor Bible (New York: Doubleday, 1962), pp. xviii–xx.
5. But see John G. Gager, *Reinventing Paul* (New York: Oxford University Press, 2000), p. 90. Against traditional readings of Paul's letters, Gager believes that the original context for such remarks should be seen as limiting their application only to the Gentiles. The history of their reception is, however, another and, for our concerns more important, matter.
6. For an excellent account of the word and its cognates in the Bible, see G. Bertram's entry in Gerhard Kittel, *Theological Dictionary of the New Testament,* 10 vols. (Grand Rapids: Eerdmans, 1951–76), 5:596–625. The word *paidagogos* compounds *paidos* and *agogos;* see H. G. Liddell and R. Scott, *A Greek-English Lexicon,* rev. ed., ed. Sir Henry Stuart Jones et al. (Oxford: Clarendon Press, 1925–30), 2:1286b. The classic treatment of the concept of pedagogy in the ancient world remains Werner Jaeger, *Paideia: The Ideals of Greek Culture,* trans. Gilbert Highet, 3 vols. (New York: Oxford University Press, 1943–45). Intriguingly, the character of the pedagogue also appears in midrashic meshalim as a figure for the interpreter of Scripture who engages in midrash; see David Stern, *Parables in Midrash: Narrative and Exegesis in Rabbinic Literature* (Cambridge, Mass.: Harvard University Press, 1991), pp. 41–42.
7. See David J. Lull, "'The Law Was Our Pedagogue': A Study in Galatians 3:19–25," *Journal of Biblical Literature* 105 (1986): 481–98.
8. Martin Luther, "A Sermon . . . concerning them that be vnder the Law, and them that be vnder Grace," *Special and Chosen Sermons,* trans. W. G. (London, 1578), p. 315.

9.   [Edmund Ferrers], *An Abstract of a Commentarie By Dr. Martyn Luther, upon the Galathians* (London, 1642), sig. C3^r.

10. John Donne, *Sermons,* ed. Evelyn M. Simpson and George R. Potter, 10 vols. (Berkeley: University of California Press, 1953–62), 8:351.

11. Stanley Fish is especially good on the ironies of this idea of self-sufficiency. See "Wanting a supplement: the question of interpretation in Milton's early prose," in *Politics, Poetics, and Hermeneutics in Milton's Prose,* ed. David Loewenstein and J.G. Turner (Cambridge: Cambridge University Press, 1990), pp. 41–68 = *How Milton Works* (Cambridge, Mass.: Harvard University Press, 2001), pp. 215–55.

12. Luther, *A Commentarie . . . vpon the Epistle of S. Paul to the Galathians,* anonymous trans. (London, 1575), fol. 164^r.

13. John Milton, *An Apology Against a Pamphlet call'd a Modest Confutation of the Animadversions upon the Remonstrant against SMECTYMNUUS* (London, 1642), sig. D1^r.

14. The "insuls rule" to which Milton alludes may be the list of variants in the Babylonian Talmud, Nedarim, 37b, the tractate Soperim (6:8–9), or the *tiqqune hasoperim,* "the eighteen cases in which scribes are said to have 'corrected' expressions which might seem disrespectful to God." See E. J. Revell, "Masorah," in *The Anchor Bible Dictionary,* ed. D. N. Freedman et al. 6 vols. (New York: Doubleday, 1992), 4:593.

15. Milton, *An Apology,* sig. H2^r. In Milton's friend George Thomason's copy, E.147.(22), which features the inscription "Ex dono Authoris" on the title page, the erratum is not corrected on sig. D1^r. Nor is it corrected in the copy I examined at the Folger Shakespeare Library. This stands out, in part, because of the manuscript corrections appearing in other tracts that Milton presented to Thomason in the period. For example, *Of Reformation* (London, 1641), British Library shelfmark E.208.(3), features manuscript alterations that bring the text in line with the errata sheet, as that on p. 7, which appears to be in Milton's hand. Thus the question of authorial intent can only further complicate the irony of this revision to the text of *An Apology:* the "correction" could not have been introduced until after the printing of that portion of the body of the text was complete, since the usual stop-press correction did not occur. Consequently, we may deduce either that the compositor failed to notice a marginal correction in Milton's hand when first setting the type, or that Milton made the change late in the printing of his tract, as "one so copious of fancie" (YP 2:532).

16. Luther, *Commentarie . . . vpon . . . Galathians,* fol. 164^r.

17. The opposition between the "marginall Keri" and "the textual Chetiv" appears in *Areopagitica* (London, 1644), where the distinction serves a similar ironic purpose. There, Milton critiques the rabbinic editorial tradition on the page facing the emendation of "wayfaring" to "warfaring." See the

copy (frequently reproduced in facsimile) of the first edition in the British Library, shelfmark C.55.22.(9), pp. 12–13.

18. Revell, "Masorah," in *The Anchor Bible Dictionary,* 4:592.

19. Augustine, *On Christian Doctrine,* trans. D.W. Robertson, Jr. (Indianapolis and New York: Bobbs-Merrill, 1958), esp. 1.35.39–1.37.41 and 3.10.15. See Kathy Eden, *Hermeneutics and the Rhetorical Tradition* (New Haven: Yale University Press, 1997), pp. 53–63; also H. R. MacCallum, "Milton and Figurative Interpretation of the Bible," *University of Toronto Quarterly* 31 (1962): 397–415.

20. See the excellent account of this method in Dayton Haskin, *Milton's Burden of Interpretation* (Philadelphia: University of Pennsylvania Press, 1994); see also Peggy Samuels, "Dueling Erasers: Milton and Scripture," *Studies in Philology* 96 (1999): 180–203.

21. Nehemiah 8:8; 2 Esdras 14:20–48. See Gerald L. Bruns, "Midrash and Allegory," in *The Literary Guide to the Bible,* ed. Robert Alter and Frank Kermode (Cambridge, Mass.: Harvard University Press, 1987), pp. 625–46.

22. E. J. Revell, "Masoretes," in *The Anchor Bible Dictionary,* 4:594.

23. Subsequent early modern English comparativists give a similar impression, despite their antipathy toward sectarianism, independency, and nonconformity. Among the more consequential are John Lightfoot, *Horae Hebraicae et Talmudicae,* 6 vols. (Cambridge, 1658–77); John Spencer, *De Legibus Hebraeorum Ritualibus et earum Rationibus* (Cambridge, 1685), which influentially set Jewish practices in the context of other Near-Eastern religions, esp. in Lib. 3, Diss. 7, "De Urim et Thummim," pp. 851–988; and John Edwards, *Polypoikilos Sophia: A Complete History or Survey of all the Dispensations and Methods of Religion,* 2 vols. (Cambridge, 1699).

24. *An Endeavour after the reconcilement of that long debated and much lamented difference between the godly Presbyterians, and Independents; About Church-government. In a discourse touching the Jews Synagogue* (London, 1647/8), sig. M4ʳ.

25. Hugh Broughton, *A reuelation of the holy Apocalyps* ([Middelburg], 1610), p. 295.

26. A similar impetus may be seen to motivate Thomas Fuller, *A Pisgah-Sight of Palestine* (London, 1650), as well as other works of antiquarian chorography, historiography, and architecture of biblical places, including John Lightfoot, *The Temple; especially as it stood in the dayes of our Saviour (*London, 1650). For other references, close to the circle of Milton's acquaintance, see Richard H. Popkin, "Hartlib, Drury, and the Jews," in *Samuel Hartlib and Universal Reformation,* ed. John Leslie, Mark Greengrass, and Timothy Raylor (Cambridge: Cambridge University Press, 1994), pp. 118–36.

27. See Lightfoot, *Horae Hebraicae et Talmudicae,* 1:79–84, esp. 83, where he seeks to quell anxiety concerning the suspicion that the text of the Law was not preserved perfectly. The "jot and tittle" to which Jesus alludes, therefore,

must not be confused with the issue raised by *qere / ketib* variants (*variae lectiones*), which preserve the sacred text in its fullness, since they record the collated variants for the two most authoritative copies of the Torah at the time of post-Exilic canonization.

28. Broughton, *A reuelation*, p. 297.

29. Hugh Broughton, *Daniel his Chaldie visions and his Ebrew* (London, 1596), sig. Kij^r.

30. Broughton, *A reuelation*, p. 297.

31. *An Endeavour after the reconcilement of . . . Presbyterians, and Independents*, sig. M3^v.

32. Broughton, *A reuelation*, p. 297.

33. *An Endeavour after the reconcilement of . . . Presbyterians, and Independents*, sig. M3^v.

34. See Nigel Smith, "The Uses of Hebrew in the English Revolution," in *Language, Self, and Society: A Social History of Language*, ed. Peter Burke and Roy Porter (Cambridge: Polity Press, 1991), pp. 51–71, esp. 56–7 and 63, for a discussion of the use among Independents and Baptists of "Hebrew originals and translations from them in order to control their own interpretation of the text and to enter into a literal understanding of Hebraic identity and meaning, as represented in the language."

35. Erich Auerbach, "Figura," *Scenes from the Drama of European Literature*, trans. Ralph Manheim (New York: Meridian Books, 1959), pp. 56, 57. For compelling evidence of the ways in which typology influenced Milton's major poems, see Edward W. Tayler, *Milton's Poetry: Its Development in Time* (Pittsburgh: Duquesne University Press, 1979). For a massively documented account of the widespread practice of typological interpretation as it relates to the poetry of the period, see Barbara Lewalski, *Protestant Poetics and the Seventeenth-Century Religious Lyric* (Princeton: Princeton University Press, 1979), esp. pp. 111–44. For an excellent account of the paradoxes induced by typological rendering of history, see Thomas H. Luxon, *Literal Figures: Puritan Allegory and the Reformation Crisis in Representation* (Chicago: University of Chicago Press, 1995).

36. Frank Kermode, *The Genesis of Secrecy: On the Interpretation of Narrative* (Cambridge, Mass.: Harvard University Press, 1979), p. 45.

37. William Guild, *Moses Vnuailed* (London, 1620), explains typology "To confirme the CHRISTIAN, and conuince the IEVV: very profitable and full of comfort." The layout of the manual is telling: the pages consist of parallel columns (separated by a rule) in which an anticipatory passage from the Hebrew Bible is "unveiled" in a fulfilling or answering passage from the New Testament, followed by a synoptic paragraph describing "the Disparitie."

38. William Robertson, Epistle Dedicatory, *The Hebrew Text of the Psalmes and Lamentations but Published (for to encourage and facilitate Beginners in their*

way) with the Reading thereof in known English Letters (London, 1656), sigs. a2^r–a3^r.

39. "The Translators to the Reader," *The Holy Bible* [KJV] (London, 1612), sig. B3^v.

40. On the centrality of biblical interpretation to the radical sectarians, see Christopher Hill, *The English Bible and the Seventeenth-Century Revolution* (Harmondsworth: Penguin, 1993); on Milton's relations to the sectarians, see the excellent survey in Hill, *Milton and the English Revolution* (New York: Viking, 1977), esp. chaps. 6–8; and now see David Loewenstein, *Representing Revolution in Milton and his Contemporaries: Religion, Politics, and Polemics in Radical Puritanism* (Cambridge: Cambridge University Press, 2001).

41. *An Endeavour after the reconcilement*, E.432.5, dated by Thomason 14 March 1647/8. *The Petition of the Jewes For the Repealing of the Act of Parliament for their banishment out of ENGLAND* (London, 1648), E.537.17, dated by Thomason 6 January 1648/9. Edward Nicholas, *An Apology for the Honorable Nation of the Jews, and All the Sons of Israel* (London, 1648), E.544.16, dated by Thomason 21 February 1648/9.

42. Menasseh ben Israel, *To His Highnesse the Lord Protector of the COMMON-WEALTH of England, Scotland, and Ireland* (London, 1655), sig. D^v [p. 26].

43. Nicholas, *An Apology*, p. 4.

44. Nicholas, *An Apology*, pp. 8, 11.

45. Thomas Edwards, *Gangræna*, 2nd ed. enlarged (London, 1646), pp. 14–15 (Milton at 34).

46. Edwards, *Gangræna*, p. 183. False teachers are "the greatest displeasure of God to a Church" (p. 182).

47. Jason P. Rosenblatt has found the source for this assertion in Selden's treatise, *De Synedriis;* see *Torah and Law in "Paradise Lost"* (Princeton: Princeton University Press, 1994), p. 19.

48. Matthew Biberman, "Milton, Marriage, and a Woman's Right to Divorce," *SEL* 39 (1999): 131–53, provides a helpful summary of the philological grounds of the exegesis and an interesting commentary on the gender-related aspects of Milton's argument.

49. Rosenblatt, *Torah and Law,* chaps. 1 and 2, has written eloquently and persuasively on this subject.

50. Cf. Rosenblatt's illuminating discussion of Milton's interpretation of Paul's schoolmaster, *Torah and Law,* pp. 32–35.

51. The word "classic" of course refers primarily to the structure of Presbyterian church government, which groups congregations as Presbyteries or "Classes," as explained by E. A. J. Honignmann, *Milton's Sonnets* (London: Macmillan, 1966), pp. 36, 199 and Carey, *Poems,* p. 299 (and *OED* 7). Secondarily, the word meant, as it does principally today, "Of the first class, of the highest rank or importance; approved as a model; standard, leading"

(*OED* 1, from 1613) and "belonging to the standard authors and literature of Greek and Latin antiquity" (*OED* 2, from 1628).

52. Auerbach, "Figura," pp. 11–76, counterposes Tertullian's historicism to Origen's extreme allegorizing. Paul himself equated castration with circumcision (Gal. 5:12), so that circumcision could be condemned as falsely entrusting rites and fleshly signs over faith in grace, prioritizing the institutions of the church over the operations of the spirit. See J. Louis Martyn, *Galatians,* The Anchor Bible (New York: Doubleday, 1997), p. 478.

53. On the semantic range of such terms as "Judaizer" and "Judaizing," especially as they were pejoratively applied to religious radicals in seventeenth-century England, see David S. Katz, *Philosemitism and the Readmission of the Jews to England 1603–1655* (Oxford: Clarendon Press, 1982), pp. 16–42.

54. Edward Gibbon, *The History of the Decline and Fall of the Roman Empire,* vol. 1, chap. 15, n. 96, as quoted by Anthony Grafton, *The Footnote: A Curious History* (Cambridge, Mass.: Harvard University Press, 1997), p. 2.

55. Martin Dzelzainis, "Authors 'not unknown' in Milton's *Tetrachordon*," *Notes and Queries,* new ser., Vol. 45, No. 1 (March 1998): 44–47, ironically points out the imprecision of some of the Yale editor's annotations to this section.

56. For more on this topic, see the richly suggestive essay by Stephen M. Fallon, "The Spur of Self-Concernment: Milton in his Divorce Tracts," *Milton Studies* 38 (2000): 220–42; also Annabel Patterson, "No meer amatorious novel?" in *Politics, Poetics, and Hermeneutics,* ed. Loewenstein and Turner, pp. 85–101.

57. William Kerrigan, *The Prophetic Milton* (Charlottesville: University of Virginia Press, 1974), p. 172.

NOTES TO CHAPTER THREE

1. Samuel Johnson, *The Lives of the English Poets,* ed. G. B. Hill, 3 vols. (Oxford: Clarendon Press, 1905), 1:98–101. Boswell provides some very revealing details that put Johnson's remarks about Milton's "wonder-working academy" in perspective. In 1736 Johnson set up a "private academy" of his own, which failed miserably, despite having had so remarkable a student as David Garrick. See James Boswell, *Life of Johnson,* ed. R. W. Chapman, rev. ed. (Oxford: Oxford University Press, 1970), pp. 69–73.

2. Johnson, *Lives,* 1:156–57.

3. Francis Blackburne, *Remarks on Johnson's life of Milton. To which are added, Milton's Tractate of education and Areopagitica* (London, 1780), sig. B8^v.

4. Blackburne, *Remarks,* sig. C3^r.

5. Blackburne, *Remarks,* sigs. A3^{r-v}.

6. Christopher Hill, *The Intellectual Origins of the English Revolution Revisited* (Oxford: Clarendon Press, 1997), p. 384.

7. Thomas Jordan, "The Players Petition to the Parliament," in *Poetry and Revolution: An Anthology of British and Irish Verse, 1625–1660,* ed. Peter Davidson (Oxford: Oxford University Press, 1998), No. 233, pp. 309–311, ll.65–66, 69–76.

8. I cite the accusation from Milton's own tract; for a fuller context, see the selections from *Regii Sanguinis Clamor* printed as appendix D in YP 4.2:1042–75. Milton's quotation is from the passage at YP 4.2:1050. Du Moulin also conventionally depicted the regicide as a drama in his dedicatory epistle to Charles II (YP 4.2:1042).

9. For a penetrating analysis of educational paradigms by means of a structuralist-Marxist approach, see Louis Althusser, "Ideology and Ideological State Apparatuses (Notes toward an Investigation)," in *Lenin and Philosophy and Other Essays,* trans. Ben Brewster (New York: Monthly Review Press, 1971), pp. 127–86. For a systematic educational agenda within a democratic polity, with roots in Christian traditions, see John Dewey, *Democracy and Education* (New York: Macmillan, 1916).

10. Helen M. Jewell, *Education in Early Modern England* (Houndmills, Basingstoke: Macmillan, 1998), pp. 4, 37.

11. Marchamont Nedham, *Mercurius Politicus,* No. 104 (27 May-3 June 1652), p. 1.

12. See *Samuel Hartlib and Universal Reformation,* ed. Mark Greengrass, Michael Leslie and Timothy Raylor (Cambridge: Cambridge University Press, 1994).

13. Jewell, *Education in Early Modern England,* p. 32.

14. Kenneth Charleton and Margaret Spuford, "Literacy, Society and Education," in *The Cambridge History of Early Modern English Literature,* ed. David Loewenstein and Janel Mueller (Cambridge: Cambridge University Press, 2002), pp. 24, 29, 48.

15. See the illuminating discussion in Jonathan Scott, *England's Troubles: Seventeenth-Century English Political Instability in European Context* (Cambridge: Cambridge University Press, 2000), pp. 317–24 (quotation at 317).

16. Blair Worden, "English Republicanism," in *The Cambridge History of Political Thought, 1450–1700,* ed. J. H. Burns with Mark Goldie (Cambridge: Cambridge University Press, 1991), p. 456.

17. See the elegant discussion of *The Readie and Easie Way* in William Kolbrener, *Milton's Warring Angels: A Study of Critical Engagements* (Cambridge: Cambridge University Press, 1997), esp. pp. 30–40.

18. See Nicholas von Maltzahn, *Milton's "History of Britain": Republican Historiography in the English Revolution* (Oxford: Clarendon Press, 1991), pp. 189–91.

19. Norbrook, *Writing the English Republic,* p. 191.

20. On the conundrum of naming as it relates to the regicide or tyrannicide, see Joad Raymond, "The King is a Thing," in *Milton and the Terms of Liberty,*

ed. Graham Parry and Joad Raymond (Cambridge: D.S. Brewer, 2002), pp. 69–94.

21. For a brilliant and suggestive analysis of the new figuration of epic heroism in the regicide pamphlets, see Nigel Smith, *Literature and Revolution in England, 1640–1660* (New Haven: Yale University Press, 1994), chap. 7.

22. See Martin Dzelzainis, "Milton's Classical Republicanism," in *Milton and Republicanism,* ed. David Armitage, Armand Himy, and Quentin Skinner (Cambridge: Cambridge University Press, 1995), pp. 3–24 (quotation at p. 11).

23. *The Poems and Letters of Andrew Marvell,* ed. H. M. Margoliouth, 2nd ed., 2 vols. (Oxford: Clarendon, 1952), 2:293 (letter 2). Compare YP 4.1:685. Although Margoliouth (2:349) speculates that the book must have been the *Second Defense* because of the dates of the letter and the publication, the context of the letter implies another possibility. Marvell's inclusion of Salmasius in his comments suggests that the presentation copies he is discussing may have contained the *First Defense* and the *Second Defense* bound together. Decebalus, according to the *Oxford Classical Dictionary,* ed. Simon Hornblower and Antony Spawforth, 3rd ed. (Oxford: Oxford University Press, 1996), s.v., was the shrewd and dangerous military leader of Dacia who, after several campaigns against Rome (A.D. 85–89), made peace with Domitian. Trajan subsequently went to war with Decebalus, and Decebalus committed suicide after his capture in A.D. 105. The allusion is apt particularly because of the circumstances of Salmasius's death prior to his promised response to Milton's *First Defense.*

24. William Wordsworth, "London, 1802," ll.1–6, *Poetical Works,* ed. Ernest De Selincourt (London: Oxford University Press, 1936), p. 244.

25. John Toland, *Amyntor: or, a Defence of Milton's Life* (London, 1699), p. 3. As evidenced by the *Explanatory Notes and Remarks on Milton's Paradise Lost* by Jonathan Richardson, Father and Son (London, 1734), Milton's life and works compelled rather extensive speculation about his character in novelistic terms. For an interesting speculation that Milton's self-scrutiny, as an integral part of his Christian pedagogy, participated in the emergence of the narrator of the English novel out of spiritual biography, see Michael McKeon, *The Origins of the English Novel, 1600–1740* (Baltimore and London: Johns Hopkins University Press, 1987), pp. 95–96.

26. Stephen M. Fallon, "Alexander More Reads Milton: Self-representation and Anxiety in Milton's Defences," in *Milton and the Terms of Liberty,* ed. Graham Parry and Joad Raymond, p. 122. Fallon continues: "By setting so rarefied and exalted a mark, a mark difficult for anyone to reach, Milton inevitably purchases anxiety, an anxiety that emerges in the mid-1650s in moments of surprising candor, vulnerability, and even querulousness."

27. For Hazlitt's comment, see *Lectures on English Poets* (1818), "Lecture III: On Shakespeare and Milton," in *The Romantics on Milton,* ed. Joseph A.

Wittreich Jr. (Cleveland: Case Western Reserve University Press, 1970), p. 381.

28. Quintilian, *Institutio Oratoria,* 12.1.8, ed. and trans. H.E. Butler, 4 vols., LCL (Cambridge, Mass.: Harvard University Press, 1922), 4:360–61.

29. Cicero, *On Duties,* 1.23 (78), ed. and trans. Walter Miller, LCL (Cambridge, Mass.: Harvard University Press, 1913), p. 81.

30. Petrarch, *On His Own Ignorance and that of Many Others,* in *Renaissance Philosophy of Man,* ed. Ernst Cassirer, Paul Oskar Kristeller, and John Herman Randall (Chicago: University of Chicago Press, 1948), pp. 50–51.

31. On the political implications of Milton's humanism in these years, see Martin Dzelzainis's fine introduction to Milton's *Political Writings,* ed. Martin Dzelzainis (Cambridge: Cambridge University Press, 1991), esp. pp. x, xix-xxv.

32. Homer, *Iliad,* 9.411–16, trans. Richmond Lattimore (Chicago: University of Chicago Press, 1951), p. 209. All translations of the *Iliad* are taken from Lattimore's translation. Greek quoted from Homer, *Iliad,* trans. and ed. A. T. Murray, rev. W. F. Wyatt, 2 vols., LCL (Cambridge, Mass.: Harvard University Press, 1999), 1:424.

33. Cedric H. Whitman, *Homer and the Heroic Tradition* (1958; reprint New York: W.W. Norton, 1965), p. 188. Among more recent commentators, Seth Schein, *The Mortal Hero: An Introduction to Homer's "Iliad"* (Berkeley: University of California Press, 1984), pp. 90–110, is especially good on this subject. Milton felt very strongly the volitional aspect of Achilles' heroism. We therefore need not be concerned about the contradiction between what Achilles says at 9.410–16 and at 16.50–51, where he claims that "there is no word from Zeus my honoured mother has told me" (16.51); for interpretive issues surrounding the contradiction, see Malcolm M. Willcock, *A Companion to the Iliad* (Chicago: University of Chicago Press, 1976), pp. 103–4, 177–79.

34. For Neoplatonic allegories of Homer's blindness as contemplative inwardness (by way of Plotinus and Proclus), see Robert Lamberton, *Homer the Theologian: Neoplatonist Allegorical Reading and the Growth of the Epic Tradition* (Berkeley: University of California Press, 1986), p. 200. We may be sure that Milton was familiar with the twelfth-century allegorical commentary on the *Iliad* by Eustanthius, Archbishop of Thessalonia, first printed in 1546, since Milton mentions the commentary in his Euripides marginalia (see CM 18:304–5). The comments of Eustanthius on the passage are to be found in the *Comentarii ad Homeri Iliadem Pertinentes,* ed. M. van der Valk, 4 vols. (Leiden: E. J. Brill, 1976), 2:746.

35. I rely here, as in my use of the phrase "specifically divine anger," on the interpretation of *menin* in Richard Sacks, *The Traditional Phrase in Homer* (Leiden: E. J. Brill, 1987), pp. 3–4, 7–9, which lists all of the Homeric attestations as well as several corroborating instances in other early Greek sources.

36. Apollonios Rhodios, *The Argonautika,* 2.181–84, trans. Peter Green (Berkeley: University of California Press, 1997), p. 84. In his excellent introduction, Green appositely remarks, "Phineus demonstrates the inadequacy of human prophecy, the ineluctable force of divine vengeance" (p. 39). Again, I quote from an accessible modern translation rather than the Latin translation printed with the Greek in the first edition because it is uncertain whether the Latin translation is Milton's own.

37. *Argonautika,* 2.221–22, trans. Green, p. 85.

38. For a helpful explanation of the rhetorical contest and the royalists' use of Milton's blindness as a sign of divine retribution, see Nicholas von Maltzahn, "From Pillar to Post: Milton and the Attack on Republican Humanism at the Restoration," in *Soldiers, Writers and Statesmen of the English Revolution,* ed. Ian Gentles, John Morrill and Blair Worden (Cambridge: Cambridge University Press, 1998), pp. 265–85.

39. For an astute discussion of the theological implications, see Silver, *Imperfect Sense,* pp. 153–207.

40. Colin Burrow, *Epic Romance: Homer to Milton* (Oxford: Clarendon Press, 1993), pp. 244–50, brilliantly traces the motif of the elusive heroic life and the "goal that flees" Milton as he pursues a career in the early poems—namely "the desirable and unattainable fact of becoming a poet writing a romance which is not quite a romance" (250). See also his essay, "*Poems 1645:* The Future Poet," in *The Cambridge Companion to Milton,* 2ⁿᵈ ed., ed. Dennis Danielson (Cambridge: Cambridge University Press, 1999), pp. 54–69.

41. The letter to Leonard Philaras is dated 28 September 1654; the date in Thomason's copy of the *Second Defense* is 30 May 1654, and Milton presented a copy of the *Second Defense* to the Bodleian on 11 June 1654. See Gordon Campbell, *A Milton Chronology* (London and Basingstoke: Macmillan, 1997), pp. 153–54.

42. "Si modo accepteris a me unde is causas equidem quod hortaris, ne oblatam undecunque divinitus fortassis opem repudiare videar" (CM 12:66).

43. *Argonautika,* 1.151–55, trans. Green, p. 47.

44. "Teque, mi Phiara, quocunque res ceciderit, non minus forti & confirmato animo, quam si Lynceus essem, valere jubeo" (CM 12:70–71).

45. This idea forms the central preoccupation, and the sharply defined telos, of Barbara K. Lewalski, *The Life of John Milton: A Critical Biography* (Oxford: Blackwell, 2000), esp. pp. 489–538.

46. *The Poetical Works of John Milton,* ed. Thomas Newton, 5ᵗʰ edn., 3 vols. (London, 1761), 3:188. The quotation is from the final note on *Paradise Regain'd,* which begins as a gloss on 4.624. Newton writes: "As Mr. Elwood informs us, Milton did not so much as think of it, till he was advanced in years, and it is not very likely, considering the troubles and infirmities he had long labor'd under, that his studies had been much

employ'd about that time among the sprightly Italians, or indeed any writers of that turn. Consistent with this supposition we find it of a quite different stamp, and instead of allusions to poets ancient or modern, it is full of moral and philosophical reasonings, to which sort of thoughts an afflicted old age must have turned our author's mind." Compare Newton's comment on the final two lines of *Samson Agonistes:* "This moral lesson in the conclusion is very fine, and excellently suited to the beginning. For Milton had chosen for the motto to this piece a passage out of Aristotle, which may show what was his design in writing this tragedy, and the sense of which he hath expressed in the preface, that 'tragedy is of power by raising pity and fear, or terrour, to purge the mind of those and such like passions, &c.' and he exemplifies it here in Manoah and the Chorus, after their various agitations of passion, acquiescing in the divine dispensations, and thereby inculcating a most instructive lesson to the reader" (3:305).

47. Smith, *Literature and Revolution,* p. 178.

48. This general reaction of the humanists should, however, be viewed in relation to the professional academic context created by the scholastic insistence on formal or verifiable logic still common in the universities of the time. See Jardine, "Humanist Logic," p. 175: "A humanist treatment of logic is characterised by the fundamental assumption that *oratio* may be persuasive, even compelling, without its being formally valid (or without the formal validity of the argument being ascertainable)."

49. *The Spectator,* ed. Donald F. Bond, 5 vols. (Oxford: Clarendon Press, 1965), 2:519 (No. 262).

50. John Milton, *Paradise Regain'd . . . To which is added Samson Agonistes. And Poems upon several occasions. With a tractate of education* (London, 1713), p. 371.

51. Vito R. Guistiniani, "Homo, Humanus, and the Meanings of 'Humanism,'" *Journal of the History of Ideas* 46 (1985): 167–95, seeks to historicize and thereby clear up the twentieth-century confusion arising from the several inexact applications of the term by means of a meticulous philological method, and Erik Petersen, "'The Communication of the Dead': Notes on *Studia humanitatis* and the Nature of Humanist Philology," in *The Uses of Greek and Latin: Historical Essays,* ed. A. C. Dionisotti, Anthony Grafton, and Jill Kraye (London: The Warburg Institute, 1988), pp. 57–69, historically situates the philological method itself by tracing concept of the *studia humanitatis* through usage of the term.

52. There are many excellent surveys of the field, but in particular I would identify three as the most formative to my study: *Renaissance Humanism,* ed. Albert Rabil, 3 vols. (Philadelphia: University of Pennsylvania Press, 1988); P. O. Kristeller, *Renaissance Thought and Its Sources* (New York: Columbia University Press, 1979); and *The Cambridge Companion to Renaissance Humanism,* ed. Jill Kraye (Cambridge: Cambridge University Press, 1996).

53. "Et quoniam non est nobis haec oratio habenda aut in imperita multitudine aut in aliquo conventu agrestium, audacius paulo de studiis humanitatis quae et mihi et vobis nota et iucunda sunt disputabo." (Cicero, *Pro Murena* 61, ed. Louis E. Lord, LCL [Cambridge, Mass.: Harvard University Press, 1937]). All translations from the Latin are my own unless otherwise noted.

54. "Titus Gaiusque Coponii, qui ex omnibus maxime Dionis mortem doluerunt, qui cum doctrinae studio atque humanitatis tum etiam hospitio Dionis tenebantur." (Cicero, *Pro Caelio* 24, ed. R. Gardner, LCL [Cambridge, Mass.: Harvard University Press, 1958]).

55. "Quaeso a vobis, ut in hac causa mihi detis hanc veniam, accommodatam huic reo, vobis, quem ad modum spero, non molestam, ut me pro summo poeta atque eruditissimo homine dicentem, hoc concursu hominum literastissimorum, hac vestra humanitate, hoc denique praetore exercente iudicium patiamini de studiis humanitatis ac litterarum paullo loqui liberius . . ." (Cicero, *Pro Archia,* exordium, II.3, ed. N.H. Watts, LCL [Cambridge, Mass.: Harvard University Press, 1923]).

56. *Petrarch: Four Dialogues for Scholars,* ed. and trans. Conrad H. Rawski (Cleveland: Case Western Reserve University Press, 1967), p. 31.

57. Michael D. Reeve, "Classical Scholarship," in *The Cambridge Companion to Renaissance Humanism,* pp. 20–46, at 22. Reeve's excellent survey emphasizes the transmission of manuscripts and the traditions of textual criticism, commentary, philology, and translation that this process of transmission occasioned.

58. "Bono igitur animo simus: non laboramus in irritum, non frustra laborabunt qui post multas etates sub finem mundi senescentis orientur. Potius illud metuendum est, no prius homines esse desinant, quam ad intimum veritatis archanum humanorum studiorum cura perruperit." (Petrarch, *Le familiari,* 1.9, ed. V. Rossi and U. Bosco, 4 vols. [Florence: Sansoni, 1933–1942], 1:47]).

59. "Pater me puerulum humaniorum literarum studiis destinavit"; compare his claim: "ab adolescentulo humanioribus essem studiis, ut qui maxime deditus" (CM 8:10).

60. Robert Estienne, *Dictionariolum puerorum, tribus linguis Latina, Anglica & Gallica,* trans. John Veron (London, 1552), s.v.

61. See Donald L. Clark, *John Milton at St Paul's School: A Study of Ancient Rhetoric in English Renaissance Education* (New York: Columbia University Press, 1948); Harris F. Fletcher, *The Intellectual Development of John Milton,* 2 vols. (Urbana: University of Illinois Press, 1956–61). For the best introduction to the concept of "Christian humanism" as it pertains to Milton, see Douglas Bush, *The Renaissance and English Humanism* (Toronto: University of Toronto Press, 1939); a recent effort to reassert the value of seeing Milton in relation to the thought of Renaissance humanists can be found in

William Kerrigan and Gordon Braden, *The Idea of the Renaissance* (Baltimore and London: Johns Hopkins University Press, 1989).

62. J. H. Hanford, "Milton and the Return to Humanism," *Studies in Philology* 16 (1919), reprinted in *John Milton, Poet and Humanist: Essays by James Holly Hanford* (Cleveland: Case Western Reserve University Press, 1966), pp. 161–84, at 183.

63. T. S. Eliot, "Modern Education and the Classics" (1932), in *Selected Essays* (New York: Harcourt Brace Jovanovich, 1950), pp. 452–60 (quotations on 452 and 459). It is surely extraordinary to find one of the leading "modernists" advocating "the revival and expansion of monastic teaching orders" (p. 460).

64. A learned exception to this legacy of Bush's idea of "Christian humanism" can be found in Joan S. Bennett, *Reviving Liberty: Radical Christian Humanism in Milton's Great Poems* (Cambridge, Mass.: Harvard University Press, 1989). Bennett's emphasis is placed more upon the "Christian" context than that of the classical humanist; see pp. 6–32.

65. See the brief but suggestive comparison between Milton's changing educational schemes and those advocated by John Hall and particularly Marchamont Nedham, *A Discourse Concerning Schools and School-Masters, Offered to publick Consideration* (London, 1663) in Joad Raymond, "Where is this goodly tower? Republican Theories of Education," *Critical Survey* 5 (1993): 289–97.

66. "I.B., Gent.," *Heroick Education* (London, 1656), sig. B4^v.

67. *Heroick Education,* sigs. C7^v, B8^r.

68. *Heroick Education,* sig. C6^r.

69. In this passage, at sigs. B2^{r-v}, as in many others throughout *Heroick Education,* the author closely follows the Pseudo-Plutarch, "The Education Of Children," *Moralia,* ed. and trans. Frank Cole Babbitt, LCL (Cambridge, Mass: Harvard University Press, 1927), esp. 4b-c, 7b-10c (pp. 19, 33–57).

70. James Harrington, *The Commonwealth of Oceana,* ed. J. G. A. Pocock (Cambridge: Cambridge University Press, 1992), p. 190.

71. Harrington, *Oceana,* p. 191.

72. Harrington, *Oceana,* p. 206.

73. Harrington, *Oceana,* p. 199.

74. Blair Hoxby has suggested to me that Milton's attack on the centralization of learning in the universities is best seen in relation to the metaphorical economy of his antimonopoly stance. For more on the relationship between the emerging economic theory of the liberal market and the circulation of knowledge, see Hoxby, "The Trade of Truth Advanced: *Areopagitica,* Economic Discourse, and Libertarian Reform," *Milton Studies* 36 (1998): 177–202; and, further, *Mammon's Music: Literature and Economics in the Age of Milton* (New Haven: Yale University Press, 2002).

75. Roger Williams, *The Hireling Ministry None of Christs or A Discourse touching the Propagating the Gospel of Christ Jesus* (London, 1652), p. 17. Quoted by Arthur E. Barker, *Milton and the Puritan Dilemma, 1641–1660* (Toronto: University of Toronto Press, 1942), p. 231.

76. John T. Shawcross, *Milton: A Bibliography For the Years 1624–1700* (Binghamton, NY: MRTS, 1984), pp. 71–78; Campbell, *A Milton Chronology*, p. 188.

77. Edmund Ludlow, *A Voyce from the Watch Tower* (1660–62), ed. A.B. Worden, Camden Fourth Ser., No. 21 (London: Royal Historical Society, 1978), p. 85.

78. For an excellent survey of the historical situation in which the two editions of *The Readie and Easie Way* were composed and published, see Laura Lunger Knoppers, "Late Political Prose," in *A Companion to Milton*, ed. Thomas N. Corns (Oxford: Blackwell, 2001), pp. 309–25.

79. See von Maltzahn, "From pillar to post." On the politics of Milton's use of Cicero, see Martin Dzelzainis, "Milton and the Limits of Ciceronian Rhetoric," in *English Renaissance Prose: History, Language, and Politics,* ed. Neil Rhodes (Tempe, AZ: MRTS, 1997), pp. 203–226; and idem, "Milton's classical republicanism."

80. Laura Lunger Knoppers critiques similar assumptions of figures as diverse as David Masson, Arthur Barker, Don Wolfe, Douglas Bush, J. H. Hanford, Donald Daiches, among others in *Historicizing Milton: Spectacle, Power, and Poetry in Restoration England* (Athens: University of Georgia Press, 1994).

81. At its first appearance, the sonnet was printed "with the information that it was sent to Vane by Milton 3 Jul. 1652" (*Poems*, p. 329). I should qualify my description of Milton's publication history by adding that it is uncertain whether the *Brief Notes upon a Late Sermon*, which replies to a sermon preached by Matthew Griffith on 25 March, was published before or after the second edition of *The Readie and Easie Way*. Milton's poem on Shakespeare was also reprinted in the Third Folio (1664). See Campbell, *Chronology*, pp. 189, 200.

82. Richard L. Greaves, *Deliver Us from Evil: The Radical Underground in Britain, 1660–1663* (New York: Oxford University Press, 1986), p. 208.

83. See Smith, *Literature and Revolution*, p. 194.

84. Steve Pincus, "Neither Machiavellian Moment nor Possessive Individualism: Commercial Society and the Defenders of the English Commonwealth," *American Historical Review* 103 (1998): 705–36 (at 713).

85. John Rogers, *The Matter of Revolution: Science, Poetry, and Politics in the Age of Milton* (Ithaca, NY: Cornell University Press, 1996), p. 138.

86. I dissent from the opinion of Annabel Patterson, *Early Modern Liberalism* (Cambridge: Cambridge University Press, 1997), p. 25, that Milton, in restricting "elections to those of a 'better breeding'" and not committing all to a democratic polity, is "thereby undermining the educational vision he

was groping for." This seems to me rather seriously to misrepresent Milton's "educational vision" as evidenced by his writings throughout his career, not just in *The Readie and Easie Way*. This mischaracterization of Milton's political agenda(s) continues in her discussion of the tractate *Of Education*, although the discussion of the reception of Milton among eighteenth-century transatlantic intellectuals is useful (see pp. 29, 36). The "liberall exercises" Patterson wishes to locate in *Of Education* finally have more to do with her commendable if misplaced advocacy of liberalism than with Milton's liberal arts curriculum (see YP 2:385); the phrase does not, as she contends, indicate that Milton "must have recognized that a liberal education in 1644 could be designed only in a free society, politically speaking" (p. 62). The problem inheres in the difference between what Patterson and Milton think constitutes freedom, and for whom.

87. James Madison, *Writings,* ed. Jack N. Rakove (New York: Library of America, 1999), pp. 163–65. The comparison was suggested to me by Lydia Dittler Schulman, *"Paradise Lost" and the Rise of the American Republic* (Boston: Northeastern University Press, 1992), p. 88. Schulman, emphasizing the educational commitments of several key figures, provides a helpful account of the complex relationship between Milton's works and the intellectual ferment that resulted in the American Revolution.

88. Plato, *Republic,* 595c, 606e; compare *Phaedrus,* 245a. Xenophanes (Diehl, frag.10). Werner Jaeger, *Paideia: The Ideals of Greek Culture,* trans. Gilbert Highet, 3 vols. (New York: Oxford University Press, 1943–45), 1:35, 36.

89. *The New Oxford Book of Seventeenth-Century Verse,* ed. Alastair Fowler (Oxford: Oxford University Press, 1991), No. 81, l. 30, p. 75.

90. "A Defence of Poetry," in *Shelley's Poetry and Prose,* ed. Donald H. Reiman and Sharon B. Powers (New York: W. W. Norton, 1977), p. 508.

91. Thomas Hobbes, "An Answer of Mr Hobbes to Sr William D'avenant's Preface Before *Gondibert,*" in Davenant, *Works* (London, 1673), p. 27.

92. Hobbes, "An Answer," p. 23.

93. For an extensive argument that the rhetorical force of republican writing emerged in relation to a renewed conception of sublimity, see Norbrook, *Writing the English Republic,* passim.

94. Davenant, "The Author's Preface to his much Honour'd Friend Mr. Hobs," *Works,* p. 17.

95. Davenant, "The Author's Preface," p. 6. The trope of the mob as monster was a commonplace of renaissance humanism; see, for example, Erasmus, *The Praise of Folly,* trans. Clarence H. Miller (New Haven: Yale University Press, 1979), p. 40: "Such trifles as these [i.e., fables] have an effect on that enormous and powerful monster, the mob." The identification was proverbial in England: see M. P. Tilley, *The Dictionary of Proverbs in England in the Sixteenth and Seventeenth Centuries* (Ann Arbor: University of Michigan Press, 1950), M 1308.

96. Aristotle, *Poetics,* 48a, , trans. Gerald F. Else (Ann Arbor: University of Michigan Press, 1967), pp. 17–18; see also the relevant observations in the useful survey by Joshua Scodel, "Seventeenth-Century English Literary Criticism: Classical Values, English Texts and Contexts," in *The Cambridge History of Literary Criticism: Volume 3: The Renaissance,* ed. Glyn P. Norton (Cambridge: Cambridge University Press, 1999), pp. 543–54, esp. 548–49; and, more generally, on the political implications of *mimesis* in Aristotle's thought, see Amélie Oksenberg Rorty, "The Psychology of Aristotlelian Tragedy," in *Essays on Aristotle's Poetics,* ed. A. O. Rorty (Princeton: Princeton University Press, 1992), pp. 1–22, esp. 16–18.

97. On Hobbes and Davenant, see Smith, *Literature and Revolution,* pp. 214, 240; see also Steven N. Zwicker, *Lines of Authority: Poltics and Literature in England, 1649–1689* (Ithaca, NY: Cornell University Press, 1993), pp. 20–21: "The *Preface* is an example not of aesthetic language covering a polemical position but of an intellectual structure in which aesthetics argues a polity."

98. I quote the note on the verse from *Milton's Complete Poetical Works Reproduced in Photographic Facsimile,* ed. H. F. Fletcher, 4 vols. (Urbana: University of Illinois Press, 1943–48), 2:204–5.

99. Dryden, *An Essay of Dramatic Poesy, Essays,* ed. W. P. Ker, 2 vols. (Oxford: Clarendon Press, 1900), 1:96–97.

100. The poem is sometimes attributed to Andrew Marvell; see *Poems and Letters,* 1:170, quotation at l.56; and see *Poems AM,* p. 460.

101. Harrington, *Oceana,* p. 8.

102. *Astraea Redux,* ll.46–48, *The Poems of John Dryden: Volume One, 1649–1681,* ed. Paul Hammond (London: Longman, 1995), p. 40. Quotations of Dryden's poems are taken from this edition.

103. John Dryden, *Virgil's Aeneis* (1697), 6.1177, 1173–74, in *The Works of John Dryden: Volumes 5–6,* ed. William Frost and Vinton A. Dearing (Berkeley and Los Angeles: University of California Press, 1987), 5:566.

104. P[atrick] H[ume], *Annotations on Milton's Paradise Lost* (London, 1695), p. 4.

105. YP 3:399; emphasis added. Milton uses the phrase "ancient liberty" in one other place: "I did but prompt the age to quit their clogs / By the known rules of ancient liberty" (Sonnet 12, the second on the detraction which followed *Tetrachordon*). In this context, of course, "ancient liberty" refers to the domestic freedom of divorce, according to the "known rules" of Mosaic Law. In *2 Henry VI,* Jack Cade stirs up the "base peasants" who are his followers by calling upon the same sentiment: "I thought ye would never have given out these arms till you had recovered your ancient freedom" (4.7.167–9, *The Norton Shakespeare,* ed. Stephen Greenblatt et al. [New York: W. W. Norton, 1997], p. 275). For more on the Triennial Act and its future implications, see G. E. Aylmer, *Rebellion or Revolution? England from*

Civil War to Restoration (Oxford: Oxford University Press, 1986), pp. 17–18.

106. The "ancient constitution" was a new history of the effect of common law on the polity of England, which assumed the antiquity of rights and liberties "ranging from freedom of speech in parliament to its regular meetings and, after the civil war . . . , even legal rights concerned with parliamentary representation and the role of the House of Commons in law making." See C. C. Weston, "England: Ancient Constitution and Common Law," in *The Cambridge History of Political Thought*, pp. 374–411 (at 374). In addition to Weston's article, the seminal works on the subject include J. G. A. Pocock, *The Ancient Constitution and the Feudal Law*, 2nd ed. (Cambridge: Cambridge University Press, 1987) and G. Burgess, *The Politics of the Ancient Constitution* (London: Macmillan, 1992). For Milton and the ancient constitution, see von Maltzahn, *Milton's "History of Britain,"* pp. 166–67, 177, 198–223.

107. In his provocative history of the rise of the vernaculars, Auerbach observes that "it is among the high Norman nobility that we discern the first indications that a new literary public was beginning to take form" for the first time in five hundred years in Western Europe, a development "brought about by the conquerors in the twelfth century." See Erich Auerbach, *Literary Language and Its Public in Late Latin Antiquity and in the Middle Ages*, trans. Ralph Manheim (New York: Pantheon, 1965), p. 269.

108. Thomas Warton, *The History of English Poetry*, 3 vols. (London, 1774–81), 1:vi. Warton traces the development of the language and poetry together from the Norman Conquest. The first volume reprints specimens of rhyming poetry from "just after the conquest" to 1200 with commentary on the developing style (1:7–36).

109. Thomas Hobbes, *Leviathan*, ed. Richard Tuck (Cambridge: Cambridge University Press, 1996), pp. 149–50. Dzelzainis explores the implications of a parallel passage in Hobbes's *Behemoth, or The Long Parliament* in "Milton's Classical Republicanism," pp. 3–9.

110. Hobbes, *Leviathan*, pp. 149–50.

111. *Milton: The Critical Heritage*, ed. John T. Shawcross, 2 vols. (London: Routledge and Kegan Paul, 1970–72), 1:78.

112. *Critical Heritage*, ed. Shawcross, 1:83. On the politics of Milton's representation of the origins of Creation in Chaos, see Rogers, *The Matter of Revolution*, pp. 103–76.

113. *Critical Heritage*, ed. Shawcross, 1:124.

114. *Critical Heritage*, ed. Shawcross, 1:264.

115. See von Maltzahn, "The Whig Milton, 1667–1700," in *Milton and Republicanism*, pp. 229–53.

116. *Critical Heritage*, ed. Shawcross, 1:264.

117. Thomas Jefferson, "Thoughts on English Prosody," *Writings*, ed. Merrill D. Peterson (New York: Library of America, 1984), pp. 594–622 (quotation at

618). For a richly suggestive account of Jefferson's lifelong interest in Milton, which first alerted me to the existence of "Thoughts on English Prosody," see Hugh Jenkins, "Jefferson (Re)Reading Milton," *Milton Quarterly* 32 (1998): 32–38.

118. A nearly complete list of rhymes can be found in John S. Diekhoff, "Rhyme in *Paradise Lost*," *PMLA* 49 (1934): 539–43. Frank Kermode offers some preliminary suggestions for interpretation of these and similar sonic clusters in thematically rich moments of temptation in "Adam Unparadised," *The Living Milton*, ed. Frank Kermode (London: Routledge and Kegan Paul, 1960), pp. 96–98.

NOTES TO CHAPTER FOUR

1. L. S. Vygotsky, *Educational Psychology*, trans. Robert Silverman (Boca Raton, Fla.: St. Lucie Press, 1997), p. 231.

2. William Kerrigan, *The Sacred Complex: On the Psychogenesis of "Paradise Lost"* (Cambridge, Mass.: Harvard University Press, 1983), p. 210.

3. To an extent, the epic may even be said to question and ultimately reject the orthodox version of Christian morality so despised by P. B. Shelley in *A Defence of Poetry*, in *Shelley's Poetry and Prose*, ed. Donald H. Reiman and Sharon B. Powers (New York: W. W. Norton, 1977), p. 498: "Milton's poem contains within itself a philosophical refutation of that system of which, by a strange and natural antithesis, it has been a chief popular support." In agreeing with this proposition as a principle of criticism, however, I should say that I do not wish to endorse Shelley's more notorious comment just a few sentences later: "Milton's Devil as a moral being is as far superior to his God as one who perseveres in some purpose which he has conceived to be excellent in spite of adversity and torture, is to one who in the cold security of undoubted triumph inflicts the most horrible revenge upon his enemy, not from any mistaken notion of inducing him to repent of a perseverance in enmity, but with the alleged design of exasperating him to deserve new torments." What Shelley gets right, in my view, is the sense of moral outrage, which is perfectly fit to the scale of human ethics; what he gets wrong is Milton's theology, which emphasizes how misapplication of this scale to God forces humanity to construct theodicy. Only when human beings take full cognizance of the sacrifice offered by the Son, as we shall see according to the logic of Milton's great argument, can the apparent incommensurability between God and humanity be in any way "justified."

4. That being said, it seems to me essential not to foreclose the investigation of Milton's multifarious ethical paradoxes by taking recourse in the abrupt solutions offered by Arthur O. Lovejoy, "Milton and the Paradox of the Fortunate Fall," *ELH* 4 (1937), reprinted in *Critical essays on Milton from ELH* (Baltimore: Johns Hopkins University Press, 1969), pp. 163–81. The

"happy ending" Lovejoy foresees as intrinsic to the theology of the poem must, in my view, be weighed against the enormity of the losses suffered to ensure this eventual conclusion. While the tidiness of Lovejoy's explanation is attractive, even tempting, I think the poem demands a more rigorous challenge to its formal assertions of doctrine. To streamline the poem's inquiry into the conditions of human existence in this way entails undervaluing the sacrifice responsible for the poem's expansive vision of faithful human consciousness in the wake of the Fall. Compare William Kerrigan, *The Prophetic Milton* (Charlottesville: University of Virginia Press, 1974), p. 270.

5. Two recent articles have helpfully explored the epic's scenes of pedagogy. Ann Baynes Coiro, "'To repair the ruins of our first parents': *Of Education* and Fallen Adam," *SEL* 28 (1988): 133–47, claims that the two stages of learning (concrete or experiential and abstract) depicted in *Of Education* "correspond to the division of Adam's education between Book XI and Book XII" (134). Coiro shows these correspondences in the curriculum as they relate to the shift from vision to narration and emphasizes the originality of Milton's representation of Michael as a teacher (144). Michael Allen, "Divine Instruction: *Of Education* and the Pedagogy of Raphael, Michael, and the Father," *Milton Quarterly* 26 (1992): 113–21, exploring education *in* the poem but not *by* it, briefly analyzes the differing approaches to instruction in the epic without sufficiently explaining the connections between theology and pedagogy, between Milton's task and the educative tasks of his characters. See also George Williamson, "The Education of Adam," *Modern Philology* 61 (1963): 96–109, reprinted in *Milton: Modern Essays in Criticism*, ed. Arthur Barker (London: Oxford University Press, 1965), pp. 284–307, still valuable for its account of the way "the education of Adam becomes both a structural element in the epic plot and a didactic element in the meaning of *Paradise Lost*" (p. 285).

6. For a subtle interpretation of this principle's literary implications, see Geoffrey Hartman, "Milton's Counterplot," *ELH* 25 (1958): 1–12. On the thematic range of Milton's use of *discordia concors*, see Don Cameron Allen, *The Harmonious Vision: Studies in Milton's Poetry*, enlarged ed. (Baltimore: Johns Hopkins University Press, 1970); William Kolbrener, *Milton's Warring Angels: A Study of Critical Engagements* (Cambridge: Cambridge University Press, 1997), pp. 133–35 and passim; and David Norbrook, *Writing the English Republic: Poetry, Rhetoric and Politics, 1627–1660* (Cambridge: Cambridge University Press, 1999), pp. 444, 448, and esp. 473.

7. Jeffrey S. Shoulson, *Milton and the Rabbis* (New York: Columbia University Press, 2001), p. 107. For another penetrating look at Milton's employment of exegetical models related to midrash, see Sanford Budick, "Milton and the Scene of Interpretation: From Typology toward Midrash," in *Midrash and Literature*, ed. Geoffrey H. Hartman and Sanford Budick (New Haven: Yale University Press, 1986), pp. 195–212.

8. Walter Benjamin, "Theses on the Philosophy of History," *Illuminations,* ed. Hannah Arendt, trans. Henry Zohn (New York: Shocken Books, 1968), p. 263.

9. For more on this point, see Mircea Eliade, *The Sacred and the Profane: The Nature of Religion,* trans. Willard R. Trask (New York: Harcourt, 1957), p. 207.

10. Regina M. Schwartz, *Remembering and Repeating: Biblical Creation in "Paradise Lost"* (Cambridge: Cambridge University Press, 1988), p. 3.

11. For more on the speaker of the epic and the effects of prophecy upon the poetic voice, see my article, "Place, Source, and Voice in *Paradise Lost*," *ELN* 44.1 (March 2006): 57–66.

12. Abraham J. Heschel, *The Prophets* (1962; reprint. New York: Perennial / HarperCollins, 2001), pp. 6, 214.

13. See Kerrigan, *The Prophetic Milton,* esp. pp. 12, 33–37, 173, 184–86.

14. Northrop Frye, *The Great Code: The Bible and Literature* (New York: Harcourt, 1982), pp. 73, 106–107.

15. Jacques Derrida, *Archive Fever: A Freudian Impression,* trans. Eric Prenowitz (Chicago: University of Chicago Press, 1996), p. 36.

16. Georgia Christopher, "Milton and the Reforming Spirit," in *The Cambridge Companion to Milton,* ed. Dennis Danielson, 2nd ed. (Cambridge: Cambridge University Press, 1999), p. 195.

17. Dietrich Bonhoeffer, *Creation and Fall,* trans. John C. Fletcher, *Two Biblical Studies* (1959; reprint: New York: Touchstone / Simon and Schuster, 1997), p. 10. The commentary comprises lectures delivered in the winter semester of 1932–33 at the University of Berlin, originally published in German in 1937.

18. Bonhoeffer, *Creation and Fall,* p. 94.

19. G. W. F. Hegel, *Lectures on the Philosophy of Religion* (1824), trans. R. F. Brown (Berkeley: University of California Press, 1984), p. 123. I have modified the translation slightly.

20. Jacques Lacan, "The Agency of the Letter in the Unconscious, or Reason Since Freud" (1957), *Écrits: A Selection,* trans. Alan Sheridan (New York: W. W. Norton, 1977), p. 174.

21. Recent influential proponents of this view include Gerald L. Bruns, *Hermeneutics Ancient and Modern* (New Haven: Yale University Press, 1991), pp. 139–163; and Paul Ricoeur, "Philosophical Hermeneutics and Biblical Hermeneutics" and "The Model of the Text: Meaningful Action Considered as a Text," *From Text to Action: Essays in Hermeneutics, II,* trans. Kathleen Blamey and John B. Thompson (Evanston: Northwestern University Press, 1991), pp. 89–101 and 144–67.

22. The interplay between these two positions may be seen as arising out of the English Reformation(s). There are precedents in the opposition between William Tyndale and Thomas More. See Stephen Greenblatt, *Renaissance*

Self-Fashioning: More to Shakespeare (Chicago: University of Chicago Press, 1980), pp. 74–114.

23. See James Grantham Turner, *One Flesh: Paradisal Marriage and Sexual Relations in the Age of Milton* (Oxford: Clarendon Press, 1987); Mary Nyquist, "The Genesis of Gendered Subjectivity in the Divorce Tracts and in *Paradise Lost*," in *Re-membering Milton: Essays on the Texts and Traditions,* ed. Mary Nyquist and Margaret W. Ferguson (New York: Methuen, 1987), pp. 99–127.

24. William Tyndale, *A Compendious Introduccion unto the Pistle to the Romayns* (Worms, 1526), sig. aii recto. Tyndale translates Luther's preface to the Romans, which is readily available in modern (though less powerful) English translation in Martin Luther, *Selections from his Writings,* ed. John Dillenberger (New York: Anchor / Doubleday, 1962), pp. 19–34.

25. Mary Carruthers, *The Book of Memory: A Study of Memory in Medieval Culture* (Cambridge: Cambridge University Press, 1990).

26. Alister E. McGrath, *The Intellectual Origins of the European Reformation,* 2nd ed. (Oxford: Blackwell, 2004), p. 49.

27. On this process as it relates specifically to exegetical techniques, see Brian Cummings, *The Literary Culture of the Reformation: Grammar and Grace* (Oxford: Oxford University Press, 2002), esp. pp. 57–79. See also Donald J. Wilcox, *In Search of God and Self: Renaissance and Reformation Thought* (Boston: Houghton Mifflin, 1975), pp. 288–306, for a concise account that places Luther's emphasis on inwardness in the context of the intellectual history of the period.

28. Tyndale, *Introduccion unto the Pistle to the Romaynes,* sig. aii recto.

29. George Herbert, *A Priest to the Temple, or, The Country Parson,* chap. 33, *Works,* ed. F. E. Hutchinson, corrected ed. (Oxford: Clarendon Press, 1945), p. 278.

30. Dr. Williams's Library, Gordon Square, London, Jones MS. B 62, fol. 74^r; available in facsimile as *The Williams Manuscript of George Herbert's Poems,* ed. Amy M. Charles (Delmar, NY: Scholars' Facsimiles and Reprints, 1977).

31. Augustine, *On Christian Doctrine,* 1.37–38 and 2.6, trans. D. W. Robertson, Jr. (New York and Indianapolis: Bobbs-Merrill, 1958), pp. 30–31, 38.

32. Gregorius Magnus, *Moralia,* in *Patrologia Latina,* ed. J. P. Migne (Paris, 1849), vol. 75, col. 515a. I quote from the fourth chapter of the epistle dedicatory of Gregory's exposition of Job.

33. A. J. Minnis, "The Significance of the Medieval Theory of Authorship," in *Authorship: From Plato to the Postmodern,* ed. Seán Burke (Edinburgh: Edinburgh University Press, 1995), pp. 23–30.

34. Mary Thomas Crane, *Framing Authority: Sayings, Self, and Society in Sixteenth-Century England* (Princeton: Princeton University Press, 1993), p. 162.

35. Marshall Grossman, *"Authors to Themselves": Milton and the Revelation of History* (Cambridge: Cambridge University Press, 1987), treats this theme

with great depth and sensitivity. See also the perceptive remarks in his "Milton and the Rhetoric of Prophecy," *The Cambridge Companion to Milton,* ed. Dennis Danielson (Cambridge: Cambridge University Press, 1989), esp. pp. 176–77.

36. For the historical details, I am indebted to Christopher Hill, *The English Bible and the Seventeenth-Century Revolution* (London: Allen Lane / Penguin, 1993), pp. 381–83. Hill adduces helpful context in the service of a rather too straightforwardly topical reading of the Psalm translations as antiroyalist poems. See also the further contexts provided by Margaret Boddy, "Milton's Translations of Psalms 80–88," *Modern Philology* 64 (1966): 1–9.

37. The implications of this historical fact for religious lyric in the seventeenth century are vast; see Nigel Smith, *Literature and Revolution, 1640–1660* (New Haven: Yale University Press, 1994), pp. 260–76.

38. Mary Ann Radzinowicz, *Milton's Epics and the Book of Psalms* (Princeton: Princeton University Press, 1989), p. 204.

39. Barbara Kiefer Lewalski, *Protestant Poetics and the Seventeenth-Century Religious Lyric* (Princeton: Princeton University Press, 1979), pp. 31–53, shows that the Psalms were regarded as representing "a compendium of lyric kinds" (p. 45).

40. Graham Hughes, *Hebrews and Hermeneutics: The Epistle to Hebrews as a New Testament Example of Biblical Interpretation* (Cambridge: Cambridge University Press, 1979), p. 3.

41. *The Poems of Sir Philip Sidney,* ed. William A. Ringler (Oxford: Clarendon Press, 1962), p. 278.

42. For a thorough historical explanation of this point, see Neil Forsyth, *The Satanic Epic* (Princeton: Princeton University Press, 2003), p. 183.

43. Nigel Smith, "*Paradise Lost* from Civil War to Restoration," in *The Cambridge Companion to Writing of the English Revolution,* ed. N. H. Keeble (Cambridge: Cambridge University Press, 2001), p. 263.

44. The underlined verse is Ps. 2.12. Milton cites verse 2.6 at YP 6:207 and 435 (twice) and verse 2.7 at YP 6:166, 206, 207, 235, 266, and 277, according to Michael Bauman, *A Scripture Index to John Milton's "De doctrina christiana"* (Binghamton: MRTS, 1989), p. 48. See CM 18:560–61 for evidence of Milton's underlining, bracketing, and miscellaneous marks in his copy of the 1612 KJV. See also Radzinowicz, *Milton's Epics,* pp. 200–9, for commentary on Milton's favorite Psalms.

45. Charles Dahlberg, "*Paradise Lost* V, 603, and Milton's Psalm II," *Modern Language Notes* 67 (1952): 23–24.

46. Craig R. Koester, *Hebrews,* The Anchor Bible (New York: Anchor / Doubleday, 2001), p. 199.

47. Koester, *Hebrews,* p. 222.

48. Forsyth, *The Satanic Epic,* pp. 174–75. Forsyth's analysis of Satan's rebellion in *Paradise Lost,* pp. 167–87, can be profitably supplemented by the magisterial

analysis of the motif as it recurs in ancient Near Eastern, Greek, and Hebrew mythologies down to the Church Fathers in Forsyth's first book, *The Old Enemy: Satan and the Combat Myth* (Princeton: Princeton University Press, 1987).

49. "The First Epistle of the Second Book of *Horace* Imitated" (1733), l. 102, *The Twickenham Edition of the Poems of Alexander Pope*, ed. John Butt et al., 11 vols. (New Haven: Yale University Press, 1939–69), 4:203.

50. For more on the theological perplexities, see Dennis Berthold, "The Concept of Merit in *Paradise Lost*," *SEL* 15 (1975): 153–67.

51. On the implications of contradictory and reversible etymologies in usage and representation, see Sigmund Freud, "The Antithetical Meaning of Primal Words," *The Standard Edition of the Complete Psychological Works of Sigmund Freud*, trans. James Strachey et al., vol. 11 (London: The Hogarth Press, 1957), pp. 155–61. For a freshly illuminating discussion of the evil represented in Milton's Satan's claim of self-generation and independence, see Steven Batchelor, *Living with the Devil: A Meditation on Good and Evil* (New York: Riverhead Books, 2004), pp. 35–38.

52. John Toland, *The Life of John Milton* (1698), in *The Early Lives of Milton*, ed. Helen Darbishire (London: Constable, 1932), p. 180. For more on Tomkins, see Nicholas von Maltzahn, "The First Reception of *Paradise Lost* (1667)," pp. 480–87.

53. For an excellent overview of this quality of satanic rhetoric, see David Loewenstein, "The Radical Religious Politics of *Paradise Lost*," in *A Companion to Milton*, ed. Thomas N. Corns (Oxford: Blackwell, 2001), pp. 348–62, esp. 350–53. Loewenstein quotes Walwyn, *The Fountain of Slander*, on p. 350.

54. George Steiner, *The Grammars of Creation* (New Haven: Yale University Press, 2001), p. 49.

55. Compare 1 Chronicles 21:1, the only place in the Hebrew Scripture where a figure named Satan, without the definite article preceding his designation, "stood up against Israel, and provoked David to number Israel" (KJV). See the discussion in Forsyth, *The Satanic Epic*, pp. 37–38.

56. See Janel Mueller, "Dominion as Domesticity: Milton's Imperial God and the Experience of History," in *Milton and the Imperial Vision*, ed. Balachandra Rajan and Elizabeth Sauer (Pittsburgh: Duquesne University Press, 1999), pp. 35–36.

57. The translation is that of John Carey, in *Poems*, p. 349. Juvenal (1.15–16) reads: "Et nos / consilium dedimus Sullae, privates ut altum / dormiret."

58. Tacitus, *Annals*, 1.11, 1.10, ed. and trans. John Jackson, 2 vols. LCL (Cambridge, Mass.: Harvard University Press, 1931), 1:260–65.

59. Like the blanket use of the *lex maiestatis* for which Tacitus attacked Tiberius, "reason of state" (from the Italian *ragione di stato* and the French *raison d'é-tat*) came in the Renaissance to symbolize a monarch's assumption of

absolute rule, transcending the customary allowance of the law. See Tacitus, *Annals,* 1.72, pp. 366ff. For an important cautionary note concerning the topicality of Tacitus's critique of Tiberius as an encoded censure of Domitian's abuse of the *lex maiestatis,* see R. Syme, *Tacitus,* 2 vols. (Oxford: Clarendon Press, 1958), 1:422. Peter Burke, "Tacitism, Scepticism, and Reason of State," in *The Cambridge History of Political Thought, 1450–1700,* ed. J. H. Burns with Mark Goldie (Cambridge: Cambridge University Press, 1991), pp. 479–98, provides a useful if overly general survey of Tactitus's reception in the broader European context; see also Malcolm Smuts, "Court-Centred Politics and the Uses of Roman Historians, *c.* 1590–1630," in *Culture and Politics in Early Stuart England,* ed. Kevin Sharpe and Peter Lake (Stanford: Stanford University Press, 1993), pp. 21–43, which argues that the appeal to Tacitus's authority in the English Renaissance often provided a cover for advocacy of Machiavellian statecraft.

60. See Keith W. F. Stavely, "Satan and Arminianism in *Paradise Lost,*" *Milton Studies* 25 (1989): 125–39.

61. I do not mean, by citing this poem, necessarily to concede that Milton's depiction of Satan ought to be read after the fashion of a roman à clef, though there has recently been a great deal of speculation about the possible identification of Satan and the Lord Protector. I want to resist the urge to put too much specificity into the literary Satan, though I think, following some very perceptive criticism on the part of David Norbrook (*Writing the English Republic,* pp. 442, 446, 453–4, 477), that Milton may very well have had Cromwell's more imperialistic designs and monarchical trappings in mind when he was representing Satan. On the possibility of the identification, see also Merritt Y. Hughes, "Satan and the 'Myth' of the Tyrant," *Ten Perspectives on Milton* (New Haven: Yale University Press, 1965), pp. 165–95, esp. 174–75, where he shows that Vondel, *Lucifer,* "had Cromwell's rise to power as a kind of objective correlative for the action of those first three acts"; in his edition, Hughes, p. 287n., relates that, in *Adamo caduto* 5.2, "Salandra has Satan tell the devils that they are going to corrupt mankind by inventing *ragione di stato.*" John Leonard, in his edition of *The Complete Poems* (Harmondsworth: Penguin, 1998), p. 765, insists that "'necessity' was really Cromwell's word," an essential part of Cromwell's vocabulary in his various public relations campaigns against Charles I, the Levellers, the Rump, and the Barebones Parliament. Much the best treatment of the relations between the Lord Protector and his Secretary of Foreign Tongues is that of Blair Worden, "John Milton and Oliver Cromwell," in *Soldiers, Writers and Statesmen of the English Revolution,* ed. Ian Gentles, John Morrill, and Blair Worden (Cambridge: Cambridge University Press, 1998), pp. 243–64; though Worden does not specifically discuss *Paradise Lost* there, his earlier essay, "Milton's Republicanism and the Tyranny of Heaven," in *Machiavelli and Republicanism,* ed. Gisela Bock, Quentin Skinner, and

Maurizio Viroli (Cambridge: Cambridge University Press, 1990), pp. 225–45, contains many important insights about Milton's commitment to the principles of mixed government as derived from Aristotle and Polybius and the implications of this commitment for Milton's relationship with Cromwell (e.g., p. 228). While I have learned much from Worden's evolving interpretation of Milton's politics, I think he is mistaken when he dismisses the potential for political intent in the later poetry, as on p. 244: "Milton does not merely return to his right hand, from prose to poetry: he withdraws from politics into faith." To argue thus is to disregard the fact that political truths have their place, too, amongst what Worden calls "eternal verities."

62. Thucydides, *The Peloponnesian War,* trans. Thomas Hobbes (1628), 6.18, ed. David Grene (1959; reprint Chicago: University of Chicago Press, 1989), p. 388. Alcibiades, also like Satan, epitomizes self-interest in his leadership of the oligarchic coup of 411 B.C.E.; see Thucydides, 8.48 (Hobbes, p. 530).

63. Ben Jonson, *Sejanus His Fall,* ed. Philip J. Ayres, The Revels Plays (Manchester: Manchester University Press, 1990), 3.740–41. Perhaps the best illustration of "reason of state" in the literature of the English Renaissance, the whole of Macro's speech (3.714–49) provides an excellent comparison. In fact, Jonson was one of the first in English to translate the idiom, as in *Cynthia's Revels* (1599), 1.1, and *Volpone* (1605), 4.1, though it was also surely gaining in currency as a result of Bacon's usage of the Italian in *The Advancement of Learning;* see *The Oxford Authors: Francis Bacon,* ed. Brian Vickers (Oxford: Oxford University Press, 1996), p. 128.

64. See Fowler's note to the passage (p. 516), which adduces Porphyry and St. Bernard as well as Berchorius.

65. Seneca, *On Providence,* sections 2 and 4, trans. M. Hadas, *The Stoic Philosophy of Seneca* (New York: W. W. Norton, 1958). I owe this reference to Professor Walter Englert of Reed College.

66. Fowler's groundbreaking schematic discussion of chronology is still the best help for untangling the difficulties; see his recent modification in the introduction to his second edition, pp. 29–33. For a discussion of some unresolved problems of chronology in *Paradise Lost* that challenges the tidiness of Fowler's scheme, following the suggestions of Newton and other eighteenth-century readers of the poem who thought that the chronology was flawed, see Anthony Welch, "Reconsidering Chronology in *Paradise Lost,*" *Milton Studies* 41 (2002): 1–17.

67. Forsyth, *The Satanic Epic,* pp. 6, 26.

68. Christopher Ricks, *Milton's Grand Style* (Oxford: Clarendon Press, 1963), pp. 15, 66–75.

69. Contrary to Stanley Fish, *Surprised by Sin: The Reader in "Paradise Lost,"* 2nd ed. (Cambridge, Mass: Harvard University Press, 1997), p. 148, I do not believe that most readers "forget" Raphael's mediation as narrator, so that

"The reader is alone with God and with all the thought he has brought with him from the experience of the poem." See Raphael's intrusions into his own narrative, at, e.g., 5.628–29, 5.658, 5.751ff., 5.760ff., 6.74ff., 6.91, 6.200, 6.217–20, 6.373ff., 6.501ff., 6.571ff., 6.769, 6.893–912, 7.296, 7.493f., 7.535ff., 7.561, 7.635ff.

70. Jonathan Richardson, father and son, *Explanatory Notes and Remarks on Milton's Paradise Lost* (1734), in *Early Lives*, ed. Darbishire, pp. 315–16.

71. See Richardson, in *Early Lives*, p. 326.

72. The hermeneutic paradigm I am attributing to Richardson is, in fact, a deeply traditional one, which Augustine promotes in *On Christian Doctrine* and which has been influentially reintroduced in modern theory by Ricoeur, "The Model of the Text: Meaningful Action Considered as a Text," *From Text to Action*, pp. 144–67.

73. I have treated the significance of Milton's use of anaphora more fully in "Place, Source, and Voice in *Paradise Lost.*"

74. The question seems to have been posed first by Tertullian, *Adversus Marcionem*, 1.2.2, as David Scott Kastan notes in the introduction to his revised edition of Merritt Y. Hughes, ed., *Paradise Lost* (Indianapolis and Cambridge: Hackett Pubishing, 2005), p. xxii. The phrasing gets taken up by other church fathers as well, perhaps most influentially by Augustine: "et quarebam unde malum, et malum quaerebam, et in ipsa inquisitione mea non videbam malum." *The Confessions of Saint Augustine*, ed. J.J. O'Donnell, 7.5.7. O'Donnell has made his authoritative 1992 Oxford edition, with its excellent commentary, available online, now at <www.stoa.org/hippo>. This passage, in which Augustine laments that he neglected to see the evil way of his own search for the origin of evil, employs the Vulgate's term for "evil," *malum*, which also signifies "apple." The pun, from which the identification of the fruit of the forbidden tree with the apple originally derives, can be found throughout early Christian literature on the problem of evil, but Milton makes the allusion to the fruit as an apple specific to Satan, as shown by Forsyth, *The Satanic Epic*, p. 196.

75. For a thorough and informative discussion of the topic in Plato, see Gregory Vlastos, "Socrates' Disavowal of Knowledge," *Philosophical Quarterly* 35 (1985): 1–31. Though Vlastos discourages easy resolution of the paradoxical disavowal of certainty, and instead asserts the uncertainty of metaphysical knowledge as opposed to the moral truths, my emphasis is on the effect of the Socratic dialogues upon Socrates' interlocutors rather than Socratic epistemology.

76. The dialectical interaction, as I show in the following paragraphs, is in structure thoroughly Platonic, *pace* Hugh MacCallum, *Milton and the Sons of God: The Divine Image in Milton's Epic Poetry* (Toronto: University of Toronto Press, 1986), p. 135: "Adam establishes his identity, not by introspection, but by engagement with the world around him. In this, Milton's

treatment seems more Aristotelian than Platonic, at least in the sense those terms held for the seventeenth-century reader."

77. Irene Samuel, *Plato and Milton* (Ithaca, NY: Cornell University Press, 1947), discusses the dialogue at 8.364–451, though she remarkably fails to consider the implications of the divine dissembling, preferring instead a somewhat unsystematic comparison between the idea of love in *Paradise Lost* and that propounded by Diotima in *The Symposium* (see pp. 162–68). Discussing the development of Adam's knowledge, Samuel states the belief that the sophistical structure of argumentation is merely a satanic appurtenance (see pp. 110–23, esp. 118 and 123). It is surprising, given her emphasis on the way in which the great poems have "a function other than, yet not unconnected with, the revelation of the Beautiful, a work to be done in the realms of true doctrine and social good as well," that Samuel has neglected to analyze the forms in which Plato conveyed his thought. Instead her reading is largely thematic and unphilosophical.

78. Thomas H. Luxon, "Milton's Wedded Love: Not about Sex (As We Know It)," *Milton Studies* 40 (2001): 38–60, is a notable exception, though his primary focus among the dialogues remains *Symposium*.

79. Barbara K. Lewalski, *The Life of John Milton* (Oxford: Blackwell, 2000), p. 460.

80. See Gregory Vlastos, "The Socratic Elenchus," *Oxford Studies in Ancient Philosophy* 1 (1983): 27–58, which provides useful working definitions of all the key terms and lucidly explains the structural significance for each form of Socratic argumentation.

81. Plato, *Gorgias*, 463d, in *Euthyphro, Apology, Crito, Meno, Gorgias, Menexenus,* trans. R. E. Allen (New Haven: Yale University Press, 1984), p. 248. Henceforth quotations from Plato will be cited by Stephanus page numbers parenthetically.

82. Plato, *Sophist,* trans. Seth Benardete (Chicago: University of Chicago Press, 1986). Subsequent quotations will appear in the text.

83. Plato, *Phaedrus,* trans. Alexander Nehamas and Paul Woodruff, in *Plato: Complete Works,* ed. John M. Cooper (Indianapolis and Cambridge: Hackett, 1997), pp. 506–56.

84. Plato, *The Symposium,* trans. R. E. Allen (New Haven: Yale University Press, 1991). Subsequent references to this translation will appear in the text.

85. Plato, *Theaetetus,* trans. Seth Benardete (Chicago: University of Chicago Press, 1986). Quotations from this translation will appear subsequently in the text.

86. Lewis Campbell, ed., *The Theaetetus of Plato with a Revised Text and English Notes* (Oxford: Clarendon Press, 1883), ad loc (= pp. 30–31).

87. For the connection between the method of education expounded in *Theaetetus* 148e-151b and the theory of anamnesis, or learning by recollection, best explained in the *Meno,* see the commentary in F. M. Cornford,

Plato's Theory of Knowledge: The "Theaetetus" and the "Sophist" of Plato trans-
lated with a running commentary (London: Routledge and Kegan Paul,
1935), pp. 27–28. Cornford shows that Socrates in the *Theaetetus* is quot-
ing Meno's complaint that Socrates is merely reducing others to a state of
perplexity (79e). For a thorough revaluation of the Socratic method as
evinced in the *Meno* and elsewhere, see Alexander Nehemas, *Virtues of
Authenticity: Essays on Plato and Socrates* (Princeton: Princeton University
Press, 1999), pp. 3–82.

88. Augustine, *Confessions,* 10.11.18, trans. Henry Chadwick (Oxford: Oxford
     University Press, 1991), p. 189. Henceforth I will cite this translation par-
     enthetically by section number in the text.

89. Augustine, *De Trinitate,* 14.30, as quoted in Louis L. Martz, *The Paradise
     Within: Studies in Vaughan, Traherne, and Milton* (New Haven: Yale Univer-
     sity Press, 1964), pp. xviii–xvix. Martz provides a serviceable sketch of the
     impact of Augustinian teachings upon the design of *Paradise Lost* on pp.
     102–67. Although I differ in my interpretation of the nature of Augustine's
     theory of anamnesis, which I see as more integral to the later theory of
     Augustine, and thus to Milton's inheritance of it, than Martz claims, much
     of value remains in his treatment of the epic. My position on Augustine is
     finally closer to that of Brian Stock, *Augustine the Reader: Meditation, Self-
     Knowledge, and the Ethics of Interpretation* (Cambridge, Mass.: Harvard Uni-
     versity Press, 1996), esp. chap. 8, "Memory, Self-Reform, and Time," pp.
     207–42.

90. *The Oxford Authors: Francis Bacon,* ed. Vickers, p. 120.

91. Fulke Greville, *A Treatie of Humane Learning,* 25.1–2, in *Poems and Dra-
     mas,* ed. Geoffrey Bullough, 2 vols. (New York: Oxford University Press,
     1945), 1:160.

92. See Maimonides, *The Guide of the Perplexed,* 3.23, trans. Shlomo Pines, 2
     vols. (Chicago: University of Chicago Press, 1963), 2:496–97: "But the
     notion of His providence is not the same as the notion of our providence;
     nor is the notion of His governance of the things created by Him the same
     as the notion of our governance of that which we govern. The two notions
     are not comprised in one definition, contrary to what is thought by all those
     who are confused, and there is nothing in common between the two except
     the name alone. In the same way, our act does not resemble His act; and the
     two are not comprised in one and the same definition. Just as natural acts
     differ from those of craftsmanship, so do the divine governance of, the
     divine providence for, and the divine purpose with regard to, those natural
     matters differ from our human governance of, providence for, and purpose
     with regard to, the things we govern, we provide for, and we purpose. This
     is the object of the *Book of Job* as a whole; I refer to the establishing of this
     foundation for belief and the drawing attention to the inference to be
     drawn from natural matters, so that you should not fall into error and seek

to affirm in your imagination that His knowledge is like our knowledge or that His purpose and His providence and His governance are like our purpose and our providence and our governance. If man knows this, every misfortune will be borne lightly by him."

93. Marshall Grossman, "The Rhetoric of Feminine Priority and the Ethics of Form in *Paradise Lost,*" *English Literary Renaissance* 33 (2004): 424–43 (at 431).

94. E. J. Speiser, ed. and trans., *Genesis,* The Anchor Bible (New York: Doubleday, 1964), pp. 24–25.

95. Martin Luther, *Lectures on Genesis, Luther's Works,* ed. Jaroslav Pelikan et al., 55 vols. (Saint Louis: Concordia, 1958–76), 1:173, 176.

96. But see Richard Strier, "Milton against Humility," in *Religion and Culture in Renaissance England,* ed. Claire McEachern and Debora Shuger (Cambridge: Cambridge University Press, 1997), pp. 258–86, esp. 272–273, which argues that the transformative moment is not the emotional and distinctively Christian humility of Eve so much as the classically rigorous intellectual clarity of Adam's rebuke.

97. Here I agree with Stanley Fish, *Surprised by Sin,* that the historical particularity of the postlapsarian context within which a given reader would experience the representation of paradise would, inevitably, be common to all who could conceivably read the poem.

98. "Holy irony" is a term used in *Order and Disorder* (1679) to describe God's reaction to the transgression, "Whence man the folly of his pride might see." See Lucy Hutchinson, *Order and Disorder,* ed. David Norbrook (Oxford: Blackwell, 2001), 5.293–94ff. (at p. 74).

99. I therefore disagree with the position of Stanley Fish, which sees all didacticism in the poem as stemming ultimately from a voice of authority. See the remark in Fish's recent preface to the second edition of *Surprised by Sin,* p. x: the poem's method "is to provoke in its readers wayward fallen responses which are then corrected by one of several authoritative voices (the narrator, God, Raphael, Michael, the Son)."

100. Though not, as the additions to the *Artis Logicae* suggest, without a certain degree of skepticism. For the implications of the Ramistic use of argumentation by "similars" for Miltonic simile in *Paradise Lost,* see Christopher Grose, *Milton's Epic Process: "Paradise Lost" and Its Miltonic Background* (New Haven: Yale University Press, 1973), pp. 123–87, esp., on the skepticism, pp. 128–35.

101. For more on this topic and its impact on the religious writing of the early modern period, see Geoffrey Hill, *Style and Faith* (New York: Counterpoint, 2003), esp. pp. 21–70. See also Cummings, *The Literary Culture of the Reformation.*

102. H. R. MacCallum, "Milton and Figurative Interpretation of the Bible," *University of Toronto Quarterly* 31 (1962): 407, 412.

103. It should be clear that I am not entirely convinced by the effort to devalue Milton's consideration of the Analogy of Faith in Georgia Christopher, *Milton and*

the Science of the Saints (Princeton: Princeton University Press, 1983), pp. 4–14 and passim. In my reading, Christopher has overstated the difference from traditional exegetical methodology. It is not so much the technique or means, I think, as the end to which such means were put that differentiates between the "evangelical" and scholastic uses of allegorical interpretation. For more on the relationships among Michael's pedagogy, typology, allegory, exegesis, and the structure of the last two books, which "must be seen as almost geometrical in its exactness," see Edward W. Tayler, *Milton's Poetry: Its Development in Time* (Pittsburgh: Duquesne University Press, 1979), pp. 71–72ff.

104. Jason P. Rosenblatt, *Torah and Law in "Paradise Lost"* (Princeton: Princeton University Press, 1994), p. 42. Rosenblatt further argues that "Before the Fall, the Miltonic bard had diplomatically excluded from paradise the reader's determining knowledge of fallen history, thus preserving our first parents' freedom and dignity" (ibid.).

105. There are several good treatments of the exegetical task in Books 11 and 12, but probably the most influential interpretation of Milton's reliance upon Reformation messianic glosses on Gen. 3:15 is that of Christopher, *Milton and the Science of the Saints,* esp. pp. 138–40, which explains the specific strategic importance of the fact that the Son delivers the *protevangelium* in Book 10.179–81 as a representation of the Reformers' sacramental connection "between Christ and the verbal promise about him." Another very learned source for information on the subject is C. A. Patrides, "The 'Protevangelium' in Renaissance Theology and *Paradise Lost,*" *SEL* 3 (1963): 19–30, as well as the more condensed treatment in his *Milton and the Christian Tradition* (Oxford: Clarendon Press, 1966), pp. 123ff.

106. Luther, *Lectures on Genesis, Works,* ed. Pelikan, 1:162.

107. G. W. Leibniz, *Theodicy,* trans. E. M. Huggard, in *The Problem of Evil: A Reader,* ed. Mark Larrimore (Oxford: Blackwell, 2001), p. 198.

108. John Hick, *Evil and the God of Love,* rev. ed. (1966; New York and San Francisco: Harper Collins, 1977).

109. Tyndale, *A compendious introduccion . . . to the pistle off Paul to the Romayns,* sig. aiii verso.

110. William Hayley, *Conjectures on the Origin of the 'Paradise Lost,'* appended to *The Life of Milton,* 2nd ed. (1796), facsimile ed. Joseph Anthony Wittreich, Jr. (Gainesville, Fla.: Scholar's Facsimiles and Reprints, 1970), p. 276. Milton's indictment of the use of force as a lesser form that reveals a greater form of heroism may be illuminated through an intuitive link to that of Simone Weil, "The *Iliad,* or the Poem of Force" (1939), in *War and the Iliad,* trans. Mary McCarthy (New York: New York Review Books, 2005), pp. 3–37.

111. Emmanuel Levinas, "Useless Suffering," trans. Richard Cohen, in *The Problem of Evil,* ed. Larrimore, pp. 371–80 (quotations at 378 and 376).

112. Martz, *The Paradise Within,* p. 115.
113. I find much to agree with in Anthony Low, "The Fall into Subjectivity: Milton's 'Paradise Within' and 'Abyss of Fears and Horrors,'" in *Reading the Renaissance: Ideas and Idioms from Shakespeare to Milton,* ed. Marc Berley (Pittsburgh: Duquesne University Press, 2003), pp. 205–32, which argues that both a darker internalization and a redemptive interiority become possible after the Fall.
114. For a more topical reading of the "paradise within" as an antimonarchical challenge to the "spectacle of state," see Laura Lunger Knoppers, *Historicizing Milton: Spectacle, Power, and Poetry in Restoration England* (Athens: University of Georgia Press, 1994), p. 10. For an excellent contextual account of the religious history, see N. H. Keeble, *The Literary Culture of Nonconformity in Later Seventeenth-Century England* (Athens: University of Georgia Press, 1987), chap. 6.

NOTES TO THE CODA

1. Aristotle, *Metaphysics,* 980a, 981b, *The Basic Works of Aristotle,* ed. Richard McKeon (New York: Random House, 1941), pp. 689, 690.
2. Montaigne, "Of Experience," *Essayes,* trans. John Florio (1603; reprint.: New York: Modern Library, n.d.), p. 967.
3. Francis Bacon, "Of Studies," *Essays* (1625), *The Oxford Authors: Francis Bacon,* ed. Brian Vickers (Oxford: Oxford University Press, 1996), p. 439.
4. Samuel Johnson, *The Adventurer,* No. 85 (28 August 1753), *The Oxford Authors: Samuel Johnson,* ed. Donald Greene (Oxford: Oxford University Press, 1984), p. 273. Johnson's quotation reads "conversation" in place of Bacon's "conference," p. 269.
5. Sir Thomas Browne, "To the Reader," *Pseudodoxia Epidemica, The Major Works,* ed. C. A . Patrides (Harmondsworth: Penguin, 1977), p. 165.
6. This debate attracted a great deal of attention in Milton criticism. See in particular G. F. Sensabaugh, "Milton on Learning," *Studies in Philology* 43 (1946): 258–72; and Irene Samuel, "Milton on Learning and Wisdom," *PMLA* 64 (1949): 708–23. Francis C. Blessington, *"Paradise Lost" and the Classical Epic* (Boston and London: Routledge and Kegan Paul, 1979), p. xii, ably deflects the attack on classical contexts for interpreting Milton's epic.
7. For more on this aspect of *Paradise Regained,* see my entry, "John Milton," *The Oxford Encyclopedia of British Literature,* ed. David Scott Kastan et al. 5 vols. (New York and Oxford: Oxford University Press, 2006), 3:505–15.
8. Douglas Bush, *The Renaissance and English Humanism* (Toronto: University of Toronto Press, 1939), p. 125.
9. Hans Blumenberg, *The Legitimacy of the Modern Age,* trans. Robert M. Wallace (Cambridge, Mass.: MIT Press, 1983), p. 163.

10. On the problem of locating Milton within conventional periods of intellectual history, see most recently Jack Lynch, "Betwixt Two Ages Cast: Milton, Johnson, and the English Renaissance," *Journal of the History of Ideas* 61 (2000): 397–413. The climax of Renaissance culture, as William J. Bouwsma has argued, may be seen as having been simultaneous with the decline of that same culture. See *The Waning of the Renaissance 1550–1640* (New Haven: Yale University Press, 2000).

Bibliography

PRIMARY

An Endeavour after the reconcilement of that long debated and much lamented difference between the godly Presbyterians, and Independents; About Church-government. In a discourse touching the Jews Synagogue. London, 1647/8.

Apollodorus. *The Library.* Trans. J. G. Frazer. 2 vols. LCL. Cambridge, Mass.: Harvard University Press, 1921.

Apolonios Rhodios. *The Argonautika.* Trans. Peter Green. Berkeley: University of California Press, 1997.

Aquinas, Thomas. *Selected Writings.* Trans. Ralph McInerny. Harmondsworth: Penguin, 1998.

Aratus. *Phainomena kai diosaemia.* Ed. Guillaume Morel. Paris, 1559.

Aristotle. *Basic Works.* Ed. Richard B. McKeon. New York: Random House, 1941.

———. *Nichomachean Ethics.* Trans. Roger Crisp. Cambridge: Cambridge University Press, 2000.

———. *Poetics.* Trans. Gerald F. Else. Ann Arbor: University of Michigan, 1969.

Ascham, Roger. *The Schoolmaster (1570).* Ed. Lawrence V. Ryan. Charlottesville: University of Virginia Press, 1967.

Augustine. *Confessions.* Trans. Henry Chadwick. Oxford: Oxford University Press, 1991.

———. *On Christian Doctrine.* Trans. D. W. Robertson, Jr. New York and Indianapolis: Bobbs-Merrill, 1958.

———. *City of God.* Trans. Henry Bettenson. Harmondsworth: Penguin, 1972.

Bacon, Francis. *The Oxford Authors: Francis Bacon.* Ed. Brian Vickers. Oxford: Oxford University Press, 1996.

Blackburne, Francis. *Remarks on Johnson's Life of Milton. To which are added, Milton's Tractate of education and Areopagitica.* London, 1780.

Broughton, Hugh. *Daniel his Chaldie visions and his Ebrew.* London, 1596.

———. *A reuelation of the holy Apocalyps.* Middelburg, 1610.

Browne, Sir Thomas. *The Major Works.* Ed. C. A. Patrides. Harmondsworth: Penguin, 1977.

Calvin, Jean. *Institutes of the Christian Religion.* Trans. Henry Beveridge. 1845. Reprint. Grand Rapids: Eerdmans, 1995.

Castiglione, Count Baldassare. *The Book of the Courtier.* Trans. Sir Thomas Hoby. Ed. Virginia Cox. London: Everyman, 1994.

Cicero. *On Duties.* Ed. and trans. Walter Miller. LCL. Cambridge, Mass.: Harvard University Press, 1913.

———. *Pro Archia.* Ed. and trans. N. H. Watts. LCL. Cambridge, Mass.: Harvard University Press, 1923.

———. *Pro Caelio.* Ed. and trans. R. Gardner. Rev. ed. LCL. Cambridge, Mass.: Harvard University Press, 1965.

———. *Pro Murena.* Ed. and trans. Louis E. Lord. LCL. Cambridge, Mass.: Harvard University Press, 1937.

Cicero, Pseudo-. *Rhetorica ad Herennium.* Ed. and trans. H. Caplan. LCL. Cambridge, Mass.: Harvard University Press, 1954.

Comenius, John Amos. *The Great Didactic* (1657). Trans. M. W. Keatinge. 2nd ed. 1910. Reprint. New York: Russell and Russell, 1967.

Darbishire, Helen, ed. *Early Lives of Milton.* London: Constable, 1932.

Davenant, William. *Works.* London, 1673.

Davidson, Peter, ed. *Poetry and Revolution: An Anthology of British and Irish Verse 1625–1660.* Oxford: Oxford University Press, 1998.

Donne, John. *Devotions upon Emergent Occasions.* Ed. Anthony Raspa. Montreal: McGill-Queens University Press, 1975.

———. *The Divine Poems.* Ed. Helen Gardner. Oxford: Clarendon Press, 1952.

———. *Sermons.* Ed. Evelyn M. Simpson and George R. Potter. 10 vols. Berkeley: University of California Press, 1953–62.

Dryden, John. *Essays.* Ed. W. P. Ker. 2 vols. Oxford: Clarendon Press, 1900.

———. *The Poems of John Dryden: Volume One, 1649–1681.* Ed. Paul Hammond. London: Longman, 1995.

———. *Virgil's Aeneis.* Ed. William Frost and Vinton A. Dearing. *The Works of John Dryden: Volumes 5–6.* Berkeley and Los Angeles: University of California Press, 1987.

Edwards, Thomas. *Gangræna.* 2nd ed. enlarged. London, 1646.

Elyot, Sir Thomas. *The Boke Named the Gouernour.* Ed. Henry Herbert Stephen Croft. 2 vols. London: Kegan Paul, 1883.

Erasmus. *De Libero Arbitrio. Luther and Erasmus: Free Will and Salvation.* Ed. and Trans. E. Gordon Rupp and Philip S. Watson. Library of Christian Classics. Philadelphia: Westminster Press, 1969.

Estienne, Robert. [Stephanus]. *Dictionariolum puerorum, tribus linguis Latina, Anglica & Gallica.* Trans. John Vernon. London, 1552.

Euripides. *Euripidis fabulae.* Ed. James Diggle. 2 vols. Oxford: Clarendon Press, 1981–84.

————. *Euripidis Quae Extant Omnia: Tragoediae nempe XX . . .* Ed. Joshua Barnes. Cambridge, 1694.

————. *Euripidis Tragoediae.* Ed. Paulus Stephanus. 2 vols. Geneva, 1602.

————. *Hippolytos.* Ed. W. S. Barrett. Oxford: Clarendon Press, 1964.

————. [*Works*]. Ed. and trans. David Kovacs. LCL. 5 vols. Cambridge, Mass.: Harvard University Press, 1994–2002.

[Ferrers, Edmund]. *An Abstract of a Commentarie By Dr. Martyn Luther, upon the Galathians.* London, 1642.

Fowler, Alastair, ed. *The New Oxford Book of Seventeenth-Century Verse.* Oxford: Oxford University Press, 1991.

Grene, David and Richmond Lattimore. *The Complete Greek Tragedies.* 4 vols. Chicago: University of Chicago Press, 1959.

Greville, Fulke. *A Treatie of Humane Learning. Poems and Dramas.* Ed. Geoffrey Bullough. 2 vols. New York: Oxford University Press, 1945. 1:154–91.

————. *A Discourse opening the Nature of that Episcopacy which is Exercised in England.* 1641. 2nd ed. London, 1642.

Greville, Robert. *The Nature of Truth, its Union and Unity with the Soule, which is one in its essence, faculties, acts; one with truth.* London, 1640.

Guild, William. *Moses Vnuailed.* London, 1620.

Harrington, James. *The Commonwealth of Oceana and A System of Politics.* Ed. J. G. A. Pocock. Cambridge: Cambridge University Press, 1992.

Hayley, William. *Conjectures on the Origin of the 'Paradise Lost.' The Life of John Milton.* 2nd ed. 1796. Facsimile ed. Joseph Anthony Wittreich, Jr. Gainesville, Fla.: Scholar's Facsimiles and Reprints, 1970.

Hegel, G. W. F. *Lectures on the Philosophy of Religion.* Trans. R. F. Brown. Berkeley: University of California Press, 1984.

Herbert, George. *Works.* Ed. F. E. Hutchinson. Corrected ed. Oxford: Clarendon Press, 1945.

Hobbes, Thomas. *Leviathan.* Ed. Richard Tuck. Rev. ed. Cambridge: Cambridge University Press, 1996.

Homer. *Iliad.* Trans. Richmond Lattimore. Chicago: University of Chicago Press, 1951.

————. *Iliad.* Ed. and trans. A. T. Murray. Revised by W. F. Wyatt. 2 vols. LCL. Cambridge, Mass.: Harvard University Press, 1999.

H[ume], P[atrick]. *Annotations on Milton's Paradise Lost.* London, 1695.

"I.B., Gent." *Heroick Education.* London, 1656.

Hutchinson, Lucy. *Order and Disorder.* Ed. David Norbrook. Oxford: Blackwell, 2001.

Irenaeus. *Against Heresies. Ante-Nicene Fathers, Vol. 1: The Apostolic Fathers, Justin Martyr, Irenaeus.* Ed. Alexander Roberts and James Donaldson. Rev. A.C. Coxe. 1885. Reprint. Peabody, Mass.: Hendrickson Publishers, 1994.

Jonson, Ben. *Sejanus His Fall.* Ed. Philip J. Ayres. The Revels Plays. Manchester: Manchester University Press, 1990.

————. [*Works*]. Ed. C. H. Herford and Percy and Evelyn Simpson. 11 vols. Oxford: Clarendon Press, 1925–52.

Johnson, Samuel. *Lives of the English Poets*. Ed. George Birbeck Hill. 3 vols. Oxford: Clarendon Press, 1905.

————. *The Oxford Authors: Samuel Johnson*. Ed. Donald Grene. Oxford: Oxford University Press, 1984.

Kant, Immanuel. "On the Miscarriage of All Philosophical Trials in Theodicy." *Religion within the Boundaries of Mere Reason and Other Writings*. Ed. and trans. Allen Wood and George di Giovanni. Cambridge: Cambridge University Press, 1998. 17–30.

Koester, Craig R., ed. *Hebrews*. The Anchor Bible. New York: Doubleday, 2001.

Larrimore, Mark, ed. *The Problem of Evil: A Reader*. Oxford and Malden, Mass.: Blackwell, 2001.

Leibniz, G. W. *Theodicy*. Selections. Trans. E. M. Huggard. *The Problem of Evil*. Ed. Mark Larrimore. 191–200.

Lightfoot, John. *Horae Hebraicae et Talmudicae*. 6 vols. Cambridge, 1658–77.

Ludlow, Edmund. *A Voyce from the Watch Tower (1660–62)*. Ed. A. B. Worden. Camden 4th ser. No. 21. London: Royal Historical Society, 1978.

Luther, Martin. *Lectures on Genesis. Luther's Works*. Ed. Jaroslav Pelikan et al. 55 vols. Saint Louis: Concordia, 1958–76. Vol. 1.

————. "Preface of the Epistle of St. Paul to the Romans." *Martin Luther: Selections from his Writings*. Ed. John Dillenberger. New York: Anchor / Doubleday, 1962. 19–34.

————. "A Sermon . . . concerning them that be vnder the Law, and them that be vnder Grace." *Special and Chosen Sermons*. Trans. W. G. London, 1578.

————. *A Commentarie . . . vpon the Epistle of S. Paul to the Galathians*. Anonymous trans. London, 1575.

Maimonides. *The Guide of the Perplexed*. Trans. Shlomo Pines. 2 vols. Chicago: University of Chicago Press, 1963.

Martyn, J. Louis, ed. *Galatians*. The Anchor Bible. New York: Doubleday, 1997.

Martindale, Joanna, ed. *English Humanism: Wyatt to Cowley*. London: Croom Helm, 1985.

Marvell, Andrew. *Poems and Letters*. Ed. H. M. Margoliouth. 2nd ed. 2 vols. Oxford: Clarendon Press, 1952.

————. *The Poems of Andrew Marvell*. Ed. Nigel Smith. London: Pearson / Longman, 2003.

Melanchthon, Philip. "Oration On Occasion of the Funeral of Doctor Martin Luther." *Orations on Philosophy and Education*. Ed. Sachiko Kusakawa. Trans. Christine F. Salazar. Cambridge: Cambridge University Press, 1999.

Menasseh ben Israel. *To His Highnesse the Lord Protector of the* COMMONWEALTH *of England, Scotland,* and *Ireland*. London, 1655.

Milton, John. *An Apology Against a Pamphlet call'd a Modest Confutation of the Animadversions upon the Remonstrant against SMECTYMNUUS*. London, 1642.

————. *Areopagitica*. London, 1644.

————. *Complete Poems*. Ed. John Leonard. Harmondsworth: Penguin, 1998.

————. *Complete Poems and Major Prose*. Ed. Merritt Y. Hughes. New York: Odyssey Press, 1957.

————. *Complete Prose Works of John Milton*. Ed. Don M. Wolfe et al. 8 vols. New Haven: Yale University Press, 1953–82.

————. *The Complete Shorter Poems*. Ed. John Carey. 2nd ed. London: Longman, 1997.

————. *Milton's Complete Poetical Works Reproduced in Photographic Facsimile*. Ed. H. F. Fletcher. 4 vols. Urbana: University of Illinois Press, 1943–48.

————. *Of Reformation*. London, 1641.

————. *Paradise Lost*. Ed. Alastair Fowler. 2nd ed. London: Longman, 1998.

————. *Paradise Lost*. Ed. David Scott Kastan. Indianapolis and Cambridge: Hackett Publishing, 2005.

————. *Paradise Lost*. Ed. Thomas Newton. 2 vols. London, 1749.

————. *Paradise Regain'd . . . To which is added Samson Agonistes. And Poems upon several occasions. With a tractate of education*. London, 1713.

————. *Poems of Mr. John Milton, Both English and Latin*. London, 1645.

————. *The Poetical Works of John Milton*. Ed. Thomas Newton. 5th ed. 3 vols. London, 1761.

————. *The Poetical Works of John Milton*. Ed. John Henry Todd. 6 vols. London, 1801.

————. *Political Writings*. Ed. Martin Dzelzainis. Cambridge: Cambridge University Press, 1991.

————. *The Works of John Milton*. Ed. Frank Allen Patterson et al. 18 vols. New York: Columbia University Press, 1931–38.

Montaigne, Michel de. *Essayes*. Trans. John Florio. 1603. Reprint: New York: Modern Library, n.d.

————. *Essays*. Trans. Donald Frame. Stanford: Stanford University Press, 1958.

Nedham, Marchamont. *Mercurius Politicus*. No. 104. 27 May-3 June 1652.

Nicholas, Edward. *An Apology for the Honorable Nation of the Jews, and All the Sons of Israel*. London, 1648.

Pearson, John. *An exposition of the Creed* (1659). 3rd ed. London, 1669.

Petrarch. *Le familiari*. Ed. V. Rossi and U. Bosco. 4 vols. Florence: Sansoni, 1933–42.

————. *Four Dialogues for Scholars*. Ed. and trans. Conrad H. Rawski. Cleveland: Case Western Reserve University Press, 1967.

Phillips, Edward. "The Life of Mr. John Milton." 1694. *The Early Lives of Milton*. Ed. Helen Darbishire. London: Constable, 1932. 49–82.

Plato. *Collected Dialogues*. Ed. Edith Hamilton and Huntington Cairns. Princeton: Princeton University Press, 1961.

————. *Euthyphro, Apology, Crito, Meno, Gorgias, Menexenus*. Trans. and commentary R. E. Allen. New Haven: Yale University Press, 1984.

———. *Ion, Hippias Minor, Laches, Protagoras.* Trans. and commentary R. E. Allen. New Haven: Yale University Press, 1996.

———. *Phaedrus.* Trans. Alexander Nehamas and Paul Woodruff. *Plato: Complete Works.* Ed. John M. Cooper. Indianapolis and Cambridge: Hackett, 1997. 506–56.

———. *Plato's Theory of Knowledge: The "Theaetetus" and the "Sophist" of Plato translated with a running commentary.* Trans. and commentary F. M. Cornford. London: Routledge and Kegan Paul, 1935.

———. *Republic.* Trans. Richard W. Sterling and William C. Scott. New York: W. W. Norton, 1985.

———. *Sophist.* Trans. and commentary Seth Benardete. Chicago: University of Chicago Press, 1986.

———. *Symposium.* Trans. and commentary R. E. Allen. New Haven: Yale University Press, 1991.

———. *Theaetetus.* Trans. and commentary Seth Benardete. Chicago: University of Chicago Press, 1986.

———. *The Theaetetus of Plato with a Revised Text and English Notes.* Ed. Lewis Campbell. Oxford: Clarendon Press, 1883.

Plutarch. *Moralia.* Ed. and trans. Frank Cole Babbitt. 14 vols. LCL. Cambridge, Mass.: Harvard University Press, 1927–36.

Plutarch, Pseudo-. "The Education of Children." *Moralia.* LCL. 1: 4–69.

Pope, Alexander. *The Twickenham Edition of the Poems of Alexander Pope.* Ed. John Butt et al. 11 vols. New Haven: Yale University Press, 1939–69.

Quintilian. *Institutio Oratoria.* Ed. and trans. H. E. Butler. 4 vols. LCL. Cambridge, Mass.: Harvard University Press, 1922.

Richardson, Jonathan. *Explanatory Notes and Remarks on Miltons 'Paradise Lost.' With the Life of the Author, and a Discourse on the Poem.* 1734. *The Early Lives of Milton.* Ed. Helen Darbishire. London: Constable, 1932. 199–330

Robertson, William, ed. *The Hebrew Text of the Psalmes and Lamentations but Published (for to encourage and facilitate Beginners in their way) with the Reading thereof in known English Letters.* London, 1656.

Seneca. *On Providence.* Trans. M. Hadas. *The Stoic Philosophy of Seneca.* New York: W. W. Norton, 1958.

Shelley, Percy Bysshe. *Shelley's Poetry and Prose.* Ed. Donald H. Reiman and Sharon B. Powers. New York: W. W. Norton, 1977.

Sidney, Sir Philip. *Poems.* Ed. William A. Ringler. Oxford: Clarendon Press, 1962.

Smith, G. G., ed. *Elizabethan Critical Essays.* 2 vols. Oxford: Clarendon Press, 1904.

Speiser, E. A., ed. *Genesis.* The Anchor Bible. New York: Doubleday, 1962.

Tacitus. *Annals.* Ed. and trans. John Jackson. 2 vols. LCL. Cambridge, Mass.: Harvard University Press, 1931.

Thucydides. *The Peloponnesian War.* Trans. Thomas Hobbes. 1628. Ed. David Grene. 1959. Reprint. Chicago: University of Chicago Press, 1989.

Toland, John. *Amyntor, or a Defence of Milton's Life.* London, 1699.

———. *The Life of John Milton*. 1698. *The Early Lives of John Milton*. Ed. Helen Darbishire. London: Constable, 1932. 83–197.

Tyndale, William. *A compendious introduccion, and prologe or preface un to the pistle off Paul to the Romayns*. Worms, 1526.

Vaughan, Henry. *The Complete Poems*. Ed. Alan Rudrum. Harmondsworth: Penguin, 1976.

Warton, Thomas. *The History of English Poetry*. 3 vols. London, 1774–81.

Wittreich, Joseph A., Jr., ed. *The Romantics on Milton*. Cleveland: Case Western Reserve University Press, 1970.

Woodhouse, A. S. P. *Puritanism and Liberty*. 2nd ed. Chicago: University of Chicago Press, 1950.

Wordsworth, William. *Poetical Works*. Ed. Ernest De Selincourt. London: Oxford University Press, 1936.

SECONDARY

Adorno, Theodor. *Minima Moralia*. Trans. E. F. N. Jephcott. London: Verso, 1974.

Ainsworth, O. M. *Milton on Education*. New Haven: Yale University Press, 1928.

Allen, Don Cameron. *The Harmonious Vision: Studies in Milton's Poetry*. Enlarged ed. Baltimore: Johns Hopkins University Press, 1970.

Allen, Michael. "Divine Instruction: *Of Education* and the Pedagogy of Raphael, Michael, and the Father." *Milton Quarterly* 26 (1992): 113–21.

Althuser, Louis. "Ideology and Ideological State Apparatuses (Notes towards an Investigation)." Trans. Ben Brewster. *Lenin and Philosophy and Other Essays*. New York: Monthly Review Press, 1971.

Armitage, David, et al., eds. *Milton and Republicanism*. Cambridge: Cambridge University Press, 1995.

Auerbach, Erich. "Figura." *Scenes from the Drama of European Literature*. Trans. Ralph Manheim. New York: Meridian Books, 1959. 11–76.

———. *Literary Language and Its Public in Late Latin Antiquity and in the Middle Ages*. Trans. Ralph Manheim. New York: Pantheon, 1965.

Aylmer, G. E. *Rebellion or Revolution? England from Civil War to Restoration*. Oxford: Oxford University Press, 1986.

Barker, Arthur E. *Milton and the Puritan Dilemma, 1641–1660*. Toronto: University of Toronto Press, 1942.

Bauer, Walter, ed. *A Greek-English Lexicon of the New Testament and Other Early Christian Literature*. Trans. W.F Arndt et al. 2nd ed. Chicago: University of Chicago Press, 1979.

Bauman, Michael. *A Scripture Index to John Milton's "De doctrina christiana."* Binghamton, N.Y.: Medieval and Renaissance Texts and Studies, 1989.

Beal, Peter. *Index of English Literary Manuscripts, Volume II: 1625–1700, Part 2: Lee-Wycherley*. London: Mansell, 1993.

Benjamin, Walter. "Theses on the Philosophy of History." *Illumniations*. Ed. Hannah Arendt. Trans. Harry Zohn. New York: Schocken Books, 1968. 253–64.

Bennet, Joan S. *Reviving Liberty: Radical Christian Humanism in Milton's Great Poems*. Cambridge, Mass.: Harvard University Press, 1989.

Berthold, Dennis. "The Concept of Merit in *Paradise Lost*." *Studies in English Literature 1500–1900* 15 (1975): 153–67.

Biberman, Matthew. "Milton, Marriage, and a Woman's Right to Divorce." *Studies in English Literature 1500–1900* 39 (1999): 131–53.

Blessington, Francis C. *"Paradise Lost" and the Classical Epic*. Boston and London: Routledge, 1979.

Blumenberg, Hans. *The Legitimacy of the Modern Age*. Trans. Robert M. Wallace. Cambridge, Mass.: MIT Press, 1983.

Boddy, Margaret. "Milton's Translations of Psalms 80–88." *Modern Philology* 64 (1966): 1–9.

Bonhoeffer, Dietrich. *Creation and Fall*. Trans. John C. Fletcher. *Two Biblical Studies*. Reprint. New York: Touchstone / Simon and Schuster, 1997.

Bouwsma, William J. *The Waning of the Renaissance 1550–1640*. New Haven: Yale University Press, 2000.

Bruns, Gerald L. *Hermeneutics Ancient and Modern*. New Haven: Yale University Press, 1992.

————. "Midrash and Allegory." *The Literary Guide to the Bible*. Ed. Robert Alter and Frank Kermode. Cambridge, Mass.: Harvard University Press, 1987. 625–46.

Budick, Sanford. "Milton and the Scene of Interpretation: From Typology toward Midrash." *Midrash and Literature*. Ed. Geoffrey H. Hartman and Sanford Budick. New Haven: Yale University Press, 1987. 195–212.

Burke, Peter. "Tacitism, Scepticism, and Reason of State." *The Cambridge History of Political Thought, 1450–1700*. Ed. J. H. Burns with Mark Goldie. Cambridge: Cambridge University Press, 1991. 479–98.

Burns, J. H. with Mark Goldie, eds. *The Cambridge History of Political Thought 1450–1700*. Cambridge: Cambridge University Press, 1991.

Burrow, Colin. *Epic Romance: Homer to Milton*. Oxford: Clarendon Press, 1993.

Bush, Douglas. *The Renaissance and English Humanism*. Toronto: University of Toronto Press, 1939.

Campbell, Gordon. *A Milton Chronology*. London and Basingstoke: Macmillan, 1997.

Carruthers, Mary. *The Book of Memory: A Study of Memory in Medieval Culture*. Cambridge: Cambridge University Press, 1990.

Caspari, Fritz. *Humanism and the Social Order in Tudor England*. Chicago: University of Chicago Press, 1954.

Chartier, Roger. *The Order of Books*. Trans. Lydia G. Cochrane. Stanford: Stanford University Press, 1994.

Christopher, Georgia. "Milton and the Reforming Spirit." *The Cambridge Companion to Milton*. Ed. Dennis Danielson. 2nd ed. Cambridge: Cambridge University Press, 1999. 193–201.

————. *Milton and the Science of the Saints.* Princeton: Princeton University Press, 1982.

Clark, Donald L. *John Milton at St. Paul's School.* New York: Columbia University Press, 1948.

Coiro, Ann Baynes. "'To repair the ruins of our first parents': *Of Education* and Fallen Adam." *Studies in English Literature 1500–1900* 28 (1988): 133–47.

Corns, Thomas N., ed. *A Companion to Milton.* Oxford: Blackwell, 2001.

Cummings, Brian. *The Literary Culture of the Reformation: Grammar and Grace.* Oxford: Clarendon Press, 2002.

Curtius, Ernst Robert. *European Literature and the Latin Middle Ages.* Trans. Willard R. Trask. Princeton: Princeton University Press, 1953.

Dahlberg, Charles. "Paradise Lost V, 603, and Milton's Psalm II." *Modern Language Notes* 67 (1952): 23–24.

Daiches, David. "The Opening of *Paradise Lost.*" *The Living Milton.* Ed. Frank Kermode. London: Routledge and Kegan Paul, 1960. 55–69.

Danielson, Dennis, ed. *The Cambridge Companion to Milton.* 2nd ed. Cambridge: Cambridge University Press, 1999.

Darbishire, Helen. "The Chronology of Milton's Handwriting." *The Library.* 4th ser. 14 (1933): 229–35.

Davies, David and Paul Dowling. "'Shrewd books, with dangerous Frontispieces': *Areopagitica*'s Motto." *Milton Quarterly* 20 (1986): 33–37.

Derrida, Jacques. *Archive Fever: A Freudian Impression.* Trans. Eric Prenowitz. Chicago: University of Chicago Press, 1996.

Dewey, John. *Democracy and Education: An Introduction to the Philosophy of Education.* New York: Macmillan, 1916.

Diekhoff, John S. "Rhyme in *Paradise Lost.*" *PMLA* 49 (1934): 539–43.

Dobranski, Stephen B. *Milton, Authorship, and the Book Trade.* Cambridge: Cambridge University Press, 1999.

DuRocher, Richard J. *Milton Among the Romans: The Pedagogy and Influence of Milton's Latin Curriculum.* Pittsburgh: Duquesne University Press, 2001.

Dzelzainis, Martin. "Authors 'not unknown' in Milton's *Tetrachordon.*" *Notes and Queries.* New ser. Vol. 45, No. 1 (March 1998): 44–47.

————. "Milton's Classical Republicanism." *Milton and Republicanism.* Ed. David Armitage et al. 3–24.

————. "Milton and the Limits of Ciceronian Rhetoric." *English Renaissance Prose: History, Language, and Politics.* Ed. Neil Rhodes. Tempe, AZ: MRTS, 1997. 203–226.

————. "Milton and the Protectorate in 1658." *Milton and Republicanism.* Ed. David Armitage et al.181–205.

Eden, Kathy. *Hermeneutics and the Rhetorical Tradition: Chapters in the Ancient Legacy and Its Humanist Reception.* New Haven: Yale University Press, 1997.

————. *Friends Hold All Things in Common: Tradition, Intellectual Property, and the "Adages" of Erasmus.* New Haven: Yale University Press, 2001.

Eliade, Mircea. *The Sacred and the Profane: The Nature of Religion.* Trans. Willard R. Trask. New York: Harcourt, 1957,

Eliot, T. S. *Selected Essays.* New York: Harcourt Brace Jovanovich, 1950.

Fallon, Stephen M. "Alexander More Reads Milton: Self-representation and Anxiety in Milton's Defences." *Milton and the Terms of Liberty.* Ed. Graham Parry and Joad Raymond. Cambridge: D. S. Brewer, 2002. 111–24.

———. "The Spur of Self-Concernment: Milton in his Divorce Tracts." *Milton Studies* 38 (2000): 220–42.

Festa, Thomas. "John Milton." *The Oxford Encyclopedia of British Literature.* Ed. David Scott Kastan et al. 5 vols. New York and Oxford: Oxford University Press, 2006. 3:505–15.

———. "Milton's 'Christian *Talmud.*'" *Reformation* 8 (2003): 79–115.

———. "Place, Source, and Voice in *Paradise Lost.*" *English Language Notes* 44.1 (2006): 57–66.

———. "Repairing the Ruins: Milton as Reader and Educator." *Milton Studies* 43 (2004): 35–63.

Fish, Stanley. "Driving from the letter: truth and indeterminacy in Milton's *Areopagitica.*" *Re-membering Milton: Essays on the Texts and Traditions.* Ed. Mary Nyquist and Margaret W. Ferguson. New York: Methuen, 1987. 234–54.

———. *How Milton Works.* Cambridge, Mass.: Harvard University Press, 2001.

———. *Is There a Text in This Class? The Authority of Interpretive Communities.* Cambridge, Mass.: Harvard University Press, 1980.

———. *The Living Temple: George Herbert and Catechizing.* Berkeley: University of California Press, 1978.

———. *Surprised By Sin: The Reader in "Paradise Lost."* 1967. 2nd ed. Cambridge, Mass.: Harvard University Press, 1997.

———. "Wanting a Supplement: The Question of Interpretation in Milton's Early Prose." In *Politics, Poetics, and Hermeneutics in Milton's Prose.* Ed. David Loewenstein and James Grantham Turner. Cambridge: Cambridge University Press, 1990. 41–68.

Fletcher, Harris Francis. *The Intellectual Development of John Milton.* 2 vols. Urbana: University of Illinois Press, 1956–61.

Forsyth, Neil. *The Old Enemy: Satan and the Combat Myth.* Princeton: Princeton University Press, 1987.

———. *The Satanic Epic.* Princeton: Princeton University Press, 2003.

Freedman, D.N. et al., eds. *The Anchor Bible Dictionary.* 6 vols. New York: Doubleday, 1992.

French, J. Milton, ed. *The Life Records of John Milton.* 5 vols. New Brunswick: Rutgers University Press, 1949–58.

Frye, Northrop. *The Great Code: The Bible and Literature.* New York: Harcourt, 1982.

Gadamer, Hans-Georg. *Truth and Method.* 2nd ed. Trans. Joel Weinsheimer and Donald G. Marshall. New York: Continuum, 1994.

Gager, John G. *Reinventing Paul.* New York: Oxford University Press, 2000.

Gallagher, Catherine, and Stephen Greenblatt, *Practicing New Historicism.* Chicago: University of Chicago Press, 2000.

Gentles, Ian, et al., eds. *Soldiers, Writers and Statesmen of the English Revolution.* Cambridge: Cambridge University Press, 1998.

Gould, Stephen Jay. "Father Athanasius on the Isthmus of a Middle State: Understanding Kircher's Paleontology." *Athanasius Kircher: The Last Man Who Knew Everything.* Ed. Paula Findlin. New York: Routledge, 2004. 207–37

Grafton, Anthony. *Commerce with the Classics: Ancient Books and Renaissance Readers.* Ann Arbor: University of Michigan Press, 1997.

———. "Humanism and Political Theory." *The Cambridge History of Political Thought, 1450–1700.* Ed. J. H. Burns with Mark Goldie. Cambridge: Cambridge University Press, 1991. 9–29.

———. *Joseph Scaliger: A Study in the History of Classical Scholarship.* 2 vols. Oxford: Clarendon Press, 1983–93.

Greenblatt, Stephen. *Renaissance Self-Fashioning: From More to Shakespeare.* Chicago: University of Chicago Press, 1980.

Greengrass, Mark, Michael Leslie, and Timothy Raylor, eds. *Samuel Hartlib and Universal Reformation.* Cambridge: Cambridge University Press, 1994.

Grose, Christopher. *Milton and the Sense of Tradition.* New Haven: Yale University Press, 1988.

———. *Milton's Epic Process: "Paradise Lost" and Its Miltonic Background.* New Haven: Yale University Press, 1973.

Grossman, Marshall. *"Authors to Themselves": Milton and the Revelation of History.* Cambridge: Cambridge University Press, 1987.

———. "Milton and the Rhetoric of Prophecy." *The Cambridge Companion to Milton.* Ed. Dennis Danielson. Cambridge: Cambridge University Press, 1989. 167–81.

———. "The Rhetoric of Feminine Priority and the Ethics of Form in *Paradise Lost.*" *English Literary Renaissance* 33 (2004): 424–43.

Guistiniani, Vito R. "Homo, Humanus, and the Meanings of 'Humanism.'" *Journal of the History of Ideas* 46 (1985): 167–95.

Hale, John K. "*Areopagitica*'s Euripidean Motto." *Milton Quarterly* 25 (1991): 25–27.

———. "Milton's Euripides Marginalia: Their Significance for Milton Studies." *Milton Studies* 27 (1991): 23–35.

———. *Milton's Languages.* Cambridge: Cambridge University Press, 1997.

Hanford, James Holly. *John Milton, Poet and Humanist.* Cleveland: Case Western Reserve University Press, 1966.

Hankins, James. "The 'Baron Thesis' after Forty Years and some Recent Studies of Leonardo Bruni." *Journal of the History of Ideas* 56 (1995): 309–228.

———. "Humanism and the origins of modern political thought." *The Cambridge Companion to Renaissance Humanism.* Ed. Jill Kraye. Cambridge: Cambridge University Press, 1996. 118–41.

Hartman, Geoffrey. "Milton's Counterplot." *ELH* 25 (1958): 1–12.

Haskin, Dayton. *Milton's Burden of Interpretation*. Philadelphia: University of Pennsylvania Press, 1994.

Heschel, Abraham J. *The Prophets*. 1962. Reprint. New York: Perennial / Harper Collins, 2001.

Hill, Christopher. *The English Bible and the Seventeenth-Century Revolution*. Harmondsworth: Penguin, 1993.

———. *The Intellectual Origins of the English Revolution Revisited*. Oxford: Clarendon Press, 1997.

———. *Milton and the English Revolution*. New York: Viking Press, 1977.

Hill, Geoffrey. *Style and Faith*. New York: Counterpoint, 2003.

Hornblower, Simon and Antony Spawforth, eds. *Oxford Classical Dictionary*. 3rd ed. Oxford: Oxford University Press, 1996.

Hoxby, Blair. *Mammon's Music: Literature and Economics in the Age of Milton*. New Haven: Yale University Press, 2002.

Hughes, Graham. *Hebrews and Hermeneutics: The Epistle to the Hebrews as a New Testament Example of Biblical Interpretation*. Cambridge: Cambridge University Press, 1979.

Hughes, Merritt Y. "Satan and the 'Myth' of the Tyrant." *Ten Perspectives on Milton*. New Haven: Yale University Press, 1965. 165–95.

Hughes, Merritt Y. et al., ed. *Variorum Commentary on the Poems of John Milton*. 5 vols. to date. New York: Columbia University Press, 1970-.

Jaeger, Werner. *Paideia: The Ideals of Greek Culture*. Trans. Gilbert Highet. 3 vols. New York: Oxford University Press, 1943–45.

Jardine, Lisa. "Humanist Logic." *The Cambridge History of Renaissance Philosophy*. Ed. Charles B. Schmitt and Quentin Skinner. Cambridge: Cambridge University Press, 1988. 173–98.

Jenkins, Hugh. "Jefferson (Re)Reading Milton." *Milton Quarterly* 32 (1998): 32–38.

Jewell, Helen M. *Education in Early Modern England*. Houndmills, Basingstoke: Macmillan, 1998.

Kahn, Victoria. "Allegory and the Sublime in *Paradise Lost*." *Milton*. Ed. Annabel Patterson. London: Longman, 1992. 127–52

Kastan, David Scott. *Shakespeare after Theory*. New York: Routledge, 1999.

Katz, David S. *Philosemitism and the Readmission of the Jews to England 1603–1655*. Oxford: Clarendon Press, 1982.

Keeble, N. H. *The Literary Culture of Nonconformity in Later Seventeenth-Century England*. Athens: University of Georgia Press, 1987.

Kelley, Maurice, and Samuel D. Atkins. "Milton's Annotations of Euripides." *JEGP* 60 (1961): 680–687.

———. "Milton's Annotations of Aratus." *PMLA* 70 (1955): 1090–1106.

Kermode, Frank. *The Genesis of Secrecy: On the Interpretation of Narrative*. Cambridge, Mass.: Harvard University Press, 1979.

———. "Adam Unparadised." *The Living Milton*. Ed. Frank Kermode. London: Routledge and Kegan Paul, 1960. 85–123.

Kerrigan, William. "Milton's Place in Intellectual History." *The Cambridge Companion to Milton.* 2nd ed. Ed. Dennis Danielson. Cambridge: Cambridge University Press, 1999. 253–266.

———. *The Prophetic Milton.* Charlottesville: University of Virginia Press, 1974.

———. *The Sacred Complex: On the Psychogenesis of "Paradise Lost."* Cambridge, Mass.: Harvard University Press, 1983.

Kerrigan, William, and Gordon Braden. *The Idea of the Renaissance.* Baltimore: Johns Hopkins University Press, 1989.

Kittel, Gerhard. *Theological Dictionary of the New Testament.* 10 vols. Grand Rapids: Eerdmans, 1951–76.

Knoppers, Laura Lunger. *Historicizing Milton: Spectacle, Power, and Poetry in Restoration England.* Athens: University of Georgia Press, 1994.

———. "Late Political Prose." *A Companion to Milton.* Ed. Thomas N. Corns. Oxford: Blackwell, 2001. 309–25.

Kolbrener, William. *Milton's Warring Angels: A Study of Critical Engagements.* Cambridge: Cambridge University Press, 1997.

Kraye, Jill. "Moral Philosophy." *The Cambridge History of Renaissance Philosophy.* Ed. Charles B. Schmitt and Quentin Skinner. Cambridge: Cambridge University Press, 1988. 303–86.

Kraye, Jill, ed. *The Cambridge Companion to Renaissance Humanism.* Cambridge: Cambridge University Press, 1996.

Kristeller, P. O. "Humanism and Moral Philosophy." *Renaissance Humanism.* Ed. Albert Rabil. 3 vols. Philadelphia: University of Pennsylvania Press, 1988. 3:271–309.

———. *Renaissance Thought and Its Sources.* New York: Columbia University Press, 1979.

Lacan, Jacques. *Écrits: A Selection.* Trans. Alan Sheridan. New York: W. W. Norton, 1977.

Lamberton, Robert. *Homer the Theologian: Neoplatonic Allegorical Reading and the Growth of the Epic Tradition.* Berkeley: University of California Press, 1986.

Levinas, Emmanuel. *Basic Philosophical Writings.* Ed. Adriaan T. Peperzak, Simon Critchley, and Robert Bernasconi. Bloomington: Indiana University Press, 1996.

———. "Useless Suffering." Trans. Richard Cohen. *The Problem of Evil: A Reader.* Ed. Mark Larrimore. Oxford and Maldon, Mass.: Blackwell, 2001. 371–80.

Lewalski, Barbara K. "Milton and the Hartlib Circle: Educational Projects and Epic *Paideia.*" *Literary Milton: Text, Pretext, Context.* Ed. Diana Treviño Benet and Michael Lieb. Pittsburgh: Duquesne University Press, 1994. 202–219.

———. *Protestant Poetics and the Seventeenth-Century Religious Lyric.* Princeton: Princeton University Press, 1979.

———. *The Life of John Milton.* Oxford: Blackwell, 2000.

Lewis, C. S. *A Preface to Paradise Lost.* London: Oxford University Press, 1942.

———. *The Allegory of Love: A Study in Medieval Tradition.* 1936. Reprint. London: Oxford University Press, 1958.

Liddell, H.G. and R. Scott. *A Greek-English Lexicon.* Rev. ed. Ed. Sir Henry Stuart Jones et al. 2 vols. Oxford: Clarendon Press Press, 1925–30.

Loewenstein, David. "The Religious Politics of *Paradise Lost.*" *A Companion to Milton.* Ed. Thomas N. Corns. Oxford: Blackwell, 2001. 348–62.

———. *Representing Revolution in Milton and his Contemporaries: Religion, Politics, and Polemics in Radical Puritanism.* Cambridge: Cambridge University Press, 2001.

Lovejoy, Arthur O. "Milton and the Paradox of the Fortunate Fall." 1937. *Critical Essays on Milton from ELH.* Baltimore: Johns Hopkins University Press, 1969. 163–81.

Low, Anthony. "The Fall into Subjectivity: Milton's 'Paradise Within' and 'Abyss of Fears and Horrors.'" *Reading the Renaissance: Ideas and Idioms from Shakespeare to Milton.* Ed. Marc Berley. Pittsburgh: Duquesne University Press, 2003. 205–32.

Lubac, Henri de. *Exégèse médiévale: les quatre sens de l'écriture.* 4 vols. Paris: Aubier, 1959–64.

Lull, David J. "'The Law Was Our Pedagogue': A Study in Galatians 3:19–25." *Journal of Biblical Literature* 105 (1986): 481–98.

Lynch, Jack. "Betwixt Two Ages Cast: Milton, Johnson, and the English Renaissance." *Journal of the History of Ideas* 61 (2000): 397–413.

MacCallum, H. R. "Milton and Figurative Interpretation of the Bible." *University of Toronto Quarterly* 31 (1962): 397–415.

———. *Milton and the Sons of God: The Divine Image in Milton's Epic Poetry.* Toronto: University of Toronto Press, 1986.

Martin, Catherine Gimelli. *The Ruins of Allegory: "Paradise Lost" and the Metamorphosis of Epic Convention.* Durham, NC: Duke University Press, 1998.

Martz, Louis L. *The Paradise Within: Studies in Vaughan, Traherne, and Milton.* New Haven: Yale University Press, 1964.

McGrath, Alister E. *The Intellectual Origins of the European Reformation.* 2nd ed. Oxford: Blackwell, 2004.

McKeon, Michael. *The Origins of the English Novel, 1600–1740.* Baltimore: Johns Hopkins University Press, 1987.

Morgan, John. *Godly Learning: Puritan Attitudes towards Reason, Learning, and Education, 1560–1640.* Cambridge: Cambridge University Press, 1986.

Mueller, Janel. "Dominion as Domesticity: Milton's Imperial God and the Experience of History." *Milton and the Imperial Vision.* Ed. Balachandra Rajan and Elizabeth Sauer. Pittsburgh: Duquesne University Press, 1999. 25–47.

Nehemas, Alexander. *Virtues of Authenticity: Essays on Plato and Socrates.* Princeton: Princeton University Press, 1999.

Norbrook, David. *Writing the English Republic: Poetry, Rhetoric and Politics, 1627–1660.* Cambridge: Cambridge University Press, 1999.

Nuttal, A. D. "Everything is over before it begins." Review of *How Milton Works,* by Stanely Fish. *London Review of Books.* 21 June 2001. 19–21.

Nyquist, Mary. "The Genesis of Gendered Subjectivity in the Divorce Tracts and in *Paradise Lost.*" *Re-membering Milton: Essays on the Texts and Traditions.* Ed.

Mary Nyquist and Margaret W. Ferguson. New York: Methuen, 1987. 99–127.

Parker, William Riley. *Milton: A Biography.* 2nd ed. Ed. Gordon Campbell. 2 vols. Oxford: Clarendon Press, 1996.

———. *Milton's Contemporary Reputation.* Columbus: Ohio State Unversity Press, 1940.

Parry, Graham and Joad Raymond, eds. *Milton and the Terms of Liberty.* Cambridge: D. S. Brewer, 2002.

Patrides, C. A. *Milton and the Christian Tradition.* Oxford: Clarendon Press, 1966.

———. "The 'Protevangelium' in Renaissance Theology and *Paradise Lost.*" *Studies in English Literature 1500–1900* 3 (1963): 19–30.

Patterson, Annabel. "No meer amatorious novel?" In *Politics, Poetics, and Hermeneutics in Milton's Prose,* ed. David Loewenstein and J. G. Turner. Cambridge: Cambridge University Press, 1990. 85–101.

———. *Early Modern Liberalism.* Cambridge: Cambridge University Press, 1997.

Peterson, Erik. "'The Communication of the Dead': Notes on *Studia Humanitatis* and the Nature of Humanist Philology." *The Uses of Greek and Latin: Historical Essays.* Ed. A. C. Dionisotti, Anthony Grafton, and Jill Kraye. London: The Warburg Institute, 1988. 57–69.

Piaget, Jean. "The Significance of John Amos Comenius at the Present Time." *John Amos Comenius on Education.* Ed. Lawrence A. Cremin. New York: Teachers College Press, 1967. 1–31

Pigman, G. W., III. "Versions of Imitation in Renaissance Literature." *Renaissance Quarterly* 33 (1980): 1–32.

Pincus, Steve. "Neither Machiavellian Moment nor Possessive Individualism: Commercial Society and the Defenders of the English Commonwealth." *American Historical Review* 103 (1998): 705–36.

Popkin, Richard H. "Hartlib, Dury, and the Jews." *Samuel Hartlib and Universal Reformation.* Ed. John Leslie, Mark Greengrass, and Timothy Raylor. Cambridge: Cambridge University Press, 1994. 118–36.

Porter, William M. *Reading the Classics and "Paradise Lost."* Lincoln: University of Nebraska Press, 1993.

Rabil, Albert, ed. *Renaissance Humanism.* 3 vols. Philadelphia: University of Pennsylvania Press, 1988.

Radzinowicz, Mary Ann. *Milton's Epics and the Book of Psalms.* Princeton: Princeton University Press, 1989.

———. "The Politics of *Paradise Lost.*" *John Milton.* Ed. Annabel Patterson. London: Longman, 1992. 120–41.

Rajan, B. "'Simple, Sensuous and Passionate.'" *Review of English Studies* 21 (1945): 289–301.

Rawls, John. *Justice as Fairness: A Restatement.* Ed. Erin Kelly. Cambridge, Mass.: Harvard University Press, 2001.

Raymond, Joad. "Where is this goodly tower? Republican Theories of Education." *Critical Survey* 5 (1993): 289–97.

———. "The King is a Thing." *Milton and the Terms of Liberty.* Ed. Graham Parry and Joad Raymond. Cambridge: D. S. Brewer, 2002. 69–94.

Raylor, Timothy. "New Light on Milton and Hartlib." *Milton Quarterly* 27 (1993): 19–31.

Ricks, Christopher. *Milton's Grand Style.* Oxford: Clarendon Press, 1963.

Ricoeur, Paul. "The Model of the Text: Meaningful Action Considered as a Text." *From Text to Action: Essays in Hermeneutics, II.* Trans. Kathleen Blamey and John B. Thompson. Evanston, Ill.: Northwestern University Press, 1991. 144–67.

———. "Philosophical Hermeneutics and Biblical Hermeneutics." *From Text to Action.* Trans. Kathleen Blamey and John B. Thompson. 89–101.

Riggs, William G. "Poetry and Method in Milton's *Of Education.*" *Studies in Philology* 89 (1992): 445–69.

Rogers, John. *The Matter of Revolution: Science, Poetry, and Politics in the Age of Milton.* Ithaca, NY: Cornell University Press, 1996.

Rorty, Amélie Oksenberg. "The Psychology of Aristotelian Tragedy." *Essays on Aristotle's Poetics.* Ed. A. O. Rorty. Princeton: Princeton University Press, 1992. 1–22.

Rorty, Richard. *Philosophy and the Mirror of Nature.* Princeton: Princeton University Press, 1979.

Rosenblatt, Jason P. *Torah and Law in "Paradise Lost."* Princeton: Princeton Univeristy Press, 1994.

Rumrich, John Peter. "Milton's Concept of Substance." *English Language Notes* 19 (1982): 218–33.

———. *Milton Unbound: Controversy and Reinterpretation.* Cambridge: Cambridge University Press, 1996.

Samuel, Irene. "Milton on Learning and Wisdom." *PMLA* 64 (1949): 708–23.

———. *Plato and Milton.* Ithaca, NY: Cornell University Press, 1947.

Samuels, Peggy. "Dueling Erasers: Milton and Scripture." *Studies in Philology* 96 (1999): 180–203.

Sauer, Elizabeth. "Religious Toleration and Imperial Intolerance." In *Milton and the Imperial Vision.* Ed. Balachandra Rajan and Elizabeth Sauer. Pittsburgh: Duquesne University Press, 1999. 214–30.

Schulman, Lydia Dittler. *"Paradise Lost" and the Rise of the American Republic.* Boston: Northeastern University Press, 1992.

Schultz, Howard. *Milton and Forbidden Knowledge.* New York: MLA, 1955.

Schwartz, Regina M. *Remembering and Repeating: Biblical Creation in "Paradise Lost."* Cambridge: Cambridge University Press, 1988.

Scott, Jonathan. *England's Troubles: Seventeenth-Century English Political Instability in European Context.* Cambridge: Cambridge University Press, 2000.

Sensabaugh, G. F. "Milton on Learning." *Studies in Philology* 43 (1946): 258–72.

Shawcross, John T. *John Milton: The Self and the World*. Lexington: University of Kentucky Press, 1993.

———. *Milton: A Bibliography For the Years 1624–1700*. Binghamton, N.Y.: Medieval and Renaissance Texts and Studies, 1984.

Shawcross, John T., ed. *Milton: The Critical Heritage*. 2 vols. London: Routlege and Kegan Paul, 1970–72.

Shoulson, Jeffrey S. *Milton and the Rabbis: Hebraism, Hellenism, and Christianity*. New York: Columbia Unversity Press, 2001.

Sherman, William H. *John Dee: The Politics of Reading and Writing in the English Renaissance*. Amherst: University of Massachusetts Press, 1995.

Shuger, Deborah Kuller. *The Renaissance Bible: Scholarship, Sacrifice, Subjectivity*. Berkeley: University of California Press, 1994.

Silver, Victoria. *Imperfect Sense: The Predicament of Milton's Irony*. Princeton: Princeton University Press, 2001.

Skinner, Quentin. "John Milton and the Politics of Slavery." *Milton and the Terms of Liberty*. Ed. Graham Parry and Joad Raymond. Cambridge: D. S. Brewer, 2002. 1–22.

———. *Liberty before Liberalism*. Cambridge: Cambridge University Press, 1998.

———. *Reason and Rhetoric in the Philosophy of Hobbes*. Cambridge: Cambridge University Press, 1996.

Smith, Nigel. "*Areopagitica:* voicing contexts, 1643–5." *Politics, Poetics, and Hermeneutics in Milton's Prose*. Ed. David Loewenstein and James Grantham Turner. Cambridge: Cambridge University Press, 1990. 103–122.

———. *Literature and Revolution in England, 1640–1660*. New Haven: Yale University Press, 1994.

———. "*Paradise Lost* from Civil War to Restoration." *The Cambridge Companion to Writing of the English Revolution*. Ed. N. H. Keeble. Cambridge: Cambridge University Press, 2001. 251–67.

———. "The Uses of Hebrew in the English Revolution." In *Language, Self, and Society: A Social History of Language*. Ed. Peter Burke and Roy Porter. Cambridge: Polity Press, 1991. 51–71.

Smuts, Malcolm. "Court-Centered Politics and the Uses of Roman Historians, c.1590." *Culture and Politics in Early Stuart England*. Ed. Kevin Sharpe and Peter Lake. Stanford: Stanford University Press, 1993. 21–43.

Stavely, Keith W. F. "Satan and Arminianism in *Paradise Lost*." *Milton Studies* 25 (1989): 125–39.

Steiner, George. *The Grammars of Creation*. New Haven: Yale University Press, 2001.

Stern, David. *Parables in Midrash: Narrative and Exegesis in Rabbinic Literature*. Cambridge, Mass.: Harvard University Press, 1991.

Stock, Brian. *Augustine the Reader: Meditation, Self-Knowledge, and the Ethics of Interpretation*. Cambridge, Mass.: Harvard University Press, 1996.

Stillman, Robert E. "Hobbes's *Leviathan:* Monsters, Metaphors, and Magic." *ELH* 62 (1995): 791–819.

Strier, Richard. "Milton against Humility." *Religion and Culture in Renaissance England.* Ed. Claire McEachern and Debora Shuger. Cambridge: Cambridge University Press, 1997. 258–86.

Syme, R. *Tacitus.* 2 vols. Oxford: Clarendon Press, 1958.

Tarcov, Nathan. *Locke's Education for Liberty.* Chicago: University of Chicago Press, 1984.

Tayler, Edward W. "Milton's Grim Laughter and Second Choices." *Poetry and Epistemology: Turning Points in the History of Poetic Knowledge: Papers from the International Poetry Symposium, Eichstätt, 1983.* Ed. Roland Hagenbüchle and Laura Skandera. Regensburg: Verlag Friedrich Pustet, 1986. 72–93.

———. *Milton's Poetry: Its Development in Time.* Pittsburgh: Duquesne University Press, 1979.

Teskey, Gordon. "Allegory." *The Spenser Encyclopedia.* Ed. A. C. Hamilton et al. Toronto: University of Toronto Press, 1990. 16–22

———. *Allegory and Violence.* Ithaca: Cornell University Press, 1996.

Toulmin, Stephen. *Cosmopolis: The Hidden Agenda of Modernity.* 1990. Reprint. Chicago: University of Chicago Press, 1992.

Turner, James Grantham. *One Flesh: Paradisal Marriage and Sexual Relations in the Age of Milton.* Oxford: Clarendon Press Press, 1987.

Van der Kolk, Bessel A. and Onno van der Hart. "The Intrusive Past: The Flexibility of Memory and the Engraving of Trauma." *Trauma: Explorations in Memory.* Ed. Cathy Caruth. Baltimore: Johns Hopkins University Press, 1995. 158–82

Vickers, Brian. *In Defence of Rhetoric.* Oxford: Clarendon Press, 1988.

Viswanathan, Gauri. "Milton and Education." *Milton and the Imperial Vision.* Ed. Balachandra Rajan and Elizabeth Sauer. Pittsburgh: Duquesne University Press, 1999. 273–93.

Vlastos, Gregory. "Socrates' Disavowal of Knowledge." *Philosophical Quarterly* 3 (1985): 1–31.

———. "The Socratic Elenchus." *Oxford Studies in Ancient Philosophy* 1 (1983): 27–58.

Von Maltzahn, Nicholas. "The First Reception of *Paradise Lost* (1667)." *Review of English Studies.* New ser. 47 (1996): 479–99.

———. "From Pillar to Post: Milton and the Attack on Republican Humanism at the Restoration." *Soldiers, Writers and Statesmen of the English Revolution.* Ed. Ian Gentles, John Morrill, and Blair Worden. Cambridge: Cambridge University Press, 1998. 265–85.

———. "Laureate, Republican, Calvinist: an Early Response to *Paradise Lost.*" *Milton Studies* 29 (1992): 181–98.

———. *Milton's "History of Britain": Republican Historiography in the English Revolution.* Oxford: Clarendon Press, 1991.

———. "The Whig Milton, 1667–1700." *Milton and Republicanism.* Ed. David Armitage et al. Cambridge: Cambridge University Press, 1995. 229–53.

———. "Wood, Allam, and the Oxford Milton." *Milton Studies* 31 (1994): 155–77.

Vygotsky, L. S. *Educational Philosophy.* Trans. Robert Silverman. Boca Raton, Fla.: St. Lucie Press, 1997.

Watson, Foster. *The English Grammar Schools to 1660.* Cambridge: Cambridge University Press, 1908.

Welch, Anthony. "Reconsidering Chronology in *Paradise Lost.*" *Milton Studies* 41 (2002): 1–17.

Weston, C. C. "England: Ancient Constitution and Common Law." *The Cambridge History of Political Thought 1450–1700.* Ed. J. H. Burns with Mark Goldie. Cambridge: Cambridge University Press, 1991. 374–411.

Whitman, Cedric H. *Homer and the Heroic Tradition.* 1958. Reprint: New York: W. W. Norton, 1965.

Wilcox, Donald J. *In Search of God and Self: Renaissance and Reformation Thought.* Boston: Houghton Mifflin, 1975.

Williamson, George. "The Education of Adam." *Modern Philology* 61 (1963): 96–109.

Wittgenstein, Ludwig. *The Blue and Brown Books.* 2nd ed. New York: Harper and Row, 1960.

Worden, Blair. "English Republicanism." *The Cambridge History of Political Thought, 1450–1700.* Ed. J. H. Burns with Mark Goldie. Cambridge: Cambridge University Press, 1991. 443–75.

———. "John Milton and Oliver Cromwell." *Soldiers, Writers and Statesmen of the English Revolution.* Ed. Ian Gentles et al. Cambridge: Cambridge University Press, 1998. 243–64.

———. "Milton's Republicanism and the Tyranny of Heaven." *Machiavelli and Republicanism.* Ed. Gisela Bock et al. Cambridge: Cambridge University Press, 1990. 225–45.

Young, Robert Fitzgibbon. *Comenius in England.* London: Oxford University Press, 1932.

Zwicker, Steven N. *Lines of Authority: Politics and English Literary Culture, 1649–1689.* Ithaca, NY: Cornell University Press, 1993.

———. "Reading the Margins: Politics and the Habits of Appropriation." *Refiguring Revolutions: Aesthetics and Politics from the English Revolution to the Romantic Revolution.* Ed. Kevin Sharpe and Steven N. Zwicker. Berkeley: University of California Press, 1998. 101–15.

Index